NOTES ON INDIA

NOTES ON INDIA

Robert Bohm

South End Press   Boston Ma.

Cover by Mary Lea.

First printing, July 1982
Typesetting and production at South End Press
Printed in the U.S.A. by Banta Company
Library of Congress number: 81-51390
ISBN 0-89608-125-7
ISBN 0-89608-126-5

South End Press—302 Columbus Avenue—Boston Ma.02116

Table of Contents

Acknowledgements

Whatever value might be in this book comes from those people, both known and unknown, whose histories are reflected in the following pages. Although there are too many to list individually by name, I want to especially thank those who submitted to interviews, who opened their homes, who revealed some of the private details of their daily lives. Simply put, this book would not have come into existence without the cooperation of many people, and without the fact that the lives and struggles of the Indian people in general are a compelling story that demands to be heard. Therefore *Notes* rightfully belongs to those ordinary women and men who are its main subject, although any deficiencies in the writing or analysis are of course mine.

In terms of the actual writing of the book, there are a number of individuals I'd like to thank for various kinds of assistance and emotional support.

First of all my wife, Suman. Authorship is frequently more difficult to define than it might seem on the surface. In terms of gathering the information for *Notes*, Suman and I worked jointly on a large portion of the manuscript. By jointly I don't mean she played the role of technical assistant or secretary. She was an active, full-partner participant in the creation of at least half the manuscript. Her input was most crucial in those parts having to do with the cultural aspects of colonialism and psychological quality of Indian life. Together, we talked to people incessantly every day for four months. Much of the information gotten from these discussions is directly traceable to Suman's sensitivity and openness as well as to a certain tough grittiness of spirit she shared with many of those we spoke with. So, although she didn't do any of the actual writing, the book, in fact, would not have been written without her.

I'd also like to thank Earl Sandy Carter, Jamila Gaston, Jill Holloway, Bala Krishnan, Seth Rockwell, Vickie Harvey, and John Williams.

Also to be thanked are distant friends and in-laws: Malti, a gutsy woman and a survivor; Anand, whose love of life has led him down some dark roads, but who is now healthier than he has been for a number of years; and Kunda, tall Bombay woman, a stabilizing force in the world of which she is part.

INTRODUCTION

This book is about India. It's about politics and economics and about people working their butts off and cooperating and squabbling and struggling to survive. The book is also, out of necessity, about the West's tendency to misperceive India, to downgrade and underestimate and stereotype the population. The fact is that it's impossible to write about India without confronting head-on the narrowness and self-servingness of some of our lingering colonial assumptions about the nature of Indian society.

At this point in U.S. history, India's precisely the kind of place it's good for all of us to try to understand more completely. The confusion in North America about what's happening in the so-called developing countries is palpable. Reading our newspapers and watching our televisions, it seems as if these countries are always on the edge of an incomprehensible social chaos, are always close to revolution. And the word revolution scares us, conjuring up images in our heads of international instability, meaningless violence, cynical communist plots. We too often forget that these countries are inhabited by actual living people, and that it's these people who, for specific reasons, are behind the occurences we're forced to view from so far off. These people, without exception, are much like ourselves in their desire to survive with a certain amount of dignity. Once we understand this, our understanding of the world situation expands overnight. It's no longer possible, then, to view the struggles in other countries as merely distant "incomprehensible" events, or to pretend that these struggles are all set in motion by some giant computer in the Kremlin. Instead we're faced with the fact that, in different nations across the world, people like ourselves are fighting passionately for their very survival. Such a perspective deepens our approach to the question of revolution and revolutionary struggles. This is especially important given the fact that our own government frequently supplies us with misleading information concerning the goings-on in other countries. Right now, for instance, at the very moment I'm writing this introduction, the morning paper has two articles on U.S. involvement in Central America and one on the Reagan administration's increasing political coziness with South Africa. All three articles mention, in one form or another, the need to ward off the mounting "communist threat." The millions of South Africa blacks oppressed by apartheid and the millions of working people and peasants in Central America aren't mentioned in any significant way. Instead they are made to seem like bit players and stage-props in a big drama in which U.S. interests are the main important star. This is the kind of thing we're up against: the systematic reduction of living human beings to *things*. If we want to retain any semblance of morality, we have to fight this tendency.

This book is of course specifically about India, an attempt to provide some clarity concerning what life is like there. I've tried to employ a broader rather than a narrower approach. By this I mean that although I hoped to write a book about the political structure of Indian life, I didn't want it to be merely an economic or a political science treatise. I wanted it, also, to be sensuous, human. Subsequently the manuscript contains not only political commentary, but also an attempt to communicate the imagery of everyday life.

I remember the first time I was in India, in 1968. I was with my wife, Suman, who is from India. There are moments from that first trip that still stick with me. Little signals of that first confrontation.

One afternoon I was returning from a walk outside the village where we spent most of our time. I was on a hillside. I could see, over to the right at the hill's base, a spot where women were washing clothes in a stream. I looked at them and then out over the land. An amazingly radiant noon light coated everything: rocks, gulleys, sugarcane fields, people. I felt connected, perfectly at peace with my surroundings. Then I walked to the bottom of the hill and stood for awhile, relaxed and lazy, looking at a yellow-flowering cassia tree.

But things, unfortunately, weren't always that simple, that nice.

One evening we were in Bombay. The sun was setting over the Arabian Sea, leavng a bloodred highway of fire on the water. After it set, we walked in the dusk's growing bluish darkness through a lightbulb lit bazaar along the beach. Suman wanted something to eat, from one of the vendors. Suddenly I felt like I was tagging along, that all this was too new for me. In the air: smell of coriander and curried chickpeas and onions. I looked around. There seemed to be a flood of human strangeness. There were holy men, Shivites, their foreheads marked with lines of greyish ash. There were beggars swarming through the narrow aisles between the vendors' stands. Young streetwise kids, maybe seven or eight years old, were hanging out, yelling, running errands for some of the stallkeepers. For a moment, everything seemed weird and ingraspable. India seemed to me totally incomprehensible, alien, frightening.

I mention this particular incident for a reason. In retrospect, I recognize how on that Bombay night many years ago I was displaying the symptoms of someone who suddenly feels threatened when they enter a new, culturally different environment. Rather than relaxing and seeing the new environment for what it was, I projected my feelings of alienation onto that environment and therefore saw it as strange and ingraspable. It isn't particularly pleasant for me to acknowledge that this is what happened, and yet, if I didn't admit it, this would have the effect of being misleading, by making it appear that this book was written by someone who sees himself as always objective and therefore "above" making certain kinds of mistakes in perception. This of course isn't so. I stress this point because I feel it provides one of the bases upon which we—you and I, reader and writer—can establish serious contact. We're both equally capable of having insight and we're both equally capable of giving into our cultural limitations. This is the link that binds us together. If this isn't understood, then a good deal of this book can't be understood, since one of the book's primary messages is that we—the little people, the nobodies, the workers, the average struggling-to-survive U.S. woman and man—have to make a collective effort to overcome our limitations and to acquaint ourselves with our counterparts on the other side of the world. If we don't make this effort, no one will do it for us. Then we'll be left stranded, our intelligences like lumps of clay easily molded by the powers that be into whatever attitudes they feel it's necessary for us to have.

This is the last thing we want. We have to commit ourselves to achieving clarity.

Whatever human power we have comes from our ability to
seek out the truth and hold onto it. It doesn't come from our
capacity to accept easy answers, or to deceive ourselves, or to
adopt the aims of a super-sophisticated cynicism.

I should say something here about the fact that a significant
portion of Notes was written four years ago, during a ten-month
period ending in September 1978. I mention this because it
means that, inevitably, there are certain events and conditions
referred to in the following chapters that should be looked at in
the light of subsequent events. For instance, one pertinent aspect
of Notes is that it was written during the period following Indira
Gandhi's ouster from the Prime Ministership in March 1977.
Because of this, the book implies in places that the Indian people
no longer had any tolerance for the kind of repressive measures
Ms. Gandhi had employed in subduing discontent within the
population. But now it's a number of years later and she's back in
office. This might seem to indicate that Indians are either willing
to accept some sort of totalitarian leadership or that they have no
"real" desire for political change.

Such an interpretation of Ms. Gandhi's reelection is
incorrect. This is because it refuses to look at the context in
which she was returned to office. As is documented in the
following text, in many ways the Janata Party government that
followed hers was as unsuccessful as her own. India continued to
be wracked by serious economic and unemployment problems,
and the government had to resort to police and military control
of dissidents, demonstrators, workers. Subsequently when elections were held again in 1980, people were in fact being given
little choice. Because of this, it's impossible to read the mood of
the Indian population simply in terms of how that population
expresses itself through the electoral system. As in so many
countries, in India it is in the arenas outside the electoral system
that we often have to hunt down the people's true mood.

I think it's pertinent here to quote the concluding para-
graphs of Part 3, Section 7. These paragrpahs were written
while Indira Gandhi was out of office and the Janata Party had
power:

As each day passes and the government displays 1) its
continuing inability to stabilize the economy or eradi-

cate class inequities, and 2) its willingness to resort to violent methods for repressing people, the outlines of the near future become clearer. The days of Janata Party power are numbered.

What will happen as the Janata Party declines bears watching. This will require some reading between the lines. The maneuverings of the officially recognized power blocs, including the Congress Party and Indira Gandhi, will probably be fairly well reported here in the West. But such coverage of traditional politics runs the risk of obscuring the real pulse of subcontinent life: the people themselves, especially in the form of the workers' and peasants' movements. These movements, unfortunately, aren't likely to be overly emphasized by our press. The reason this is problematic is because, on the subcontinent, occurences at the top of the political pyramid—at the so-called official level—don't necessarily accurately reflect the moods being generated at the base, among the millions. At the top, famous faces will fade and reappear, depending on the political winds of the moment. At the bottom, often independently of traditional political life, there will be the emotional creation of dreams and plans for a radically different subcontinent future.

Inevitably, there will be detours and setbacks. Still, it is true: the day of the final confrontation is approaching.

The fact is that although Indira Gandhi is presently back in office, her reelection hasn't changed either the economic or psychological conditions that make India a hotbed of potential upheaval.

That this is so is shown by the fact that even now, four years after the writing of some of this book, the kinds of incidents reported in the following chapters are still occuring, with regularity.

Take, for instance, Ms. Gandhi's recent reinauguration of "special measures" to curb working class dissent. Strikes in all essential services as well as most other significant industries have been declared illegal. Jailterms of up to a year are the penalty for supporting or sponsoring strike-related labor agitations. The reason for this? The frail state of the Indian economy (the economy had a negative growth rate in 1980) and the expectation of mounting organized discontent. Largescale unemployment, a subsistence level existence for millions of people, soaring food prices—these are some of the facts that have convinced India's present leadership that serious restraints must be put on the people's ability to collectively demonstrate their anger and shared concerns.

Other recent occurences also indicate the seriousness of the divisions within Indian society. One of these has to do with the revolutionary group, the Naxalites. Not long ago in a certain area of northern India, they launched raids on a number of villages for the purpose of confiscating guns and ammunition (from the wealthy) in order to build up their arms supply for their continuing "war" with local landlords, who wield feudallike power over their subordinates: landless laborers, tenant farmers, etc. This threat of armed conflict is no mirage, and it isn't isolated in a single part of India. In the southern state of Kerala, there was a recent gun battle between farmworkers and well-off landowners, concerning the rights of the rural poor.

I mention such incidents in order to establish that the need for Westerners to understand India is as urgent today as it was three or even forty years ago. The incidents just described, of course, may seem at first glance a little confusing. They may inspire questions like "Why do such things happen?" or "Why is their such violence on the subcontinent?" Questions like these are appropriate: they're a first step toward gaining understanding. Hopefully this book will provide the answers, or at least the bases for answers, to such questions.

Now for a few words about the book's structure.

The book is called *Notes on India* because that's what it is: a series of notes, observations and reflections on India and the West's attitude toward India. Some of the writing—specifically in Parts 1 and 4—was done quickly, impressions being jotted down either immediately after the incidents described or when some particular event kicked off a series of sudden, spontaneous thoughts that I chose to record. In writing the manuscript I favored the notes format because it gave me, I felt, the freedom to jump around a little, to try to create an interesting arrangement of descriptions and comments, and yet at the same time to sustain a certain cohesiveness. I also chose this structure because I think it's the one best suited to my abilities: neither sociologist nor political scientist, I'm simply a writer trying to present a clear picture of certain human realities. In this light, my main goal has been to try to present India as a tangible place where knowable people live and work, and also to get at some of the underlying social structures that determine the nature of people's lives there.

The book is divided into five sections.

Part I is an account of life in the particular area of India I'm most familiar with: Belgaum District, Karnataka State. A variety of related subject matters are dealt with here: village life, marketplace activity, people working, capsulated personal histories, a few glimpses into the lives of the Western-oriented upper clases, labor-management conflicts, etc. When necessary, the subjects dealt with in this section are expanded upon by giving relevant historical background—for instance, information is given on both the labor and peasant movements in order to put into an intelligible context certain contemporary events that are described.

Part II attempts to incorporate Indian myths, portraits of people's personal lives and some sociological information in an effort to explain the significance, and deeply engrained nature, of caste and sexual divisions within Indian society. Yet at the same time I try to make clear how these divisions, so often used by Westerners to "prove" the backward nature of Indian society, are in fact no more weird or bizarre than some of our own social contradictions.

Part III is a condensed overview of Indian economic/political life since Independence in 1947. Details are presented concerning the negative impact of many of India's economic policies on large portions of the Indian population. Examples are also given of the insensitive nature of much U.S. economic assistance to India—insensitive in that it attempts to "control" rather than to help the subcontinent. Also explored in this section, through the narration of specific events, is the government's repression of anti-government forces up to and including the Emergency period that ended in 1977.

Part IV discusses the distorting colonial quality of many Western views of India. To show that a number of the old colonial attitudes have persisted into modern times, some analysis is given of the relationship of the U.S. counterculture to India. This relationship is explored in such a way as to show that many of the counterculture's attitudes toward subcontinent life (fascination with yoga, gurus, etc.) have been in fact a continuation of, as opposed to a departure from, certain classical colonial attitudes. Also discussed, in this light, is the West's attitude toward Mohandas Gandhi, the proponent of nonviolence.

Part V, the concluding section, presents a series of final images of Indian life.

Readers should feel free to either read straight through the book or, instead, to begin with whatever section seems most interesting to them individually.

There are no footnote designations in the text. Rather, there's a Notes Section at the back of the book where all references to particular sources are appropriately acknowledged.

One final comment.

Last night, while watching a sports event on tv, I had a conversation with my friend Junior Walker, who works with my wife at the Chevette plant on Boxwood Road, here in Wilmington, Delaware. Junior was saying he was afraid we might slip back into the kinds of labor-management relations prevalent in the "old days" when more workers than now were unorganized, unprotected, and vulnerable to the owners' weirdest whims. He said he couldn't figure out why many working people didn't understand that the present swing to the political right, under Reagan's guidance, represented a serious attack on ordinary people across the nation. Junior also, as he'd done other times, spoke passionately about the myths that negatively describe, and get some folks angry at, poor people, blacks and unemployed. Junior is black and when he was young he used to be a streetkid, so he knows the full human significance of such myths. They irk him—he didn't like them in the past and he doesn't like them now.

I mention Junior's remarks because they're relevant. The fact is that the same forces—those with political and economic power, the "official" decision makers, the supporters of the status quo—benefit from both domestic and international stereotypes.

Domestically, stereotypes of the poor, blacks, working people, the unemployed, women—all serve the purpose of reinforcing a social vision that says that those on the lower rungs of the economic ladder are incapable of making sensible political decisions or wielding any kind of political power. Likewise, international stereotypes concerning the populations of countries like India serve a similar purpose: they reinforce the view that the populations of those countries are backward and therefore need guidance, from the wealthy sectors of the so-called advanced nations, in order to get ahead.

Once we know this, it should make certain things clearer. For instance, if we accept the myths about a nation like India without making the effort to strip them away and to get at the realities behind the illusions, then we're basically saying yes to the same process by which we ourselves are stereotyped and downgraded and written off by those in power. In other words, when we support colonial attitudes about people from other countries, we're bolstering up the strength of those (the corporations, the big banks, etc.) who benefit from such attitudes and who just as readily propagate stereotypes about ourselves.

Whether or not we want this kind of thing to continue, is up to us.

1
LIFE SLABS

SETTLING DOWN

From my window I see two women walking slowly in the hot sun. I hear, on the main road at the bottom of the hill, the tinkle of a bull's bell collar: somewhere down there, a cart is being pulled.

If I were in a daydreamy sort of mood, a convenient image might form itself in my mind now. It might seem to me that the bullock cart symbolized India's rhythm, the bull's ass swaying slowly back and forth as it drags the cart with its lazy-looking driver down the road. Also, I might begin to feel that this was the subcontinent's basic pace: slow motion. And that this, in turn, was a reflection of something inside the people: a fundamental laid-backness, a refusal to go too fast, a suicidal attempt not to move, to hold onto the past. In such a vision the bullock cart, of course, would represent the past.

I see something else through the window: a water buffalo grazing on the side of the hill. A boy, standing next to the buffalo, swats its hip with a stick to get it going. The buffalo moves forward two slow steps, then stops and starts grazing again. The boy, looking around absent-mindedly, waits a minute, then swats the animal with a stick again. And again the same pattern is repeated: the buffalo takes a few slow steps forward, stops and starts grazing.

On the basis of the almost somnambulistic quality of this scene, it might be possible to feel that this is another proof of the fact that everything in India moves slowly, that it's become, even, a racial characteristic of the people. They luxuriate in bodily tranquility, in not overdoing anything. One rationale for accepting such a vision could be that the hot sun, beating on the population over the centuries, has forged such passivity into the single most noticable national attribute.

An interesting approach, but stupid, meaningless.

The image of universal Indian slowness is typical, not in the sense that it's an accurate portrayal of either India or Indian people, but in the sense that it's a typical western appraisal of what India and the Indian people are like—unchanging India, static, tropical, somehow fundamentally reluctant to move. This is the commodity sold to the unwary. It comes from all sides. As one contemporary writer says in a recent book, "In India...everything proceeds at the rate of the slowest member." His basic point is that in traveling to India one is, strangely, traveling into the past. He talks about the "ancient, unchanged spectacle of raw endurance." The reader is drawn into a falsely poeticized dreamworld in which even the simple magpie—described as an "archaeopteryxian snakebird" in order to persuade the reader that it's some sort of holdover from prehistory—becomes a symbol of India's ancientness, its unchangingness. The message is that once the foreigner steps onto Indian soil he/she becomes "part explorer, part time-traveler." The final consequence of such self-indulgent poeticization is the dehumanization of the people. Marketplace crowds made up of distinct individuals are transformed in this western writer's fantasy into "crowds...like a vast grey ameoba." Certainly no one's going to have a human relationship with an amoeba. The stage is set for the degrading objectification of a whole population.

As mentioned above, typical is one word for such a picture. Colonialistic is another. But such a picture can only exist in disregard of the historical data. It robs the people of their history as an active world-changing people; it robs them of the fact that like all people of all nations their very presence in the world has changed the world, has transformed nature, has resulted in the evolution of the productive forces, has moved history itself in certain irreversable directions.

But the fact is that for Westerners interested in India, the correct historical data isn't always easy to come by. First one has to scrape away the crap, the crud that has been carefully built up into an almost impregnable sediment by the so-called experts. Even upper class Third World intellectuals have been drafted for the purpose of falsifying India. Take, for example, V.S. Naipaul's writings on India which first appeared in the *New York Review of Books*, the prestigous journal of U.S. academics. How pleased these people must have been to find out from Naipaul's essays that the working classes of India were just as worthless (when compared to intellectuals) as the laboring classes of the United States: truckdrivers, hardhats, secretaries, clerks, etc. Naipaul's claim is that after studying Indian history and examining the residue of that history as it exists in the modern era, one discovers that all the subconinent has been left with "is a peasantry that cannot comprehend the idea of change."

Such attitudes, unfortunately, aren't exceptions. There are many distorted pictures of India available in the West and they all serve a political purpose: hauling India into the U.S. dominated capitalist orbit. Every portrait of India which depicts the country as a backward nation, seething with a dangerously dense population strangling on its own blind self-multiplication, serves this purpose, the implications of such portraits being that in order for India to achieve even minimal stability it needs the West's guidance. Even the picture the counter-culture has drawn serves the same purpose in a convoluted sort of way. By characterizing India as a land of gurus and wandering holy men it has emphasized India as an historical artifact left over from some primitive stage of human development. Neither of these portraits really gets close to the basic question: what is India like? Certainly Allen Ginsberg's meaningless metaphysical comment about India, that it's "the wonderworld where Man knows he's in a dream," is no help in getting at the real India.

I'm presently living—with my wife and two children—in Karnataka State, in southern India. We live in Vijaynagar, a village a few miles outside of Belgaum City on the Vengrula Road. After Vijaynagar, Vengrula Road heads west toward the coast, which is about a hundred miles away. On the way to the coast, the road passes through Chandrakar where bauxite is mined, loaded onto lorries and hauled back to Belgaum where it's processed into aluminum. Chandrakar is thirty miles away.

All day on Vengrula Road, the lorries pass. They speed by leaving large breeze-blown clouds of pale reddish dust in their wakes. The village children love to watch the lorries pass. Their cabs are painted bright colors—red, yellow, maroon, green—as are the side panels in the back. Other than the lorries, the traffic on the road consists mostly of peasants on bicycles, walking women from nearby villages, bullock carts, someone leading a herd of water buffalo to a grazing spot up the road. Also, there are the inevitable drab grey or dirty red government busses.

Vijaynagar's a small village with a population of only a few hundred. It's situated toward the bottom of a long sloping hill, on the last ridge before the hill descends to the road. Looking up from the road, one can see that the village consists of two house-clusters. The houses to the right are older. Most of them are sturdy-looking structures made of brick and cement, with flat roofs that can be used for sleeping on hot nights. These houses are what we would call middle class homes. To the left, divided from the first group of houses by a narrow dirt road, is the second house-cluster. These houses are newer and are owned by poorer peasants. The houses range from very small to medium-sized. They are constructed of mud brick and have either bricktile or thatched roofs. There are a few huts made of straw, mud and cowdung; these huts are held together by bamboo frames. Some of the plots of land on which the homes in this second house-cluster are built were sold cheaply by the government to the people here as part of its (for the most part ineffectual) land-distribution program. Only a few such plots exist. According to one villager, many more plots of land were scheduled for low-price distribution, but the distribution was stopped by a bottom-level government bureaucrat who hatched a plan for keeping the land unsettled and then selling it later at a more profitable under-the-table rate to well-off peasants. This second house-cluster is built on bare hill. There's no vegetation: no flowering shrubs, no trees. This is unlike the first house-cluster which is shaded by bananna, palm and tamarind trees and which is thick with purple-flowering bougainvillea bushes. We live in the second group of houses.

On the far side of the Vengrula Road there's farmland: rice paddies, vegetable plots and, in the distance, broad stretches of tall-growing sugarcane. All day men and women can be seen working in these fields: plowing, planting, cutting grass in the uncultivated areas, loading bullock carts. In the furthest distance, there's a line of blue hills. After sunset, as the day dissolves into dusk, one can watch these hills grow bluer, darker by the minute, until at last the night, with its first stars, covers the land.

Nearby there are three larger villages, all of them older than Vijaynagar. The first of these villages, Hindalga, is a half mile

down the Vengrula Road, to the west. It's situated on the far side
of the road. The second village is Ambavadi. It's two miles
behind Hindalga, to the north. For the most part the families of
these two villages are bound to the soil, although some of the
younger sons have now secured jobs in the city, Belgaum. The
third village is Ganeshpur. It's not on the Vengrula Road. It's on
the road at the top of the hill that Vijaynagar's built toward the
bottom of. There are a number of dirt paths leading up the hill to
Ganeshpur. Many of the people in this village originally came
from one of the tribal areas and are very poor. None of them own
farmland. Survival, for them, is a day-to-day affair.

This is my third time here and it still takes time to adjust.
Coming back, at first everything exists at the level of
physical sensation. For instance, the sensation of color. Bright
silk and cotton saris, the pale reddish orange of the soil, blond
bales of hay in the middle of pale green fields, sunlight drenching
the dark stones on the dirt path in front of our house, white
jasmine or yellow marigolds in the black hair òf many of the
women, peasants (men and women) spitting quick spurting
streaks of tobacco juice onto the roads. Color, all around.
Also there's the sensation of new smells. In the fields and in
the vegetable markets, the pungent odor of coriander. Or, in both
city and countryside, the inescapable smell of roaming animals—
goats, sheep, water buffalo, cows. And in the villages, as well as
in certain sections of the cities, there's the sometimes vague,
sometimes strong stench of open-ditch sewage systems.
But the basic sensation is the sheer feeling of existence,
human existence. People doing things. What exactly are they
doing? Some of the activity of course is immediately identifiable.
For example, Laxshmi, a woman who lives in a small mud brick
hut in Vijaynagar, is using her knife to shave thin strips of
bamboo from a bamboo pole. She does this crouched inside the
doorway of her house. The bamboo strips will be used to weave
baskets that she'll sell. She's a widow with eight children and this
is how she makes a living. Therefore, what Laxshmi is doing
crouched inside the doorway of her hut is no mystery: she's
working to survive.

But there are other activities that aren't so easily identifiable. For instance, on a street in Belgaum a man beats a crude flat drum (it looks something like a tambourine) with a stick. The simple regular beating of the stick against the drum makes a surprisingly lively music. The man's surrounded by young children. I go closer. Next to him, on a small wooden platform, is a tiny chair decorated like a throne—a chair just big enough, maybe, for a two year old child. Sitting in this chair, a bright garland of flowers around its neck and a small hat of flowers on its head, is a dead monkey stiff with rigor-mortis. Some passers-by put coins in a small box that the drummer has placed on the platform next to the monkey. The exact reason for the dead monkey's enthronement is unclear to me. It has something to do with an old Indian myth concerning Hanuman, the monkey god. One thing is certain: this is precisely the kind of image, exotic and apparently bizarre, that's been hawked in the West as typical of Indian life. But for the moment this doesn't interest me. The fact is that the scene is just raw sensation to me; my attention is caught, I note the details, but I don't quite understand.

The reality, however, is that most of what one sees is recognizable. Definable.

Take, as an example, the Saturday market in Belgaum. Wide mats are spread out on the ground, piled with grains, vegetables, fruits. The marketplace streets are jammed, people bumping into each other, shouting, trying to find out where they can get the best buy. Coolies, pulling long flat handcarts stacked with different kinds of merchandise, try to make their way through the crowds. Inevitably, they get stuck behind tight knots of pedestrians. Eventually, though, they maneuver themselves free and are on their way again. All the while they're trying to wend their way through the crowds, they're talking to people: get out of my way, stand over on the side, I'm coming through, watch out. All over—activity, noise.

Yes. The marketplace is buzzing with life. The air is filled with chaff from rice, wheat and barley. On the ground, great piles of red chilies sprawl like rolling hills of fire on straw mats, while nearby women haggle over potential prices with potential customers. You move through the crowd, amazed by the action, the color. Large mounds of white onions brightly reflect the sunlight. A man weighs a bunch of grapes on a scale. Three women vegetable sellers get up and chase away a stray cow that has started nosing around their cauliflowers and cabbages. People step aside as a bullock cart, loaded with grainsacks, makes its way haltingly through the packed streets. Then, quickly glimpsed, an isolated image: in a group of women sitting on the ground selling vegetables, there's one heavyset woman with a weather-beaten brown basket turned upside down over her head, blocking the sun. Yes, the heat, the light, are intense. It's impossible to describe the intensity. It's almost as if you can see the light drilling thin holes into everything it touches. One woman shouts at Suman: "Buy my last dozen bannanas so I can get out of this sun and go back to my village. I've been sitting here all morning; I can't take it anymore."

This, then, is the so-called mysterious East, the supposed paradise of slowness.

Look: a man carries a 150 lb. grainsack on his back. He's bent over in such a way that his chest is almost parallel to the ground. He's struggling to hold onto the end of the sack nearest his neck. To do this, his arms are positioned so that the elbows jut out sideways like two knobby wings. He's a middle-aged man, a few days' white stubble on his chin and cheeks. Eyes darting this way and that, he looks for little tunnels in the thick Saturday crowd that he can pass through. When he gets bottled up in the crowd, he makes a few quick hissing sounds, a signal to people that he's trying to get by. Up close, one can see the face's tightness, a sign of the physical strain.

And similarly: in the wholesale section of the market, a man's backed up against the side of a truck. He has on nothing except a pair of torn khaki shorts. Above him, the lorry's loaded with big sacks filled with coconuts. Two men have seated themselves on some of these sacks, while a third is in the process of lifting one of the sacks over the wooden side-panels and lowering it onto the shoulders of the man below. The coolie in the khaki shorts bends forward slightly, preparing to receive the sack. The man above lowers the sack as far as he can while still retaining his balance, then lets it drop the final half a foot to the waiting coolie's back. When the full weight of it lands, for a split second the coolie's face is twisted into a teeth-gritting grimace. Then he throws his hands over his shoulders, secures the sack with two iron hooks and, bending further forward in order to keep the sack balanced on his back, walks toward the cab end of the truck where another worker helps him dump the sack onto a pile of similar sacks. Relieved of his burden now, the coolie stands up straight and stretches his back. Then he returns to the other end of the truck and the same process is repeated.

From one end of the street to the other: work. The street's crammed with lorries whose cargoes are being unloaded: wheat, salt, barley, coconuts, limes, betel nuts. There are also trucks with large cylindrical tanks on the back, some filled with cooking oil, others with kerosene. On the back-end of the tanks, there are spigots from which metal drums are being filled. When a drum's filled and then sealed shut with a soldering iron, someone rolls it off down the street. As the drum rolls, it makes a thumping thunder-like noise. In one place, just outside a shopfront, a sack of salt is broken open and a man weighs out a large quantity of it on a set of six foot high scales. In another place, the same process occurs with red chilies. All this time, men with heavy burlap bags on their backs try to make their way between parked trucks and walking people. The temperature's 101 degrees. Someone cuts open a sack of flour, a white dry powder floats in the air like visible heat. You look around and you think to yourself: in a place like this, a quart of sweat should sell for a thousand rupees. But no it doesn't. According to the lean-faced accountant in the wholesale grain shop, "Some people are born to be pack animals, mules."

Born to be. A familiar phrase. A cheap rationale.

So we are here: India. The process of settling down has begun.

The land outside our door—Vijaynagar, Hindalga, Ambavadi, Ganeshpur—is one small, but typical, fraction of a gigantic nation with a population of over 600 million. It's important to walk around, to get the feel of things, to become familiar with the details of people's work, to listen to what they have to say. It's only at the mundane level of the daily routine of people living and working that one begins to develop a clear picture of what life here is all about.

Morning. We're in Hindalga. At the north end of the village, we stand for about ten minutes watching some workers building a house—six men and one woman. There's a pile of bricks about fifteen yards in front of the house. In a basket carefully balanced on her head, the woman carries bricks into the half constructed house and deposits them in a corner. Two men are using the bricks to finish the wall that will separate the front room from the second room. The woman comes out again to the brickpile, bends down, lifts eight bricks one by one into the basket on her head, stands upright again and returns to the house, deposits the bricks in the same corner and once more comes out. While this pattern is being repeated again and again at ground-level, men are working on the one story high roof. Each movement they make—fitting a brick into mortar and then scrapping the excess mortar away with a trowel, etc.—occurs against a background of cloudless blue sky. At one point, one of the men yells down at the woman brick-carter that they need some more bricks on the roof, quick. He calls to her just as she is going through the doorway with another basket-load of bricks balanced on her head. She snaps back at him. "Hold on! You'll get them!"

Another Day. In the fields of a wealthy landlord, two men shove sugarcane stalks into a grinding machine in which the stalks are crushed and the juice squeezed out. Once squeezed out, it's piped up onto the boiling platform about ten yards away. On the platform there are two huge vats, each about seven feet in diameter. Under the platform, directly below these vats, a fire is kept burning so that the juice boils and the water is steamed off. The more it boils, the more it becomes a swirling yellowish froth. When it has been sufficiently heated, eight men carry the vats (first one, then the other) to the other side of the platform, which is under a canopy, and pour the purified sugarcane juice into a shallow square tank built into the platform floor. Once the juice has been poured in, the men take turns stirring it with a hoe-like instrument that they push back and forth from one side of the tank to the other. While the men are doing this, the juice crystalizes and thickens, becomes heavier. When the crystalization process is completed, the men scoop the finished product (*jagari*) out of the tank and put it into buckets, where the final solidification process will occur. Then it will be ready for sale. For this *jagari*, the U.S.-educated landlord who owns these fields will get a price in excess of one hundred rupees ($12.50) per bucket. The highest paid worker, on the other hand, earns ten rupees ($1.25) a day. The average worker makes significantly less: five rupees (63¢) per day.

For the most part, of course, the people you meet aren't quiet. They talk. They have stories to tell, grievances to unload.

For instance, one afternoon we're in a field on the north side of the Vengrula Road, near Hindalga. In the distance, about a hundred yards away, two peasants sit in the grass while a water buffalo grazes nearby. We approach them. A conversation starts. One man is about sixty. The other's younger, maybe forty. After we talk awhile, the younger man goes to get our children, Adriana and Nikos, some sugarcane from an adjacent field. While he's gone, the older man talks about the political situation in India. About the Janata Party (which defeated Indira Ghandi in the March, 1977 elections) he says: "To people like me in the farming areas, all these parties are the same. Whether it be Indira the woman or the Janata Party as a whole, it comes to the same thing for us: nothing. Janata Party means 'People's Party' and yet they don't care what happens to the poor, all they're interested in is making money for themselves. The poor don't benefit. The only ones who benefit are those who already have positions of influence."

At this point, the younger peasant comes back with two sugarcane stalks. The kids love it, sucking the juice from the sticks after the green bark has been peeled off. Meanwhile, the older man keeps talking, his emotion increasing.

> Let me tell you what things are like here. Right now we're sitting in some fields. Whereas in the past, without modern machinery, these fields produced only about ten sacks of rice a year, now, with the new methods, they produce a lot more. Yet people still don't get enough to eat. Things remain the same; nothing changes. Do you know why? It's not true that in India there isn't enough to eat. There's enough, but the ones who own the biggest tracts of land stash away what they grow waiting for the prices to go up, and if

the prices don't go up the crops just stay stashed away until they rot. So what's the use of increasing the amount grown, when it doesn't get to the people it was originally intended for? After all these years, I'm still forced to buy foodstuffs on the black market. But now I've gotten to the point where I'm tired of working all day and then at night, when I come home, having to go to the black market for grain. And let me tell you, I'm just like everybody else: an average man, not well off, worn out by all this corruption. Why is there no effective price control, so that everybody would be able to buy what they needed? You used to pay seventeen rupees ($2) for manure and now you pay three hundred rupees ($37.50) for the same amount. Believe me, things aren't going to be able to go on like this. Someday soon something's going to happen.

One tirade by an old man met accidentally in a field near a godforsaken village called Hindalga.

You listen. Not knowing what else to do, you casually nod your head while he talks. You remember his face, long afterwards.

PEOPLE

In discussing a country like India, there's a danger; statistics (we'll get to these later) can be quoted endlessly. This percentage of the rural population is in debt to moneylenders, this percentage is suffering from malnutrition, and so on. Such numbers are important. They indicate concrete things about the quality of life. But sometimes the numbers obscure precisely what they're intended to indicate—human realities. And so certain basic questions arise. What are the people actually like? What are the details of their daily lives? How do they go about the business of survival?

To begin answering such questions, not much is necessary. You step out of the door, into Vijaynagar and the surrounding area...

Holika and Family

A light breeze blows down the side of the hill, between the houses and huts. The sky's sprinkled with hard clear stars.

Malava and Shoba, Holika's two daughters, stand holding hands in front of their house, singing. Laxshman, the girl's father, stands a few feet away from them, giving instructions between songs about what to sing next. It's *poornima*, night of the full moon. At moments like this, history seems to dissolve. Vijaynagar seems the perfect hiding place, tranquilly isolated from the rest of the world. It's like a field mouse nestled cozily in its dark hole in the middle of a huge otherwise uninhabited field. The girls' singing moves like the breeze, lightly between houses and huts. Vijaynagar, the perfect refuge. Or so it appears.

When the singing's done, we go inside. The room we sit in is lit by a single oil wick. Near the wall opposite the entrance, we sit on the hardened cow-dung floor. The talk's spirited, gossipy; there's a *jatara* (fair) tomorrow in Hindalga, and everybody's guessing what it will be like. There are fourteen of us: adults, children, grandchildren. Laxshman, who's sitting on the floor directly in front of me, facing me, suddenly insists that everyone should be quiet while his son, Vishnu, a high school graduate, shows us how well he knows English. The father's leaning forward, thrusting his narrow, thin-nosed face toward the center of the group. His serious expression, however, is offset by the fact that his turban, which is coming undone, gives him a comical, disheveled appearance. He has been drinking cashew liquor and is slightly drunk. His son is embarrassed by his insistance; the boy doesn't want to speak English. Finally Vishnu is saved by Holika, who intervenes, leading the dialogue in another direction.

Laxshman smokes his *beedie* (cigarette) in silence, but only for awhile. Then, disregarding the talk about who's going to wear what to the fair tomorrow, he announces that he wants another drink. Holika, overhearing him, tells him she doesn't want him drinking anymore, especially in front of the children. A momementary confusion arises as they begin to argue back and forth. Then Laxshman proclaims that we are all obligated to drink with him since we are guests in his house and are therefore expected to accept his hospitality. Holika, fit to be tied,

yells at him that if he keeps on drinking his stomach is going to
get as big as a water buffalo's. Finally, the argument subsides,
Laxshman retreating into a stubborn silence. He has a look on
his face that says he's tired of everybody trying to bamboozle him.
     The next morning, Suman and Holika get into a conversa-
tion on the path that leads between our two houses. I see them
from the window. Holika's right hand punctuates the air as she
speaks. An almost stream-of-consciousness torrent of words
pours from her mouth. She has time to talk because today is fair
day, and she doesn't have to go to the construction site where she
has been working lately. It's still early, 7:30, and there's time yet
before she has to get ready for the fair. The way she's talking,
there's no doubt some trouble's brewing.
     When Suman comes in, she says Holika's still angry because
Laxshman drank so much last night. After we left, their son-in-
law and two of his friends came and everybody sat down to eat.
Laxshman, having had a few more swigs before the meal, sat
sullen and quiet through most of the dinner. But then, just before
everyone was done eating, he flew into a rage and shouted at
Holika to stop chattering, since like all women the only thing she
was good for was fucking. Once again they went at it, back and
forth. To Suman, Holika said it wasn't just the comments that
upset her, but also the fact that Laxshman, who seems especially
frustrated and moody recently, didn't appreciate the fact that she
also got frustrated from overwork. "After all," she said, "after
doing construction work yesterday, I came home and made
dinner for everybody, and the only thing I got for it was a few
insults." She also told Suman, "He (Laxshman) drinks too much
lately, as if that's the only way he can make himself happy."
     What's Laxshman's life like? What's *he* like?
     Every morning by seven he's out in front of the house
hitching his cow to the cart. His trade is hauling goods for hire.
"One day," he says, "it's carrying sacks of rice from some village
into the market in Belgaum, another day it's carrying bricks,
another day it's something else." In reality, Laxshman's a serious,
low-key man, friendly once he gets to know you, but slow to open
up. He has two kinds of laughter. The first, mouth wide open and
head thrown back, is unselfconscious and spontaneous. This
laughter comes at predictable times: when someone, man or

woman, tells an earthy joke, or when someone, including himself, does something clumsy, revealing a sort of slapstick awkwardness in the face of life's realities. But the second kind of laughter is entirely different, coming as it does through a tight, only half-opened mouth. He seems to spit it out; it's a forced laughter that can take on the tone of either self-mockery or outward directed hatred, depending on his mood. It's this laughter, more than the other, that punctuates his narration when he talks about his life history.

One morning, while he's hitching the cow to the cart, Suman and I get into a conversation with him. Soon Holika comes to join us. She's a strong sinewy woman, both her forearms covered, in peasant fashion, with tatoos. For some reason, on this particular morning, it's in Laxshman's blood to talk about himself. In the slightly exaggerating tone a person sometimes adopts when trying to establish their worth, he talks pridefully about his early (in fact minimal) education. "I studied drama at the school and was good at it too. My father had big dreams for me. I was going to be a success. I was also a trained wrestler, a champion, able to beat anyone my weight in the village." Then, laughing his second kind of laugh, he adds: "Of course, my father's plans didn't work out quite the way he thought. When we had trouble holding onto our land because of some money he owed, it was my future that was the first thing to go. My father needed me to help him work, and that was final."

It's the image of the young, physically fit wrestler that strikes the listener the most, offering as it does a contrast with Laxshman's present condition. For instance, you look at his bare brown legs which are always giving him trouble: each one is covered with lumpy knotted-looking varicose veins. And then (still thinking of his youth) you notice how he's constantly trying, unsuccessfully, to avoid straining his back, which is always in pain. "Just what I need, all this lifting and loading," he says self-consciously, arching his head back and trying to sooth his back muscles.

On the average, forty-eight year old Laxshman makes about ten rupees ($1.25) each working day, about two hundred and fifty rupees ($31) a month. When talking about his business and about the money he takes in, his voice is characterized by a tone of self-respect; he wants you to understand that he's doing well. But whenever his talk goes beyond his job, touching instead upon the larger world of which he and his work are only a small part, the tone of self-respect fades, replaced by hefty doses of cynicism and bitterness. His meaning at such moments is clear. Somewhere, somehow, something in his life went wrong.

Socially and psychologically, Holika is different from her husband. Far from being laid back and slow to open up, she's outgoing, is quick to give her opinion and seems to have eyes in the back of her head. People in the village say about her: If you don't want Holika to know you've done something, then don't do it to begin with, because if you do, she'll see it, she'll know.

But for all her outgoingness and sly humor, Holika's not a funny lady. What she is—and she's the first one to tell you this—is a hardworking woman. On the one hand, she oversees a household that still includes, after marrying off one duaghter, four children from nine to sixteen. On the other hand, according to the season and the jobs available, she hires herself out as unskilled labor: cutting hay, mixing cement and carrying bricks at construction sites, digging wells, etc. At most she gets three rupees ($.38) a day for such work. Working an average of twenty days a month, her monthly contribution to the family earnings is sixty rupees ($7.50). Not unpredictably, Holika is prone to complaining about being overloaded, of "working and working and never having a chance to rest." Also she's concerned that a suitable marriage hasn't yet been arranged for her oldest unmarried daughter, Munjala, who's fifteen. Then there's Laxshman who, according to her, has started drinking too much and too often.

Although Holika and her husband aren't members of the most exploited sector of the rural population, this hasn't resulted in any sense of well-being. It's one of her contradictions that although Holika's willing, when angry, to castigate those lower than she on the social scale, the fact is that when projecting her vision of the world, it's them she identifies with: all of them working and all of them getting nothing in return, while "those who run society get rich."

Working for pay isn't something reserved only for the adults in the household. Of the four children still living at home, three work for wages. The son, Vishnu, having just completed highschool and being unemployed at the moment, is the only exception. All three girls—nine year old Shoba, eleven year old Malava, and fifteen year old Munjula—are part of the family wage-earning unit, all of them doing domestic work in the home of the well-off, either in Vijaynagar or the surrounding area. Although the two younger girls work less than Munjala, they all perform the same kinds of tasks: washing dishes and clothes, cleaning house, etc. Munjala works five hours a day, seven days a week, while the two younger girls work no more than three hours a day, also seven days a week. Between them, their monthly contribution to the family income is about seventy-five rupees ($9).

When talking about the girl's work hours, it's important to point out that we've so far only been referring to their wage-earning work hours. If we include the household work that's required of them in their home, we discover that although the jobs they do might be "simpler," their number of work hours is almost equivalent to their parents'. For instance, Shoba and Malava, the youngest girls and the ones home the most, are involved in a variety of household tasks all day long: drawing water from the well on the side of the hill, gathering cow-dung and making cow-dung patties for fuel, washing dishes and preparing a significant portion of each meal, grazing the water buffalo and so on. On top of this, as the oldest children in a group of four houses, they're constantly at the disposal of the adults in these houses, to be used, when necessary, as babysitters. It isn't at all unusual to see one of the girls grazing the water buffalo or walking towards the well with a three year old perched on her hip.

Vishnu, the son, is a sixteen year old high school graduate who's presently trying to decide whether he should get a job or attempt to go to college. As mentioned before, he is at the present moment the only exception to the life-is-work formula that dominates the house. To both his parents, Vishnu symbolizes the possibility of social motion, of transcending through education the kind of life they feel mired in. As the repository of his parents' dream of success, Vishnu's position within the family is a privileged one. In spite of this, there's no apparent tension between him and his sisters. He, as well as they, responds to his situation with basic acceptance; as the son, it was inevitable that such responsibility should fall on his shoulders and no one else's. But Vishnu does feel under pressure. This is most noticeable when either his mother or father talk about the great care they've taken to see that he has every chance to succeed in life. When such a statement is made in front of him, his face is likely to assume a dull tired look as if to say he's heard this before, too often. At such moments it isn't Vishnu's privileged position within the house that one thinks of, but the frail architecture of his parents' dream. For they know, as well as their son does, that there is a high unemployment rate even among the educated.

Devki

Devki is a thirty year old servant working in the home of a man who owns a medium-sized cement factory. She has strong arms, a mole on the tip of her nose, and in general a trim but solid build. She's the senior servant in the house, having been with the family over ten years.

From sunup till about ten o'clock at night, Devki works. She does all the food preparation for the three main meals, as well as afternoon tea for the adults and snacks for the children. In an Indian house where all vegetable chopping and much grinding (with a rotary quern and muller) is still done by hand, and where the family numbers seven people (three adults and four children), and where it's frequent to have guests for either lunch or dinner or both, the job of being primary cook is far more complicated and time-consuming than the analogous position would be in the West. Not only do the specifics of each meal have to be prepared, but there's also the preparation of foods that are meant to carry over from one meal to another, day to day, month to month: pickles (mango, lemon, chile) and chutneys (garlic, onion, coconut, ground nut) must be made and jarred; a perpetual supply of curry (which is made by a tedious process of cleaning and then grinding into powder a varied combination of spices) must be kept on hand; and also the grain and rice supplies must be maintained. On top of this is the fact that the preparation of each single meal may entail the preparation of more than one menu. For instance, the wife and mother-in-law will usually eat a traditional vegetarian meal, whereas the husband, who was educated in England, is likely to have a western style meal with meat (imported ham, fried eggs, home-fried potatoes, with maybe a side dish of German cheese). The children (ranging in age from four to thirteen) are also free to demand any variation on the prepared meal they desire. For Devki, what all this entails is a sort of technical flexibility which enables her to cook more than one meal at once.

But this isn't all. In terms of work, Devki also has other duties. For instance the two teenage girls who come daily to do the wash, the peasant woman who comes when necessary to clean the grain, the teenage boy who washes dishes and does general errands—all have to be supervised by Devki. Then there are the children who, before and after school, have to be catered to: a snack prepared whenever they call for it, someone in a fit of tears to be calmed down.

According to her employers, Devki's given ample free time to satisfy "whatever needs she has." This free time amounts to maybe four hours one afternoon, once a month. She's now trying to negotiate two weeks off (at one time) each year, but she isn't sure whether this will work out in reality, although she's been tentatively told it might be possible. In terms of resting during the day, her rest periods are coincident with her meals, which of course she has to eat after everyone else is done. This means that on the average day, she eats lunch at about 2:30. At most, she gets between a half hour and forty-five minutes to relax over this meal. She eats dinner between 9:30 and 10. Theoretically, after eating dinner, she has the rest of the night free. What this means in reality is that after eating—and maybe taking a little time to daydream over her life—she goes to sleep. According to members of the family, she's recently started to moan out loud in her sleep "as if she were in pain or crying out for help." They're concerned about this, since "everybody needs a good night's rest."

What is Devki's personal history? What do we find, when we scrape the surface?

Devki doesn't remember her father, who died when she was very young. She does, however, remember her stepfather, although she doesn't like to think about him. He raped her when she was sixteen. At the time, it was a scandal both in her family and in their neighborhood. Since, for the most part, Indian society still retains a semi-feudal obsession with a woman's sexual purity, the fact that Devki was raped, although it brought her a certain amount of abstract sympathy from those near her, essentially resulted in her being socially stigmatized as a woman whose future had been ruined. At this point, emotionally crushed and carrying with her an ineradicable feeling of shame, she struck out on her own, going through a series of live-in domestic jobs and in this way putting herself out of her stepfather's reach.

Because she was a good, obedient, dedicated worker who never forced her own needs on her employers by requesting more pay or time off, she earned a reputation as a trustworthy and reliable servant. At the age of eighteen she secured, as the result of her good references, what is now her present job. About a year after getting this position, feeling somewhat secure and also feeling that she had finally overcome the worst of the self-torment that had begun with her rape, she fell in love with a worker from her employer's factory. She got pregnant. At first she felt an attack of her old shame, but she decided to overcome it by legalizing her relationship with her lover and getting married. When she informed him of this, however, he told her that marriage had never been mentioned and wasn't a possibility, since he had entered into the relationship with her only because he knew that she was a "free" woman, having been profaned by her stepfather. She had an abortion and their affair was terminated. After a few years of sexual abstinence, she again had a dead-end affair, although this one at least ended without a pregnancy. Since then (for the last seven years), she has had no interest in men. Men have nothing to offer her, she says, and she has nothing she wants to offer them.

There is no doubt that Devki's life is stunted, closeted. For all practical purposes, her existence is confined to her employers' compound. She hardly ever goes out alone. When she does (maybe a few hours one afternoon a month), she goes to the movies, then, when the picture's done, comes straight back home. She of course rationalizes the restricted nature of her life by taking a great deal of pride in her selfless devotion to the needs of her employers. But it is almost wrong to say "employers." Devki doesn't see herself as hired help. Rather, she considers herself an integral, though minor, limb of the family. The pride she takes in this (that she's indispensible), and in the fact that she has survived when all the odds seemed to be against her, provides the motive for her existence. The fact that she works harder than anyone in the house—including the husband, who spends only a few hours each day at his factory—and is therefore exploited isn't something she is inclined to talk about.

Devki's locked in life, which entails hard work almost every waking minute of the day, with only the briefest rest periods, apparently provides her with precisely the kind of rigid life-schedule she needs to protect herself from the insecurity she feels in the outside world. One sign that this is true is the change that occurs in her physical appearance when she leaves the compound. The most noticeable aspect of this change is the adoption of a stiff, almost blank facial expression that entails a tightening of the jaw muscles and a nervous tautness of the skin around the mouth. When she does this, she's obviously "blocking out" what she can of the threatening world that exists beyond the familiar compound, which provides her with an almost monastic refuge from a society that only hurt her when she was in it. There's also a strong element of self-consciousness in her physical rigidness at such times, as if she knew that people were scrutinizing her and, because of this, felt required to surround herself with a wall of emotional resistance.

But if these things are true, it's also true that Devki has good reason to take pride in her indispensibility, her ability to do a job and do it well. Also, there's no doubt she has reason to pride herself in the fact that, against the odds, she has carved out for herself what she considers a fairly comfortable life in spite of being cut off from the traditional way for an Indian woman to be assimilated into the mainstream of society—marriage. Her socially-created maternal instincts have found an object in her new "family."

But she also has the insight to know this situation isn't permanent; the time will come when she will have to retire. Already at the age of thirty, she has saved (over the last fourteen years) two thousand rupees ($250) that she will use to provide for herself when the time comes. She hopes she'll be able to save enough money so that later on in life she'll be able to buy or build a small home somewhere. Then, even if she still has a job, it

won't be a live-in one and she'll have her own private space to
return to. In this way, she has pre-imagined what her life is going
to be like and has set herself the task of making sure everything
works out as well as it can.

There are two ways of looking at Devki. One is that Indian
society has done it's best to crush her: she is an oppressed
woman. Overworked, with no real time to take care of her
private needs, and with a tendency to display uptight symptoms
when removed from her little bit of familiar turf, Devki can't be
described as a flourishing human being. But this is only one way
of looking at her. Another way is to understand that in spite of
the obvious drawbacks of her life, she has nonetheless refused to
relinquish her resourcefulness. She has survived. This survival
capacity is important. It shows she is characterized by a
nonmysterious, pragmatic inner core of strength that only she
fully comprehends. It's this part of her—secreted away and
usually nonarticulate—that occasionally, in sudden flashes,
reveals itself. The revelation is sometimes caustic, as when she
once sarcastically commented that there were "two kinds of
people who end up in jail: thieves, and any poor person who
dares open his mouth too wide."

Meeda Mamma

The early afternoon sky: a hard blue. The sunlight has the
force of a hammer-blow. The temperature is close to a hundred
degrees.

On the right of the dusty street, a woman in maroon sari
hauls a bucket of water up from a well. The sound of the pulley's
creaking fills the air like the sound of some gigantic insect.

The man with me walks alongside his bicycle, pushing it
forward. Two children sit on the crossbar that extends from the
seat to the base of the handlebars. Nearby an old woman huddles
in a doorway, the end of her white sari pulled over her head. She
calls to us that we should get out of the street, that it's too hot to
be walking. My friend disregards her instructions and breaking
his silence, points down a narrow sidestreet and tells me, "That's
where I used to live." He's pointing at a plot of land near a small
cluster of brick houses. On this small plot there are three straw
and mud huts. He hasn't lived there now for three years, since he

moved from Hindalga (where we now are) to Vijaynagar. His house in Vijaynagar is similar to the huts he has just pointed out. The only difference is that in Vijaynagar the dwellings aren't as cramped together. As he talks, he smiles a big wide-toothed grin. He's evidently remembering something pleasant about his life in Hindalga, or he's just plain happy to indicate a landmark of some importance in his personal history.

This is Meeda Mamma ("Uncle Basketweaver")—34 years old. He's in a good mood today, unlike the morning a few weeks ago when he told Suman and me : "I don't know what's happening. I never used to get depressed, but now I seem to get depressed all the time. It's nothing serious; it's just that I can't seem to let loose and laugh anymore. It worries me sometimes, but I try not to think about it too much."

Another Day. It's early evening. Suman and I have just walked back from Belgaum. On the way to our house, we stop in front of Meeda Mamma's hut to talk with him. His youngest child, a five and a half month old baby, is sick, and we want to know how he's doing. Meeda Mamma stands up, goes into the hut. Just inside the doorway, a gray woolen blanket is stretched out on the floor and the baby's lying on it crying. Meeda Mamma lifts the child up, cradling him in one arm, to show him to us. Then, kneeling down, with his free hand he points to two whitish blotches on the blanket. "He's still throwing up everything he eats," he says.

The baby isn't a pleasant sight. Five and a half months old and he's the size of a newborn: a small, emaciated, shriveled-up child, ugly from bad health. At birth the baby was normal and remained that way for about five months. Then, a few weeks ago, he got sick. At first, according to Meeda Mamma, he and his wife thought it was just a passing minor illness, and so they didn't pay much attention. But then it didn't go away and the child began to lose weight, fading away right before their eyes. Now they are scared. And if you look at the child you know why; it seems as if there is a good chance he's going to die.

By this time, Laxshmi, Meeda Mamma's wife, has come out. She says the sickness began when the shadow of a woman who was having her period fell on the child. She continues by claiming she and her husband have found a solution; they're planning to take the baby to a person in Hindalga who has a reputation for being able to diminish the negative effects of bad omens and evil spells. Suman replies that, yes, they should do that, but maybe they should also take him to a doctor in Belgaum: "Two places are better than one," she says. They agree. Meeda Mamma says that tomorrow he'll take the baby to a doctor. As we get ready to leave, I can't help but notice there's something forlorn-looking about Meeda Mamma. It has to do with the way he's standing in the hut's shadowy entranceway, cradling the baby in one arm and repeating that taking the child to a doctor is a good idea, but saying it with a look on his face that actually expresses something entirely different: that a heavy sad darkness has fallen on his life and he doesn't know if anything, now, will help.

   Two days later, late afternoon. Meeda Mamma comes to the house with two things, a manilla envelope and a small brown bottle. He has just come back from the doctor's (yesterday the office was closed). From the envelope he carefully removes an x-ray of the child's chest and shows it to us. He doesn't know if the x-ray reveals anything about the child's health, because the doctor took no time to explain it to him. Likewise with the medicine. He knows he's supposed to give the baby one spoonful six times a day, but he doesn't know what the medicine's for, again because the doctor didn't tell him. We aren't much help. The x-ray seems to be normal, but we aren't sure. As far as the medicine's concerned, the bottle label is half scraped off so it can't be read; the small fragment that remains says "of the liver," but beyond that there's no useable information. But Meeda Mamma didn't really come for additional information. He's confident that now that he's been to the doctor things will soon take a turn for the better. The impression of fatalistic despair that he gave two nights ago is gone. The very fact that he went to the doctor's, that he *acted,* seems to have resulted in a new assumption that fate can be transformed by human will. Later in the evening when we see Laxshmi, it's obvious that she also has adopted a new, more optimistic attitude.

   Two days go by. A week passes. The baby's holding down his food now, and he has also put on a little weight. The crisis seems to have passed. The child isn't going to die...

Every day Meeda Mamma and Laxshmi work; he weaves baskets, she does an endless array of household chores. But because Meeda Mamma's work is done at home, he participates in the household tasks when necessary. Frequently he can be seen watching the children or, if Laxshmi's busy or not feeling well, cooking a meal. Still, his basic work is basketweaving, hers is the house.

Almost any time between eight in the morning and six at night, you can stop in front of their house and talk to Meeda Mamma, who's crouched there working. He comes from a low-caste background. At most, he makes two hundred fifty rupees ($31) a month. If the cost of bamboo goes up, the amount he makes goes down.

Earlier I mentioned Meeda Mamma's concern with what he described as his growing depression. Part of this is due to the family's economic condition. But it would be wrong to trace his depression simply to financial problems. To understand Meeda Mamma and his sadness, we have to look more deeply into his character.

Like most people, Meeda Mamma is "philosophical." He has questions about the meaning of existence, about what determines the actual quality of an individual's life. These questions, or the answers to these questions, are never seen by him in an abstract, metaphysical way. Meaning, for Meeda Mamma, is a this-world phenomenon, discoverable in people's lives, in the flow of life. Because of this, and because he knows that he himself has nothing and is going nowhere, he inevitably wonders if his life is without meaning. One day when Laxshman (Holika's husband) is talking about the land his family lost when he was a child, Meeda Mamma butts in and says with a certain aggressiveness, "Nobody in my family ever had anything to lose." Then he immediately becomes quiet, staring off into space. He's mulling something over in his mind, trying to come to grips with something he feels deeply. As you spend more time with Meeda Mamma, you realize that such moments are typical, moments of an inward-turning meditativeness over which he seems to have little control.

Meeda Mamma's first wife killed herself by jumping in a well. He mentioned this once, as if by accident, but never again. This, along with his father's recent death, has apparently left it's imprint on him, providing at least a partial explanation for his moods as well as for the kind of fatalism he initially felt when confronted with his baby's illness.

But personal grief, although it undeniably stimulates his thoughts about life's meaning, isn't the sole source of such thoughts. This is so for the simple reason that what he observes happening to himself, personally, he also observes happening all around him, generally. Seeing himself as not significantly different or better off than his parents, he has to face the fact that his life replicates fairly closely the lives of those around him, not just those in his family but people in the village where he grew up, then in Hindalga and now in Vijaynagar. Although the seasons change and different crops are sown and harvested, although sometimes the price of a cartload of bamboo is better than at other times, the quality of life doesn't seem to change. The rhythm seems monotonous, deadening, without hope. This is why, when Meeda Mamma is feeling especially down, he says, "Life is a trap for everyone I know." This isn't merely an expression of a unique, eccentric, personal grief. It is larger and more overflowing and truth-containing than that. It springs from a world view firmly rooted in the day-to-day world Meeda Mamma is part of.

And yet, for all this, Meeda Mamma isn't at all an immobilized, passive, inactive man. Given his limited options, he cuts a fairly heavy-stepping path through the world. He finds relaxation and contentment in his work, believing that he has a "special touch" when it comes to weaving baskets and mats. This isn't only his private view; people consider him a good craftsman and also trustworthy.

Meeda Mamma also has another antidote for his depression. In his head, he makes plans for his children. "I'm going to give them all a good education," he says. "I'm going to do everything I can to help them. I'm going to do this because I've promised it to myself. And when they grow up and have been to school, they'll discover what it is that makes so many people suffer. And then they'll change the world."

This, of course, is a dream, not entirely realistic. But it is also a signal of will and persistance.

Shamabai

Shamabai has two children, a boy three and a girl six. Another daughter, who would be eight now, died two years ago. Her husband Ram, who used to be an agricultural laborer, recently got a job as an unskilled worker in a textile mill. The mill is on Vengrula Road, not far from Vijaynagar. Shamabai and Ram live in a hut the size of a small cowshed behind the mill. Unlike many rural women, Shamabai doesn't work in the fields. Occasionally, but not regularly, she does part-time domestic work for a local landowning family. For Shamabai and Ram, their present financial situation is luxurious compared to what it was before he got the mill job. They now live on two hundred and twenty five rupees ($28) a month.

Shamabai has some negative feelings about her marriage. She feels that, other than being sexually aggressive, her husband pays little attention to her. One of the consequences of this is that a few months ago she decided being sterilized might be a good idea. She developed this attitude after some local Family Planning people approached her and explained what they felt were the advantages of such an operation. After she talked to them a second time, it was agreed that a tubal ligation would be done after the completion of her present pregnancy. They didn't, however, explain to her anything about alternative methods of contraception. "I don't want anymore children," Shamabai says flatly, "after this one we'll have enough." Also involved is the fact that getting sterilized will limit the need for sexual contact with her husband. In this small way, at least, she will have some control over their relationship. In all other areas, she's resigned to sticking with the marriage more or less as it is. "He's not a bad man," she says, "he's just trapped. He's always tired, worn out."

This morning as Shamabai was walking up the hill to the road into town, she met a peasant woman named Malu. Seeing Malu made her a little anxious, because there was something she'd been wanting to talk to Malu about and she didn't know how the woman would take it. Shamabai's daughter Saluchana had complained that Malu's daughters had been teasing her lately and wouldn't stop. One result of this was that the girl didn't want to go out of the house alone anymore. Shamabai wanted to tell all this to Malu, but knowing Malu could have a fiery temper, she was hesitant. Maybe she'd get defensive and start screaming, Shamabai thought. Still, meeting Malu on the path, she decided to tell her what was on her mind. Unfortunately, Shamabai's fears came true: Malu was completely unsympathetic. But that wasn't all. Malu got angry and told Shamabai that if she didn't shut up things would get worse. She also said some great calamity was going to befall Shamabai and shatter her life.

Late this afternoon Shamabai told Suman:

When she (Malu) gets angry like that, it's as if she grows a second set of long sharp teeth. Then she bites and tears and does whatever she can to attack. I told her: 'Malu, why are you getting so angry at me like this? We're only talking about the children; you shouldn't get so vicious. I was just wondering if you knew that your daughters were teasing Saluchana.' But she still wouldn't listen. So then I said: 'Look, sometimes I do the work of a servant in people's houses. You and your daughters do the same kind of work; we shouldn't be yelling at each other. Why should we be so angry? We should be friends; we have so much in common. It's not right for you to go crazy with me. It's those others you should be getting angry at if you have to get angry.' That's what I told her. But she wasn't in the mood to listen, so we left each other. I didn't find out if she knew why her daughters were teasing Saluchana.

But that wasn't all Shambai told Suman. She also said:

It's true that if you look at it right, we're all nothing but servants. Because of this we shouldn't be arguing with each other but should be arguing with the people who've made us servants. If I have to work for people, I work for them, but I don't try to talk to them or be friendly with them. Why should I? They're not interested in me, just my work. Even you, although I don't work for you, I didn't know you a few months ago and so there's the question of why I should talk to you. But you came to me, and so we got to know each other a little. If somebody's willing to come into my house, sit

on the floor, treat me as if they don't think they own
me, then even if I'm uncertain at first about what they
want from me, I'll give it a chance, see what happens.
But even that's not enough. In the end, it's only if
people think alike that they can have any kind of
friendship. Other than that, the safest thing to do is to
stick to those you are sure of.

Narayan Ativedikar

The room's small, about twelve by nine. We're eating,
sitting on the floor, our backs against the wall. Round stainless
steel plates, piled with food, are on the floor in front of us.

While the meal goes on, Narayan Ativedikar, who is sitting
next to me, is eating and talking at the same time. He's in the
middle of a diatribe against the devotees of a local goddess,
Yellamma, whose main temple is about sixty miles from here in
the hill-village of Saundatti.

Just recently one of the low caste families from
Ambavadi married their daughter to Yellamma. Year
after year this same kind of thing goes on. Now
marrying your daughter to the goddess, that's an
interesting thing. You know what happens? The
priest, knowing that this young child has been given to
the goddess and will therefore never be married to a
man and have a family, remembers her. When she
comes of age, when her menstrual cycle starts, he sends
one of his agents to her and she's taken and given to
some upper class gentleman for his use. The family
doesn't object because their daughter's sexual degradation is, in their superstitious minds, somehow connected with service to the goddess. Then, after the girl
has been used by a number of these upper class people
and her youth has wilted, the priest and his agent and
the men who've used her lose their interest in her. At
this point, her life spoiled, the girl migrates to some
city and becomes the companion of prostitutes, selling
her services where she can. Once in the city, the
original religious thinking behind her degradation

fades away. The only thing left for her now is the life of the street and the cheap bed and an endless variety of men who couldn't care less for her, except to use her briefly for their own pleasure...

Narayan's a thin man in his late forties. There's a strange contrast between his surprisingly boyish face and his pure silver hair, shiny with oil. But there's nothing boyish about the well-informed seriousness he brings to the two main questions at hand: superstition and the government's failure, over the last thirty years, to live up to its promise to educate people. Stuffing some food in his mouth, he continues talking:

It's not the people's fault, the fact that they're superstitious. Thirty years ago the government promised it would get rid of illiteracy. And today, all these years later, seventy percent of the people are still illiterate. With hardly anyone able to read or write or understand anything other than the daily drudgery of their lives, what else can you expect? People are gripped by a thousand fears. You go out into the fields and what do you see? In the corner of each field there's a stone with some *kum-kum* on it, and somewhere in the village there's an old grandmother or grandfather who swears that the stone in their particular field has magical powers. The only answer to these superstitions is education, and the government hasn't been able to provide it. It hasn't been able to provide education, and it hasn't been able to provide much of anything else either. It gets you angry; after a while you begin to feel like you'd do *anything* to change things. The other day I read in the local paper that one of our government ministers, who's abroad in either Europe or America, said that India is in the process of making important changes. When I read it, I wondered what India he was talking about. It certainly wasn't the one I live in. Anyone who lives here can see how mired down the people are, how the wretchedness, rather than decreasing, increases, or at best stays the same...

Narayan is a local, not very well known writer, who prides himself in writing about serious issues. Last year he wrote a play that won some recognition, or maybe the better word for it is infamy. It was an attack on superstition, and some of the people in the area thought it was too anti-traditional. When it was performed in Ambavadi, it caused an uproar and Narayan found himself simultaneously attacked and praised.

Narayan isn't the only one in his family who has strong beliefs. So does his wife, Indu. For instance, when Yellamma devotees come to the door looking for donations, she tells them to go away, that she has no use for them. "If the goddess is in you, that's fine," she says, "because the goddess is in all of us. Now go away and leave me alone." The result of such behavior and of the fact that she enjoys acting in Narayan's plays is that Indu has had to learn to deal with some open hostility from certain individuals within the community. At one time the situation developed to the point where even going to the well to draw water could culminate in harsh words and bad feelings. But she has been able to handle it, she insists. To Suman she says: "At first I didn't believe in these things as deeply as my husband. But as time went on, I began to understand and respect what he was doing. Now, although it isn't always easy, I have similar goals."

One aspect of Narayan's character that Indu especially respects is his attitude toward women. She says he has an honestly high regard for them and believes in their equality. "This carries over into his writing," she adds. "When he writes, he refuses to do what so many of the famous writers do: make women into stupid creatures or treat them as if the only interesting thing about their lives is the sexual part."

Both Narayan and Indu come from poor backgrounds. When he was growing up in Ambavadi, his family lived off the produce from one acre of land. Now his father and older brother work three acres between them, but, he says, it's difficult for them to survive. As the younger brother, he considers it his duty to help out, and so he gives them a small amount of money each month. The money doesn't come from his writing, from which he makes nothing. It comes from his teaching (he has a high school education and teaches grammar school) as well as two other sources of family income. One of these other income sources is the small sewing jobs he and Indu do for people. The other one is a shop they operate out of the front room of their three room house. In this shop they sell cooking oil, biscuits, puffed rice, candy and cigarettes. The shop is always thinly stocked, and what stock they do have is kept in makeshift boxlike wooden cupboards. The shop area is very small, about eight feet square. All told, their income is about three hundred rupees ($38) a month. Although they aren't wealthy, they make ends meet. They don't complain.

When questioned about the anger stirred up against him by certain local priests and landlords who feel threatened by hs attacks on superstition and feudal social structures, Narayan responds: "What can you do? You learn to live with it."

He sums up his personal ambitions by saying, "I want to do something good for society."

Rebelling Against a Tradition: Raja and the Priest

A loud drumming sound comes from somewhere in the village. Adriana and Nikos, who've been playing outside, run into the house. Adriana yells: "A man's going from house to house swinging a stick and telling people he wants money. There's a woman with him and she's banging a drum. Come see!"

Suman and I go with the children. A little beyond Meeda Mamma's hut, in an open space at the center of the village, there's a group of about thirty people. They've gathered around a man who's sitting on the ground. His face and bare chest are smeared with yellow *haldi*. Next to him is a box, about four feet square, painted with religious symbols. It's a portable temple. The door's open and inside is a red-painted *devi* or goddess. In front of the man and the *devi* are gifts for the goddess that have been placed there by some of the villagers. The gifts include rice and grain as well as two saris.

One of the *devi's* wooden arms is stretched forward, hand open, palm downward. The man encourages a young girl to sit in front of the goddess, and to hold her small hand under the *devi's* hand. As the girl does this, the man's female companion (she's sitting behind him on the ground) begins beating both ends of her two-ended drum with sticks. She also starts chanting, as does the man. Suddenly from a tiny trap door in the goddess's palm, a coin drops into the little girl's hand. The *devi*, supposedly, has blessed her. The priest then tells the girl to go and encourages another villager, a man named Raja, to take her place.

Unshaven Raja, in his blue cotton shirt, squats on the ground in front of the *devi*. The same process is repeated as with the child, except that no coin appears in his hand. The priest says to him, "Do you want to know why you didn't get anything?" Raja looks at him cynically (he also looks around at the crowd, either in search of support or in order to make sure everyone's ready for what he's about to say) and replies: "No, I'm not interested. I thought if I could get a few *paise* (pennies) fine, but since I didn't, that's fine too. I guess your piece of wood just didn't like me, that's all."

Predictably, the priest doesn't like Raja's response. Even so, the animosity of his reply is startling. "Listen to me, friend," he says. "At some point in your life, you promised the goddess something big, maybe a thousand rupees. You broke your vow, and she's angry with you. You have to live up to your promise, or her anger will grow. Today she refused to give you a few *paise*, but tomorrow her resentment will take another form. You have children; they will all die. You'll be left with no son to cremate you, to oversee your passage into the other world. I suggest you make up for your previous lack of responsibility. Live up to your vow; give the goddess the rupees you promised.

With a certain amount of self-assurance, Raja answers: "I never made any promise to the *devi*. I never had anything to give and I still don't and I would've had to be crazy to promise. Leave me alone."

"But maybe it wasn't you," the priest persists. "Maybe it was your mother or father or one of their mothers or fathers. Now the job of fulfilling the promise has fallen on you. It makes no difference if it wasn't you yourself who made the original promise. What makes a difference is that you're the one who'll have to suffer if the vow isn't kept."

"But I don't have anything to give. This is foolish."

"Are you so selfish, so willing to let your children die, just because you aren't willing to share even the little you have with the *devi*? If you don't have a thousand rupees, she'll understand. But there must be something you can give, some saris maybe, or maybe you could give one of your children to the goddess. I would watch the child in the goddess's behalf."

At this point, although Raja's initial bravado has been somewhat shaken by the priest's prediction that his children will die, he angrily gets up and leaves, having refused to give in."

Intermittently throughout the dialogue, the priest's companion has been banging her drum and singing. When Raja leaves, the priest also begins singing. His tightly braided ponytail swings back and forth, as his head sways in rhythm to the music. Then he invites someone else to sit down before the *devi*. A young woman in a lime-green sari steps forward and sits down. The crowd has grown sparser now, mostly teenage girls and a few children. There are only a few adults.

The drummer continues playing. She seems only half conscious of what's going on, as if she has been through all this too many times to remember or care. While she plays the drum, her baby, wearing a little hat kept on by a string tied under the chin, sucks at her breast.

Meanwhile the woman in the lime-green sari waits for some money to drop from the *devi's* wooden hand.

TWO PLACES
DAMBAVADI AND THE HUTMENT COLONY

Dambavadi

A stony dirt path passes in front of our house, circles around the house next to us, then winds its way toward the top of the hill. On the ridge at the top of the hill, there's a road. A short distance down this road is the Dambavadi section of Ganeshpur.

Dambavdi means "place of the gypsies." The people who live in Dambavdi resent the name that has been given to their area of Ganeshpur. Beginning with their ancestors, they've been settled here for over a hundred years. They see no reason why, as a group, they should be referred to as a rootless, gypsy-like people, especially when the Marathi phrase "Dambavadi" contains a direct connotation of disdain, disapproval. It's bad enough, they say, that they have all they can do to eke out a wretched economic existence; but to have piled on top of this the implication that their poverty is somehow their own fault, a result of their gypsy-like natures, is an insult that has no basis in reality. Gypsies, they say, don't sink roots in a single place looking for stability, security, order.

Dambavdi consists of two hundred and fifty families. Out of these, only fifteen men have regular employment. The others work part time, usually for no more than six months out of the year. The kind of work they do is low-skilled manual labor; road repair work, digging sewage ditches, agricultural labor. When unemployed, many of the men make wallhangings out of boar and deer antlers. They do this by hollowing the horns out, filling them with wood shavings, polishing them and then mounting them on square boards covered with red cloth. They try to sell these wallhangings for ten rupees ($1.25) a piece, but at best they only sell a few. The men also keep pigs which they feed and fatten, then sell to local Christians who, unlike most Hindus and all Muslims, eat pork.

The actual breadwinners in Dambavadi are the women. They have a year-long, day-to-day reliable profession: begging and scavaging. By eight o'clock every morning, they're out on their rounds. Most go into the city, Belgaum, where in small groups of two or three they follow particular pre-planned routes, which include stops at certain houses and shops where they can depend on getting handouts, either loose change or foodscraps. Some of the women don't beg but instead scavenge for recyclable items: old tin cans, broken glass, bits of wire, paper. The scavenging routes are less pre-planned and more anarchic than the begging routes. Groups of women wander through the city, or through the villages surrounding the city, exploring the ground for whatever they think they can sell. Anything they find is put in baskets balanced on their heads. When the baskets are filled, they take what they've gathered to a junkyard man in town who buys it from them. When the day's work of begging and scavenging is done, the women return to the village, draw water from the well, cook the evening meal and go to sleep.

The next day the same routine occurs.

The people of Dambavadi feel their efforts to survive occur in a vacuum, with relatively little outside help or reinforcement. They consider themselves, in the words of one woman, "forgotten people." The villagers use the local school as an example of the superficial nature of government intervention in their lives. One man says: "The school exists more on paper than it does in the actual life of the village, if you know what I mean. The teacher doesn't live here, and she hardly ever comes to class on time. What work the kids do isn't done well, and they don't learn much. What's even worse than this, though, is that there are kids who've gotten up to a sixth grade education and yet this hasn't at all improved, as the government has said it would, their chances of getting a job. School or no school, able to read or not able to read, most of the people here remain without work."

A woman, continuing the conversation, says: "Some of the men at times get angry at us women because when we go begging we take the kids along with us rather than sending them to school. But what's the use of school if it doesn't come to anything, if it doesn't, like he says, help you get jobs. So we think it's better to teach them, from a young age, our profession which is begging. If we send them to school, they'll only end up not knowing what it's like to beg, and then they won't have any way to support themselves or their families when they grow up. What's the use of that? If they don't know how to beg, they won't be able to live. It's that simple."

As if to underscore the fact that the school is a meaningless phenomenon for the children of Dambavadi, one morning the schoolteacher (a young middle class woman) asks Suman and me: "Why do you come here to this place anyway? The people here are dirty and worthless. There are so many better things you could be doing with your time."

Not surprisingly, the people are emotional about their situation. One man says: "You know, the people who live here are very angry, but because of the way things are we don't even have the strength to protest. But even worse than this anger we feel is the fact that they've made us feel ashamed. We feel like nothing, like worse than nothing, like a string of shit hanging from a child's ass. But even if we had the strength, who would we protest to?" Then, pointing to a wooded area on the other side of the road that borders the village, he continues: "You see that land? It's owned by the ex-Raja of Savantwadi. I know that this man became rich not by being a good person, but by being a bastard. Yet what can we do? If one of our pigs wanders across the road and strays onto his land, he has a servant shoot the pig. If he does this to pigs, what would he do to us if we dared to go on his land? He has the gun and so he has all the power. We have none."

Regularly spending time with the people here, one hears a
lot. Always, more flesh is being added to the picture of what the
quality of life is like. For instance, one morning Suman talks to a
woman who's dressed in a torn dirt-stained sari. In the course of
the conversation, which is a long rambling one, the woman tells
this story:

Well, you see, my life's hard, but it wasn't always that
way. Up until two years ago I had it fairly good. My
husband had a regular job and I didn't have to go out
begging. I stayed home, did the work that had to be
done there and also did small jobs around the village,
like making bricks. But then something happened to
my husband's head, and he quit his job and refused to
work anymore, So, the little money we once had was
gone. But that wasn't the worst part. What was worse
was how he started acting toward me. He started
beating me. Once he even threw me inside the house
and said he was going to soak everything with
kerosene and burn the house down with me in it. I was
terrified. He'd lost his mind. He kept walking around
the village saying he would never work again, it wasn't
worth it. I went to a man in the village who's
sometimes helpful in such matters. I asked him what I
should do. I was very scared. This man—his name's
Prakash—said he would talk to my husband and find
out if there was anything that could be done. But when
Prakash went to see him, my husband pulled out a
knife and told Prakash he would kill him if he didn't
leave right away. Prakash says he's certain my husband
would have slashed him if he hadn't left. So he left. I
tried adjusting to this new life, but it was impossible. I
couldn't go on living with this man who was always
threatening me and beating me and screaming crazily
that he would never work again. It was a big decision
for me to make but I made it; I left him. With some
relatives, I built a hut and then moved in with my two
children. It was then that I started going out and
searching for things to fill my basket with. There
wasn't any other way I could live. But it was hard for

me at first, and I couldn't get used to it. My head was always filled with sad thoughts. I wanted to die. Then a day came when I decided to kill myself. I had it all planned. I would go with my two children under my arms and jump in the well. That would be the end of all of us, and at last my head would have a rest. But the other women in the village figured something was wrong. They came to me and got me to tell them what I was thinking of doing. They said it was impossible, that I couldn't do such a thing. They told me the time hadn't yet come for me to die, and that if it had, I would be dead. And they warned me that if my time hadn't come and I still tried to kill myself, something horrible would happen. I might survive and the children might die. Something like that. I listened to them and changed my mind. Now it's easier for me, although it's still a difficult life.

A difficult life.

The images can be gathered up by the handful.

Example: A typical house. Two tiny rooms. The first room is a living area. This opens up into the second room, a small kitchen and storage area. Sniffing the ground for food scraps, a baby pig wanders into the kitchen through the back door. Six people live here, two adults and four children. The man has a blood spitting cough. He is dying of tuberculosis.

Example: It's noon. On one of Dambavadi's dusty lanes, a drunk asks me for a cigarette. When I give it to him, he points up at the sky, toward the sun, and says: "For thousands of years that same sun has burned down on my ancestors. My ancestors were great warriors. But me, I'm what's left over. Nothing."

Example: A bunch of kids play around a pile of dead ashes. One of them, a boy around seven years old, wears a dust-browned white t-shirt. One forlorn word is printed vertically down the front of the shirt in red letters: LEADER. Where he got the shirt, who knows? The image has a strangely ironic, even almost prophetic quality.

Example: A woman, a two year old child clawing at the hem of her sari, pulls a bucket of water up out of the seventy foot deep well. As she tugs on the rope, her face is tilted slightly upward, drenched with sunlight. There are beads of perspiration on her brow. The child's crying. When she finally gets the bucket all the way up, she pours the water into a brass vessel. Another woman helps her put the vessal on her head, then hands her the sobbing child so she can carry him on her hip. She walks off: erect posture, back perfectly straight. She and her husband and three children live on four rupees ($.50) a day.

But there is something more here than simply the poverty. If you hang out long enough, coming back day after day, week after week, you begin to feel it. The people are tough. They've weathered too many storms to be continually cringing. They swear freely and don't show "proper respect for authority." And the humor is bawdy, down to earth, blunt, never decorated with niceties. When quarreling with the men, the women call themselves "ripe fruits" and refer to the men as "dried up, shriveled vegetables." Everybody laughs, and then the jokes get dirtier as a sort of community contest begins to determine who can come up with the best, most taste-shaking, one-liners. The air is filled with a raw egalitarianism.

The people of Dambavadi have a certain spirit. Even beaten down, they feel that they've retained a secret connection to life. Giving up isn't their idea of good sense. To them, eking out a living means learning how to be canny, shrewd, oily enough to slip through the tiniest loopholes in a social contract that's obviously stacked against them.

And while all this is going on, they have things to think about.

"See that land over there?" a man asks, pointing to the sugarcane fields beyond the village's north border. "There was a time when some of us owned part of that property. Just a little, but at least some. But in order to grow crops the right way, you need money. So we borrowed. That was the end. No one could pay back their debts on time, so in a fairly short time the land went to the person who had loaned us the money: Patil, the landlord. Now he grows sugarcane, while we sit here and look at it."

The Hutment Colony

To get up the embankment, Suman and I first have to cross a narrow sewage ditch. To do this, we step on a stone in the middle of brownish green water, then jump to the other side. As we cross the ditch, a water buffalo is to our right, sunk up to its knees in the sewage, head down slurping.

Finally we come to the top of the embankment, to the railroad tracks. From here we can look around. On the other side of the tracks, down the embankment's far slope, there's a large field. In the middle, there's a pond of muddy water; some children are playing in it. To both the pond's left and right there are crude tent-like structures in which people live.

We go down the embankment toward the huts on the left. When we get there, it stinks. Pig as well as human shit, swarming with flies, is on the ground near the dwellings. Once here, you feel the rush of an odd current—life at the economy's edge. Then you take one more step and you're smack in the middle of the hutment-colony world.

It's midday. Blazing sun. People are up and about. Children run and scream. Babies cry. In one spot, a young woman in a red sari talks emotionally to a laughing man who seems to be teasing her.

Worlds within worlds. Little human dramas. Work.

There's a hut. Like all the others, it has a pup tent structure and is made of pieces of burlap and cloth sewn together and held in place by a bamboo frame. Inside, a man's chiseling an animal horn into the shape of some kind of water bird with a long beak and long, thin legs. He's sitting crosslegged, and white shavings from the horn are on his knees as well as on the dirt floor. The hut's about eight feet long and four feet wide and only about five feet in height. The man's sitting near the entrance in a shaft of sunlight. At the hut's other end, barely visible in the windowless darkness, is a young boy, maybe four years old. He's eating rice and some yellow-colored *dahl* off a tin plate. Occasionally he takes a swipe at a fly with his hand.

In at least three quarters of the other huts, men are also at work carving.

For instance here's a man in a dirty white turban. He has a thick, grey, drooping mustache. With his teenage son, he's sitting on the ground immediately outside his hut's entrance. As he works, he talks, commenting on the world and the plight of the people he knows. He smiles frequently, a broad grand-fatherly smile suggestive of an indestructible optimism. When we ask him about government land grants to the poor, he says, matter-of-factly, that the land program has been mostly a failure. "Some people have gotten land, I guess," he explains, "but others like myself and the rest of the people living here, haven't. The whole process has been no good. If you want land, you still have to pay a high price for it, but now you don't pay the landlord, you pay the government official."

Other than the son he's working with, he says, he has six children: four daughters, all married, and two more sons, one blind. He also comments that the people in this part of the squatters' settlement all come from the same tribe, somewhere in Goa. But he isn't sure of the exact history, because "nothing's written down, and so knowledge of where we came from and why is disappearing." All the while he's talking, he and his son are polishing animal horns with rough-surfaced leaves soaked in water. They're readying them for carving. Their hands, pushing the leaves, slide up and down the curved lengths of horn, scraping the dullness away and slowly bringing out a slight sheen.

And so the work of the hutment colony continues.

But there are also other people, not carving. Here's a woman. Her name is Leena. She has been living in the settlement now for fourteen years. Three months ago she had her fourth child. In terms of her life, Leena has many stories to tell. One such anecdote has to do with a quarrel she recently had with a shopowner in the city's military district. Another has to do with the on-going nature of what it's like, day after day, to gnaw the few pieces of stale *bhakeri* you get after hours of begging. As she relates these things, she's friendly and unaggressive, yet there's a sign of bitterness in her voice. She emphasizes that she lives in a world without choices, where you have to take whatever you get.

As she talks, off to our right, two pigs begin squealing angrily, evidently fighting over some food. I turn just in time to see someone's foot fly forward and kick one of the pigs in the ribs, driving it off.

We talk to Leena awhile more, then go. As we're leaving, she runs ahead of us to her hut and comes out with her baby. Standing on the opposite side of the low-roofed dwelling, she lifts the child up so we can see her. The woman and the child are facing directly into the sun. The woman's mouth is a bright, wet red from the mixture of tobacco and betel nut she's chewing. Turning sideways to spit on the ground, some of the juice dribbles down her chin. As we walk away, she waves goodby.

We skirt the marshy area that surrounds the pond and go to the other part of the settlement. Here the tent-like structures are more spread out, and there's more open space. A number of women are sitting or crouched in front of their huts sewing quilts from old sections of cloth. Thin dogs, tied to stakes in the ground, bark as we approach.

This area of the settlement's larger than the other one: about eighty huts, more people. We stop to talk with a woman who's sewing. About a third of the settlement's population gather around, curious to find out what's going on. At first, a few of the children and one or two of the adults start begging. As the conversation continues, though, the begging stops. People either listen to what's being said or, if they feel the need, begin shouting so they can be heard over the voice of whoever else happens to be speaking at the moment. Everyone wants to get in on the dialogue. They discipline the children, telling them to stand back and stop making noise so the grownups can talk.

The tone here is shriller than on the other side of the pond—more heated, angrier. In the course of the discussion, the sewing woman becomes the primary articulator of the settlement's collective opinions. That what she says is representative is evidenced by the fact that the others make various hand and head gestures to signal their approval, obviously proud of their friend's ability to speak so directly and without fear. Gradually a story is pieced together.

The place where the settlement is located is a lousy place to live, the woman says. From June through August, during the rainy season, the field becomes one huge puddle, and they have to move their huts closer to the tracks where the ground level's higher. But even there they aren't safe, since rain water is continually pouring down the side of the embankment. But they aren't a defeated people, in spite of what the world has tried to do to them, the sewing woman emphasizes. Proudly she adds that their tribe was originally based in the Kohlapur area, and that all of the people here are direct descendents of King Shivaji, who used to rule all of southern India. Pointing to the far side of the pond, to the other, smaller section of the settlement, she says: "Those are the real gypsies; they're low caste makeshifts. But not us. We're the children of Shivaji."

But she doesn't spend much time concentrating on what's obviously a long-standing clan rivalry between the two parts of the settlement. She redirects her energy toward the vast "they" of the "outside" world: the officials and bureaucrats of India's government. When she speaks of them, her loathing is unfeigned and scathing. "They don't care what happens to people like us, not the least bit," she claims. "What they really want is that all the poor people should die. That way they wouldn't have any problems with us. Us dead, dead as possible, that's the only thing that would make them feel good. But as you can see, we don't like dying, not if we can help it."

By this time a slight tension's in the air, something diffuse stirred up by the conversation. The sewing woman's thin hardboned face appears to say it silently for them all. "If you're gonna come down into the pits," her look seems to imply, "then don't expect any fancy poetry, just bluntness, since that's all you're gonna get." Throughout the discussion there's been a definite element of aggressiveness in her honesty, a sort of daring, an insistent refusal to soften the ragged edges of her opinions.

The message is clear: strangers with unknown motives, who wander through the encampment asking questions, aren't going to be treated with any special decorum.

When we leave, there's no escaping the feeling that in the hutment colony, at the bottom of the railroad embankment, there's a live fuse that even the monsoon rains won't be able to extinguish once it's lit.

DIFFERENT WORLDS

Wherever you go, one thing is striking: there's no absence of articulateness.

Take Ganesh as an example. Ganesh is a clerk in a machine shop. He took this job after retiring from the army as a sergeant. He's fifty-two years old and about five feet five inches tall. His confident, rapid way of talking is in contrast with his unhealthy, jaundiced-looking eyes. As he speaks, his open left hand slices the air: quick, nervous, brief cuts that punctuate what he's saying. Coming originally from an extremely poor background, Ganesh communicates, while talking, a stoical pride in the fact that the little he now has is the direct result of his own hard work and his commitment to providing for his wife and children. Yet he also knows, and says, that the road to "real" success has been blocked to him. He feels that what he has has been torn from the teeth of a resisting society. Like many Indians, he talks easily about his personal problems. But, also like many Indians, his vision of his personal life isn't that it's unique in an individualistic way, but rather that it's representative of the lives of many others. Because of this, he sees himself as typical of a majority of Indians: economically disenfranchised, trapped in the lower levels of society, born to struggle (and only be partially successful) against enormous odds.

His attitude toward the Independence Movement in the pre-1947 period is that it was a good, hard, worthwhile struggle, but that its basic premise—giving India back to the Indians—was contradictory from the start. He stresses that this became especially clear after independence was actually achieved.

For the first ten years after independence, people were willing to wait as the government, under the leadership of the Congress Party, attempted to reorganize the country. But it soon became obvious that although the government was doing what it could to modernize the country, by bringing new farming techniques and electricity into the villages and also by encouraging the growth of industry, it was doing very little in terms of actually bettering the lives of the poor people who are a large majority of the population. Power and wealth remained in the hands of only a small group. If on the one side you had the landlords losing a little (but only a little) of their power in the farming areas, then on the other side you had the birth of a new group of industrialists who had control over industry and the profits that came from that part of the economy. It soon became clear that India wasn't controlled by the Indian people, but rather by a club of rich Indians. It was their needs, not ours, that were being satisfied.

Throughout our conversation, Ganesh is extremely energetic and determined to make himself clear. He seems obsessed with guaranteeing that what he says isn't misunderstood as a series of merely personal—and therefore "uninformed"—grievances. He wants the outsider to know that what he's saying isn't whimsical but is grounded in reality. Another interesting characteristic of his is that in spite of the fact that he belongs to no political group and therefore has no particular sectarian ideology to proselytize, he has the passion, the concrete analysis and the phrase-turning ability of the most confirmed grassroots activist. Ganesh: the ordinary man, politically conscious.

In India the situation is bad. The poor remain poor, and the fact is that many of them are worse off now than they were a few years ago. There's no price-control, and the cost of food keeps going up. On top of this, the black market is still a major problem. Even in a good year, when the crops are plentiful, many crops are hidden away from the people who need them the most and then are black-marketed later for huge profits.

Whichever way you turn, you find no concern for the average man, the average woman. Use land reform as example. The government comes along and says to a landless peasant: "Here's a small plot of land for you to farm. The government is generous; it wants you to work and survive." But at the same time that it says this, the government does nothing at all to insure that this transaction will, in the end, turn out all right. And what happens? The peasant's happy for two days, the thrill of owning land briefly filling his life. Then on the third day he realizes he has none of the farming implements—tools, bullock, etc.—necessary for working the land. All this time the local landlord in his big house has his eye on this peasant. He knows that soon enough the peasant will have to come to him to borrow money, which he'll then lend the peasant at a very high rate of interest. Then when the peasant can't pay the money back, the landlord takes over the land. This is what land reform has meant in India. The government, knowing full well what it's doing, has chosen to be superficial, to change things on paper by passing new laws without attempting to change the basic social inequality which insures that, in the end, the laws will fail.

For thirty years now the national government has shown itself completely incapable of solving the country's problems. For how many years have they been putting money into agriculture? And do you think this means that people now have enough to eat? No, of course not. Also, they've allowed corruption to eat into every part of society. Getting a good job, for instance, is impossible. My son went to apply for a position in the bank as a clerk, but they wanted him to pay them twelve thousand rupees [$1500] for the privilege of getting a job there. Now who can afford twelve thousand? But even if you pay the bribe, there's still no guarantee the job will be given. Anyway, he didn't get the job, and so now he's gone into the army like I did before him. This is the way it is all over, asking for bribes. Maybe for somebody who knows his way around important places, getting work or living well isn't such a big problem. But for people like me it's often impossible. That's how it is all over the country; if you want a good job, you have to pay for it. Corruption is the crown on the head of India.

Later, I ask him how he thinks all this can be corrected. Without fanfare, he says: "Listen, since I've been talking to you so freely, I'll tell you what my own personal opinion is. The only way things will change is through revolution. A bloody revolution."

When I ask him if he can elaborate a little, he replies: "What I'm talking about is a vast people's revolution, a revolution that throws all the government officials in jail and that disregards the existing political parties and puts control of the country into the hands of regular people. This is the only kind of revolution that will do anyone any good. The only way things will change is in this way: the people raising up their different voices into one single cry and taking for themselves what rightly belongs to them."

When I ask if there are others who feel like him, he moves his hand in a gesture as if it were sweeping across the whole of the land and says: "Yes, there are many. All over."

But, in spite of Ganesh's confident analysis, not everyone shares his concerns. The longer you're here the clearer it becomes that depending on who you talk to, depending on what economic class they're from, you get a particular version of what the caliber of life is like. In the countryside, the stories of the poorer peasants and the laborers are likely to share certain common perceptions, as are the stories of more well-off peasants and landlords. And in the city there's a similar phenomenon. Certain basic attitudes are held by industrialists, wealthy merchants and professionals. In contrast to this are the stories of the workers or of the owners of small thinly-stocked shops, stories that tend to be characterized by despair over an economy and a form of social organization that have increasingly shown themselves incapable of meeting the needs of the common person.

One of the ways to detect the difference between the rich and the poor is in the symptoms of a continuing colonialism. Classical colonialism is certainly dead; the British were sent back to England in 1947. Yet we live in the age of what has been called neocolonialism—the "new" colonialism. No longer do the western colonial powers, led by the U.S., rely for their power on the establishment of colonial administrations within the dominated countries. Instead, through multinational corporations as well as through selected agencies like the United States Information Service (USIS) and the Agency for International Development (AID), significant control is gained over key sectors of the indigenous economy as well as over the development of a "modern" culture. This process of westernization, of continuing psychological as well as economic dependence on the west, can be seen in the way the more privileged sectors of Indian society talk and behave.

An example. It's noon. I'm in the house of a man who runs an electronics plant. At the moment I'm involved in a conversation with his friend, a visitor from out of town who owns another electronics plant somewhere to the north, in the adjoining state of Maharasthra. In the middle of our dialogue, he interrupts what he's saying in order to introduce me to a young woman, twenty-two years old. She's his niece, Leela. He wants to know if it would be possible for her to attend school in the U.S. He encourages her to speak for herself, to let me know her aspirations, her ambitions. "This is your chance," he says to her, "maybe our friend here will be able to give you some advice."

In impeccable English, with a noticeable private school polish, she tells me that she's an economics major at college and that at the conclusion of the present school year she'll receive her B.A. Then she proceeds to talk about her future. She says she wants

to go abroad and continue my studies I think it is important that I broaden my understanding of the world, not just in terms of academic work, but also from the standpoint of gaining greater sophistication. This is why I would prefer to go to America. It is the center of world activity. If I can go there, I would like to study business administration. Then when I return to India—and after I have been married—I might be able to manage one of the smaller factories that supply my father's larger units with parts. My mother has just recently begun to do this herself, and I also would like to aim for such a goal. But I would like not to have to wait until middle age to begin. I want to start earlier, and with all the advantages that living in America will have given me: a modern sense of the world, advanced ideas on how to run a business, and all the rest. This is all very important to me.

For the next half hour, she and her uncle and I talk. As the conversation continues, it becomes clear that her desire to go to the West is of fairly recent origin and was, in fact, initially suggested to her by her parents. She is being appropriately prepared for her future as a well-situated upper class woman.

Another example. It's early evening. Suman and I are in the home of Mr. and Mrs. Patil. He's a retired army colonel, a man enormously proud of his military past. While in the service, he studied law and became a lawyer. He now works for a law firm in Belgaum. As a specialist in business law, he is a consultant for a number of local enterprises. The Patils live in the catonment area of the city so that Mr. Patil can remain close to the military element he's so fond of.

Mr. Patil comes across as a simple but fairly well-cultivated man. He envisions himself as a successful middle class person who has developed, over the years, social skills worth emulating. He knows, he says, when to express an opinion and when not to.

After being with him for awhile, it becomes evident Mr. Patil enjoys giving, in a gossipy sort of way, information about other people's lives. From the nature of his talk, it's clear that he gauges human value primarily in terms of (1) a person's academic rank at school, or (2) their present business or professional status in terms of annual salary and future promise of promotion, or (3) if the person concerned is a woman, whom she married and how he rates in terms of the two previously mentioned criteria. An example of this is that when discussing the recent marriage of his youngest daughter, Patil mentions at least three times that her husband stood first in his class at medical school and is already, at the young age of twenty-nine, established with a respected medical clinic in the area. Patil, however, gives no clue at all concerning what either his daughter or son-in-law are like as persons, with reference to their goals, hopes, motives, etc.

It turns out that the Patils also have two other daughters, both living abroad in the U.S. For both Mr. and Mrs. Patil, the fact that these two daughters live out of the country, in the West, is undeniable proof of their value as human beings and of the fact that they've married extremely well, since (according to the Patil's logic) only men "with special abilities are able to secure positions in the western countries, like America." The depth of their identification with western life and their employment of western criteria for determining both social and economic value is an excellent mirror of their continuing colonialization, thirty years after independence.

They also talk about other things, however. One of these topics—brought up by Mrs. Patil—is a costume contest that was sponsored by a local social club, a sort of small scale country club that originally sprang up as a middle class Indian counterpart to the British-only clubs of the colonial era. Only professionals, military officers and solidly entrenched business people belong. The catalyst for talking about the costume contest was the fact that one young girl had been recommended by Mrs. Patil (who was one of the judges) for a consolation prize, although during the planning of the contest it had been decided not to give any consolation prizes. Nevertheless, after Mrs. Patil had talked things over with the two other judges, it was agreed that they would break their own rule and give the girl the consolation prize. After things had been arranged the way she wanted, Mrs. Patil left the contest in order to keep another appointment somewhere else in the city. The next day, much to her surprise, she discovered that through some oversight the other two judges had neglected to award the girl the prize. Mrs. Patil was enraged, since the girl in question was the daughter of a good friend. She tells this story as an example of the "problems you have to deal with when trying to keep up an active social life."

It isn't without interest, in terms of this story, that there's an element of unintended symbolism in regard to the costume of the girl who was supposed to have gotten the consolation prize. The girl, a mill owner's daughter, was dressed as a poor peasant woman. This is symptomatic of the social atmosphere of the Patil's club: snobbish. In such a context, arranging entertainments in which children of the well-to-do can win prizes for their "creativity ingenuity" by dressing up as poverty-stricken peasants is a typical and predictable phenomenon.

The fact that Mr. Patil is also a member of the local Lions Club, and his wife a member of the Lions Ladies Auxiliary, is a further indication of the interrelation between middle class life and a colonialized world vision.

The continuing colonialization of India's consciousness is, of course, far more pervasive than reference to a few families will indicate.

One way to get a sense of the extent of the hegemony of western (primarily U.S.) culture within India is to look at Indian advertising techniques, so obviously modeled on western prototypes. But what's especially insidious about these advertising techniques isn't simply that they originated in the West, but rather that their attempted application in India is so transparently meaningless. For instance, in a Belgaum ice-cream shop there's an advertisement painted on the wall in which a white, blond-haired child, dressed in blue shorts and a striped polo shirt, happily eats an ice-cream cone. It's certainly not out of place to ask: to whom, exactly, does this paleskinned, lighthaired image speak, in this culture where everyone has dark skin and no one has blond hair?

Another negative aspect of Indian advertising is its adoption of a western objectifying attitude toward women. For example, outside a shop there's a sign advertising a certain brand of table fans. The table fan is in the front right-hand corner of the tall, rectangular sign. But the biggest image on the sign, more than twice as large as the fan, is a lightskinned middle class woman wearing some sort of floorlength nightgown or dress. The dress or nightgown has a slit in its side and part of the material is being blown back by the breeze from the fan, exposing a substantial portion of leg, from the foot up to the mid-thigh. Looking at the advertisement, it's difficult to tell which is being sold, thigh or fan.

Another sign, close by on the same street, expresses the same general psychology. The sign is square, and at the top there are large block letters saying: SUN GOGGLES. Directly beneath this lettering is the lightskinned face of a woman wearing sunglasses. The only way to describe her look (the face, with slightly pouting lips, staring at you) is sultry, seductive. The message is clear: simple, traditional coyness will be instantly transformed by these sunglasses into fullblown "modern" sex appeal. Another way of phrasing this message is: if you want to be a truly sophisticated and contemporary woman, a true child of the ever more upwardly mobile middle classes, these sunglasses are just the thing for you—put them on and, in a flash, you'll become a "liberated" woman.

Such images indicate, at least in part, the powerful impact of North American culture on the subcontinent. Walking down the streets of even a medium-sized Indian city like Belgaum, you can feel it, this impact. All around you, plastered on the walls of buildings and on billboards, are advertisements and posters that unequivocally announce the presence of western sales techniques. You get the feeling of a giant country writhing in confusion, its bloodstream infused with the rough-edged shrapnel of a foreign culture. Alien images are floating like half-destroyed islands in India's blood.

Still, the fundamental question is: what part of the Indian psyche do these imported American-type images and techniques speak to? The answer, of course, is relatively easy: to that part which perceives economic salvation as coming on the platter of capitalist westernization and development. In the shopping areas here, what this concretely means is only too obvious—the Indian merchant's relentless pursuit of new commodities to sell to the ladder-climbers and the already affluent, as material symbols of their social status. Expensive cameras, cassette tape recorders, t-shirts with pictures of the U.S. flag printed on them, Indian-made brandy that claims to have "a drop of France in every sip," canned cheeses that nobody but the handful of people educated in the West eat: these are the flamboyant signs of the growing irrelevance, for a large majority of people, of the Indian marketplace. So, in a country still characterized by periodic food shortages as a result of hoarding and black marketeering and unequal distribution of land in the countryside, the market is increasingly glutted with an abundance of luxury items destined for the homes of the well-to-do.

Meanwhile, it's estimated that between fifty and sixty percent of India's six hundred million people live at, or beneath, poverty level.

THE MANAGER AND THE LAWYER

Even among the upper, more colonialized classes, there are deviations from the expected thinking and behavior patterns. In a nation that's in bad economic and social shape, sometimes even those who are members of the privileged sectors are shaken into taking a second look at how things are going. If they take this second look, it's possible they'll say—maybe haltingly, maybe clearly and systematically—that something is wrong, that the need for change is in the air.

But still there's the question: *what kind* of change and created by whom?

Prakash

Prakash is the manager of a company which produces one of the broadest varieties of pumps in India. The company also produces various kinds of valves for industrial use (for instance, for handling naptha and its derivatives in oil refineries), sugar cane crushers, planers, pillar-type drilling machines, different kinds of decorticators for shelling peanuts, seed and fertilizer distributors, plows and maize shellers.

Prakash began working for his company in 1951 as a low-level administrator. When he started, the factory complex he now manages employed approximately fifteen hundred people and had an annual budget turnover of 8.7 million rupees. Now, in 1978, the company employs four thousand workers and has a budget turnover of 300 million rupees a year. Also during this period, the company has made increasingly more sophisticated products. For instance, whereas in 1951 the factory produced mainly 6-inch-diameter low horsepower pumps, the largest pump it now produces is a 106-inch-diameter 1250 horsepower pump. It also has the largest pump-testing unit in India, with a capacity to test 5000 liters per second. Already the groundwork has been laid for increasing this testing capacity to 10,000 liters per second.

All this, of course, is big time, and Prakash, as the company's highest-paid managerial person, oversees it all...

I'm standing with Prakash at the edge of a cliff in a range of hills. Directly in front of us, there's a drop of a few hundred feet. It's late afternoon and the sun's sinking in the west, the direction we're facing. About five miles in the distance, twistings of grey smoke rise up from the flat land; after the day's processing, crushed stalks of sugarcane are being burned. Nearer, about a mile or so away, the Krishna River winds its way through the valley. The land on both of its banks is deep rich green. This part of the valley, along the river, is extremely fertile. At one point on the river, where it makes a slow S-turn, the water reflects the setting sun: brief section of blinding white light. Prakash talks about the high crop yields in the area we're looking at.

Then he turns and points to the land stretching far into the distance on the other side of the hill. This land is drier-looking, brownish in color, obviously not as fertile. Standing here at such a height, the view is truly panoramic; the land is huge. Looking down at the plain, Prakash says: "Near the river the crop yield is excellent. But on this side there isn't the same fertility, and so the farmers are lucky if they can get one sparse crop a year. No water. We'd like to change this. We've devised a plan for a large irrigation system that would bring water to this part of the valley and transform it into a high-yield area. But it will cost 60 million rupees ($7½ million), and we can't afford to do it on our own. We hope to get a loan from an international agency that's interested in such projects. To transform that barrenness, to make it fertile..." His voice trails off.

The look in his eyes as he scans the land and discusses a 60-million-rupee irrigation project is calm, clear—the look of a practical man who has carefully judged the possibilities, who has an abiding respect for his own realism. Yet the voice itself, as he describes the possibility of transforming the land, is almost visionary. He's pulling down a wall of time and gazing into the future. He loves what he sees—a chance to accelerate human progress, to move one small section of India forward into a modernized future.

Prakash is an interesting man. In his late 40s or early 50s, he has handsome silvering hair and sufficiently-sized stomach to indicate he has done well in life. But when talking to him, it soon becomes clear that the accumulation of material rewards isn't his sole ambition. He's also after something else, something less tangible: recognition of his good moral intentions.

His ascent from a 100-rupee-a-month man to being the manager of one of the largest pump-manufacturing companies in India has provided him with a solid material cushion upon which to sit and meditate "objectively" on management-labor relations and the future of India. He is aware of India's present instability and is depressed by it. At least in part because of this, he sees himself as "some kind of socialist" and is proud of his intellectual perception that it's proper "for workers, as time goes on, to combine and struggle for a larger part of the profits." When broaching the subject of wages, one of the first things he says is that "wage differentials between workers and management are too extreme." To him, providing for the workers is the only rational approach, the only hope for a nonchaotic, non-class-conflicted future.

Such attitudes don't grow out of nowhere. They spring from a worldview which is pragmatic and yet, at the same time, somewhat mystical. Part of Prakash's vision is the idea that each individual is a sensitive organism that has to be adequately cared for. In terms of this, he says:

> The workers are like everybody else. They continually take in energy from their environment, from the light of the sun, from everything. But the human body is like a reservoir, a storing place for this energy that has been accumulated from the outside. The stored energy is released during work. Because of this the worker needs time off, a period of nonproductive activity, to reaccumulate what has been drained off during work periods. We must be sensitive to these needs of the workers, must not overwork them, must be willing to give them time to re-energize themselves. Such sensitivity won't hurt production; on the contrary, it will have a positive effect on it.

But Prakash isn't always so soft-spoken, so lyrical-sounding. He is also capable of anger, especially against what he calls "the system."

Prakash speaks disparagingly and with great bitterness about the vested interests that dominate Indian political life and hold back economic and social development. Every new government plan, he says, seems to sustain or deepen the gap between rich and poor. One example he uses is how the state became involved in the purchasing of domestically produced cotton. The rationale for this, he says, is that the state's involvement was supposed to provide price stability.

This was a fine idea theoretically, but the fact is that ultimately it had a retarding effect on the cotton industry. The reason for this is simple: after it has bought up the cotton, it takes the government a year and a half to pay for it. Only those with enough capital to survive the long unpaid period can sustain production at the regular level. So, those who are already rich benefit, while the up-and-coming, struggling farmer loses. And so, once again, economic polarization is intensified.

He also speaks cynically of the government-sponsored "agricultural revolution" that's supposedly taking place in the countryside. As an example, he uses one government-supported irrigation scheme in Maharasthra. As part of this scheme, Prakash's company was given a contract to produce 200 pumps for different irrigation projects that supposedly spanned the state from one end to another. Prakash says:

Because we produced the pumps, I saw from a perfect vantage point what actually happened. Three-quarters of the pumps—150 of them—were delivered to an area that covered no more than fifteen or twenty square miles. This was because a certain state politician who was on a key committee at the time came from this particular area and, in fact, had a large amount of land there. Also, he wanted to make sure the peasants and wealthier farmers from his area would vote for him again when the next elections came. So, he arranged to have all those pumps sent there. I know this since we produced the pumps and so had the opportunity to see where they were being delivered. Unfortunately, such stories are common. The question is: how long will the government be allowed to get away with such incompetency?

This, then, is Prakash—a concerned individual capable of both idealism and anger, struggling, apparently, to be a good person in the midst of a problem-wracked world.

But is this all there is to him, or is there something more? If we scratch the surface with a little more energy, what will we find? For instance, we have heard his words, but have we looked *in between* the words? Also, we have a picture of his philosophy, but do we have an understanding of the actual context in which that philosophy exists?

An example. One night, over beer in his living room, Prakash, Suman and I talk. During our discussion, one of Prakash's two white-haired pomeranian dogs is stretched out asleep on the low coffee table in front of the sofa on which Prakash is sitting. The other one has its nose in Prakash's beer glass and is trying to slurp up the remainder of the beer. Both dogs have "sophisticated" tastes. Earlier Prakash fed them imported asparagus stalks and also expensive Bengali sweets made of milk and sugar. Sitting there, it's impossible not to fantasize that the dogs are paying close attention to what we're saying, since they have a personal stake in making sure society doesn't change too radically; they don't want anything disrupting their comfortable, pampered lifestyle.

Against this background, the three of us talk about a wide spectrum of topics: India's reliance on western technological know-how, the Taylor method for organizing work, India's need to overcome political corruption, western tourists, etc.

At a certain point, Prakash begins to speak about "the mutual interests of workers and management." There's a philosophical, moral tone to his words. As he elaborates his point, his vision of the whole nation moving towards "some kind of socialist future" is almost poetic. As a matter of fact, this is his vision's primary drawback: it seems too utopian, slightly out of touch with reality. What's missing is an understanding of the raw edge of class conflict, the bitterness, the inevitable confrontations. What he substitutes for this is an upper class notion of slow, methodical, "reasonably paced" change, a formula in which both sides, the working class and the capitalist class, gradually begin to perceive that their interests are identical. The fact is that, as well-intentioned as Prakash's "socialist" vision might be, it's still a vision hemmed in and determined by his own class position. As a manager of an extremely large Indian firm, as a man who oversees and coordinates a vast array of productive forces, he's inclined toward the belief that the most sticky human problems can be "managed" (by the "experts") into nonexistence. In this vision, workers pretty much remain a passive force willing to wait for the economic and social planners to figure out the solution to India's dramatically unequal social system. The problem with this is that one only has to look around to see how India's workers aren't displaying such passivity or patience at the moment, nor do they seem likely to do so in the near future. This is true even in Prakash's own factory complex, where during recent years production rates have been slowed down by labor-management tensions and work stoppages.

None of this is meant to imply that Prakash is a dishonest or intentionally misleading man. He isn't the kind of person who claims to believe in one thing while actually believing in another. It's obvious that, at the intellectual level at least, he believes in justice, equality, and "some kind of socialism." He's trying, confusedly, to find his way through the thicket into a better world. Yet, at the same time he's doing this, he irrevocably rides the tide of a managerial-type world vision. In his thinking, working people somehow remain rearrangeable, abstract lumps, statistical units in his overall view of the world.

Whether Prakash will persist in such a vision, or whether his desire for a better world will push him beyond it—this remains to be seen.

Arjun

The man talking has jet-black hair, a palish face and glasses rimmed with black plastic. His dark shoes are scuffed and his violet-colored cotton shirt has two or three loose threads hanging from it. He's a criminal lawyer, twenty-five years old. His name's Arjun.

He continues speaking, insisting on the frail nature of the coalition that makes up the Janata Party, the political group now in power. He's so low-key, almost shy in putting forward his ideas, that the initial impression he makes is that he wants to pleasantly while away the time skimming over the surface of things. But it soon becomes obvious that everything he says is permeated with a quiet idealism, a firm honesty that hunts down and points out hypocrisy, not because he enjoys ridiculing others, but because in a basic psychological way he finds corruption distasteful. He says:

At the most, this new government has until the next national election or possibly the one after that, and then it will disappear, because it also will have failed. In a country like ours, where most of the people still live in the rural areas, the government has to be able to speak to the needs of the peasants. By this I don't mean passing laws in Delhi; I mean it has to have the power to insure that they'll be implemented at the local level. Now the Prime Minister, Moraji Desai, speaks as if this is exactly what he plans to do. He talks about creating a government policy for supporting the development of smallscale industries in the country-side. But Desai is an old man, enormously proud of what he considers his own purity—his Gandhianism, as he calls it—and he somehow believes in his prideful way that his own purity is going to infect everyone in the country and that therefore, under his guidance, everything will work itself out. This is, of course, foolish. But it's also worse than that: it's a purposeful political blindness. Because he puts morality above politics, he robs politics of the possibility of being moral and instead ends up making political life frivolous.

Here's an example of what I mean. Desai considers himself a moral man, and part of this morality is that he doesn't believe in drinking liquor. So, from his Prime Minister's seat, he's now launching a one-man campaign to impose prohibition on the country. What a foolish fixation for the man at the head of our government to be having at this point in our history. First of all, it won't work; as in America, it will only result in the growth of a criminal-controlled liquor industry. Secondly, what about all the people who'll lose their jobs and the bad effect this will have on the economy?

We're sitting in a kitchen, on opposite sides of an old, scratched, wooden table. One end of the table is shoved up against the base of a window. Outside, bright mid-afternoon light eats into the land. It's an absolutely quiet Sunday. As he talks, Arjun takes off his glasses and puts them on again. He speaks nonaggressively, putting forward his ideas carefully, as if they were steps in a process still to be completed, a process of trying to arrive at social as well as personal truth. He says:

It was only a few years ago that I began thinking seriously about communism. I soon realized, though, that the Communist Party of India (the most conservative of the three major communist formations on the subcontinent) was too attached to the ideas of the Soviet Union. What we needed here, I felt, was a communism that was specifically related to our own conditions. Now I'm thinking of joining the Communist Party of India-Marxist (a second, slightly more radical communist group), which is trying to develop such an Indian communism.

One of the things that first moved me seriously in the direction of communism was an article I read about one of the generals of the Chinese Communist Army. He had not always been a communist. As a matter of fact, he came from a rich peasant background and I think actually owned a lot of land. He also had many women and lived extremely well: good friends, excellent wines, power over people. But as the Red Army developed more strongholds in the rural areas, he came into contact with communists and had lengthy argumentative discussions with them. Eventually he was convinced of the legitimacy of the communists' vision. Over a period of time, he gave up his material wealth and then joined the Red Army, where he finally became a fine technician and general.

When I read this article, I became fascinated by the question: what was it in the Marxist philosophy that convinced this man to sacrifice what most people will not sacrifice, all the material comforts, wine, women, power? But it was't just the sacrifice; religions get people to sacrifice worldly concerns also. It was the fact that he made the sacrifice in order to join with common people in what was essentially their struggle. In a country like ours, where the corruption of the politicians defines political life, such a sacrifice, such a commitment to the people becomes, especially when you start considering the results of the Chinese revolution, so different from the results of our own Independence Movement. Here poverty still grows worse every year; people are forced to set up their homes in the streets and to sleep in the gutters; beggars roam all the cities. In China such things no longer exist.

Anyway, I kept wondering what it was that had originally made this general accept the Marxist philosophy. I began reading about Marxism, began talking to Marxists in my own area. It was on my mind, and I wanted to know what it was that had persuaded that Chinese general—and so many others like him—to give up his interest in personal gain and instead join with the people, even accepting the people's leadership in a serious matter like how to go about organizing a national revolution.

As time went on, I began to find examples of revolutionary commitment in our own country. The Naxalite movement is one, even though it was fragmented and not, in the long run, well planned. The people involved wanted revolution too quickly. You can't just say 'now we're going to have a big change,' and then have it. Still, many of the people who joined the movemnt were uncorruptable and completely dedicated to creating a better, fairer India. I read one article about events in the Andhra Pradesh area, where there was a great deal of revolutionary activity. Again I was struck by the example of a certain organizer, a man named Narayan, who seemed to represent the fullness of commitment of so many people in the movement. He wasn't originally from that area, but he went there because people were on the move, militantly agitating for a better life. He got a job teaching children in a school. But soon he was no longer just teaching children, he was also teaching the adults. They studied together about freedom, about the relations between oppressor and oppressed. He became part of their movement against the local landlords and money-lenders and the government they controlled. But this wasn't enough for him. His understanding of what it meant to participate in a people's struggle told him that he had to join completely with the people, not just in their struggle, but also in their way of life. And so, he chose to live the rest of his life there with them, to teach them what he knew and to learn from them what they knew. In the end he even married one of the women, one of those tribal women that most people with education wouldn't dream of going close to. When the movement was finally crushed by government troops, and the people were forced into a quieter period, Narayan still stayed on, living with them, teaching, learning.

It's easy for some people to be cynical about the commitment of such a man. They claim it's a romantic dream to want to merge with people who aren't really your own people. But this isn't the part that interests me; such criticism is too easy. The real point is that India needs such people, that it's impossible to think of a better future for the country without admitting that such a future will only be created by many people, many Narayans, working together.

You know, I went to the villages as an organizer for the Janata Party when they were trying to get into office. I did this because moving the Congress Party out of power was important. But now I can see how someday soon I'll have to go back to those same villages and ask the people to throw out the Janata Party. When will it end; when will people come to power who actually speak in the interests of the downtrodden? This is what I ask myself. Recently, in one of the villages, a man told me: 'Thirty years ago, at the time of Independence, I had two acres of land. Today I still have two acres of land. On the other hand thirty years ago the head of the village *panchyat* (village council) only had three acres of land, but now he has much more. Have I done something wrong that my position shouldn't also have improved? Of course not. It's just that under Congress leadership land reform meant paying off certain people in the villages. No one else benefited. Now, although I'm glad to see the Congress Party thrown out, it doesn't look as if under the Janata Party things are going to be so different.'

You see how it is? There's an anger in people that no one really descends into, admitting its legitimacy, suggesting that it be let loose. But the time has come for us to start seeing that here, in this anger, is a force we have for changing the country. And it isn't just the anger. It's that behind the anger there's understanding. Common people understand far more than they're given credit for. They won't settle for false promises forever. The day is coming when everything is going to have to change. One way or another, everything is going to change.

THE COUNTRYSIDE

Change comes slowly. And it often comes with confusion at the edges. Confusion—and bloodshed. Four days ago in Churmuri, a village only a few miles from here, a man was killed. His name: Mense.

It was the day after a local election, and the winning party, of which Mense was a member, was having a rally to celebrate their victory. The rally began with a parade through the village streets, a parade led by women and children. After marching for only a few minutes, some bystanders started throwing stones at the women in the front of the procession. The marchers had to stop, and there was confusion at the back of the line because from there no one could see what had halted the parade. It was here, at the tail-end of the line, that Mense was marching. As soon as he saw there was some sort of mix up, he went to the head of the procession to find out what was going on. When he got there, members of the opposition party began to harass him. Hot words were exchanged, and soon the blood-dikes burst; Mense was stabbed with sticks and beaten with stones. In a short while, he was dead.

Two days after the murder, I spoke to one of Mense's relatives, a cousin. He said: "The worst thing about what happened was that there was no reason for it. Because times are bad, people get heated up about anything, and then they take it out on each other. Mense was poor, and the ones who killed him are poor, and so what's the reason? There are others who aren't poor, but too often when we get upset we don't go near them. This is how I see it. Now Mense is dead for no good reason. It's sick. Useless."

Tension builds up, then erupts brutally; no longer are such events atypical in India. The countryside's fraught with a sometimes subdued, sometimes overt, angry nervousness. And when this tension pushes itself out into the sunlight, it often has to be acknowledged that, rather than arising from isolated individual grievances, it has a distinct economic or class character. A day doesn't go by without the smell of class war growing slightly stronger.

An example. Not far from here, in the Shimoga district of Karnataka, a man was killed at the beginning of November, 1977. His name was Patre Sangappa, an untouchable. Until 1972 he had worked for a certain landlord as a bonded laborer, a fieldworker. While working for this landlord, Sangappa, feeling the need to earn extra money, sought additional part-time work. This was done in spite of his master's disapproval. Eventually the master adopted a method for insuring that Sangappa would work for no one else but him: when the laborer was at work in the fields, he was chained so that he couldn't leave; at night, when the day's work was done, he was locked up in a small room until the following morning.

Because of his harsh treatment, Sangappa ran away and secured a position with a new master. Although his old master attempted to have him returned against his will, things worked out in such a way that Sangappa remained in his new position.

But Sangappa's problems still weren't over. He had an unsettled grievance concerning the fact that while he had worked for Lokeshappa (the original landlord), he had been given one and a half acres of land by the government as part of an uplift program for the lower classes. Somehow, though, the land had fallen into the hands of the landlord and not the worker. After leaving Lokeshappa's employ, Sangappa attempted, through every available legal channel, to get possession of the one and a half acres which rightly belonged to him. But he failed. As a major landlord in the village, Lokeshappa had sufficient political power to block Sangappa's efforts to retrieve his land.

At last, totally frustrated, Sangappa returned to his village and began demanding his land in person. One night during this time he was called from his home by a group of men, including some members of his old landlord's family. They told Sangappa they wanted him to assist them in settling a local dispute. He left the house and never returned.

The next day his wife was informed that her husband had passed away in the quiet of someone's coconut grove. It was implied that he had died of natural causes. But when the body was finally located, lying face down in the grove, and then turned over, the corpse's condition indicated anything but a natural death. "Crushed and blood-stained face, green-colored neck, broken ribs, crushed testicles and blood-stained hips were seen." Although Sangappa's widow, and also his brother, maintained that his death was related to his feud with Lokeshappa, the police did nothing to investigate.

Even this, though, wasn't the end to the story. A final act, a sort of curtain call, was yet to be performed. A month after the murder, in mid-December, Sangappa's hut was burnt to the ground. This was apparently an attempt to impress on Sangappa's widow, and on anyone else interested in seeing justice done, that the hand of violence was still in excellent condition and would strike again, whenever necessary.

"Don't mess with your betters" was the message.

Life in the countryside: economically difficult, physically hard, psychologically tense, often violent. It is against this background that we observe the fact that between seventy and eighty percent of the subcontinent's population lives in the rural areas. But knowing this, knowing the massive number of people who are forced to endure deprivation and inequality, we still fall short of understanding *why* all this is so.

What, we can ask, are some of the underlying causes? And we can also ask: why haven't government efforts to offset these problems worked?

Let's take a closer look.

Since Independence in 1947, one government approach to the problem of rural poverty has been the development of programs intended to equalize land ownership in the farming areas. By and large, these programs have failed.

One example of such failure is the land-ceiling laws. The rationale for these laws was that by setting legal limits on the amount of land that could be owned by an individual, a government-controlled reservoir of surplus acreage could be created, and this land could then be distributed among the propertyless classes. But there were problems. One was that according to Indian political structure, these laws, passed at the federal level in Delhi, were handed on for implementation to the local state level. This meant that the style and pace of implementation was left to the various state governments. Given that the political machinery of the states was dominated by the very landowning classes who were supposed to be curtailed by the laws, it wasn't surprising that the laws failed. By the time the laws were ready for actual use, a sufficient number of loopholes had been written into them to effectively counteract their intended purpose. The end result was that many landlords kept possession of their land, while at the same time claiming they were adhering to the new socialist-sounding legislation that rhetorically denounced the monopolization of the land by a few people.

One major way landowners have bypassed the spirit of these laws is by artificially fragmenting their land—signing ten acres over to a four-year-old nephew, another nine acres to a brother's wife, and so on. In this way an apparent breakup of land ownership has been attained without actually reorganizing anything. In the words of one peasant acquaintance: "The government has settled for progress on paper. Other kinds of progress don't interest them."

Other methods for legally exempting oneself from the laws were also available. For instance, rich peasants who were willing to mechanize their farms (through the use of tractors, chaffing machines, tubewells, etc.) were considered exceptions to the land-ceiling regulations and were allowed to keep their lands. The justification for this was that mechanization, because it would inevitably increase crop yields, would also increase the food supply for the whole population. This, officials argued, was good reason for creating exceptions to the laws. Unfortunately, there were, as usual, negative side-effects. As many of the rural elite, in an attempt to keep their land, pursued the path of mechanized farming, the immediate effect was an increase, not in crop yields, but in economic polarization. While well-to-do landowners invested in modern machinery and kept their lands, those with middle-sized holdings and little capital lost sizeable portions of their land and were pushed economically downward. So, although the land-ceiling laws did have an effect on the rural population, it wasn't the intended effect. Rather than increased equality, intensified inequality was the result.

Another example of the same negative pattern can be found in the tenancy reforms that were enacted in the 1960s. The supposed purpose of these laws was to allow tenants who had rented or sharecropped land the right to legal ownership of that land. But again because of loopholes, the tenancy reforms failed and many peasants found themselves losing rather than gaining security. The major weakness in the reforms was the so-called "self-cultivation" clauses. These clauses enabled landlords to keep their land if they cultivated it by themselves. So, in the rush to be self-cultivators, many landlords drove tenants off land that had been tilled by their families for generations. In this way, almost overnight many peasants were uprooted and trans-formed into landless agricultural laborers.

None of this should be too much of a surprise. Laws that are programmed to self-destruct don't exist without reason; they aren't mere flukes or accidents. The influence of the landowning classes extends from the remotest rural areas to the capital, Delhi. Subsequently, there's a certain predictability to the central government's unwillingness to intercede, in clear and unambiguous ways, in behalf of the poorer classes.

All this has influenced, of course, the mood of the more deprived sections of the rural population.

If these poorer sectors displayed at least minimal patience in the immediate post-Independence period, waiting to see if the hopes aroused in them by the government's "socialist" rhetoric of equality would be realized, it's also true that by the end of a decade there had developed a widespread cynicism concerning the government's good intentions. Increasingly, there were flare-ups in the countryside, as the poor peasantry tried to take what had been promised to them but not given. As they became more conscious of themselves as an exploited group, to some degree the power of the old caste divisions began to diminish. The long slow process of struggling toward class unity had begun.

One example of the growth of militance was the Darjeeling district in West Bengal, in northern India. The time: May, 1967.

In the Darjeeling district, as in other areas of the country, land reform legislation had proven ineffectual. Both poor peasants with small landholdings and landless laborers were frustrated. Land that was theoretically to be redistributed under the new laws remained in the grip of the already well-to-do. The situation was volatile. Given the Bengali peasantry's history of struggle, it was predictable that some weak link in the chain of oppression would eventually crack. And it did.

In May, in a place called Naxalbari, peasants occupied a certain section of land on a large tea plantation. They claimed the land they were occupying was rightfully theirs, since the plantation covered acreage in excess of the legally allowed limits. The occupation wasn't sweet and peaceful. The peasants' aggression against private property resulted in police intervention. The police were instructed to have the land vacated as rapidly as possible. The peasants—maintaining that they weren't breaking the law but were, on the contrary, putting the redistribution laws into effect—refused to leave. In the ruckus that followed, one policeman was killed. Because class interests were at stake, because the question at hand was who should and who shouldn't have control of the land, the response to the bow-and-arrow murder of the single policeman was disproportionately violent. Seven women and three children were shot dead. Still, the peasants refused to vacate.

From the perspective of the dominant classes, the situation grew worse daily. Not only had the peasants siezed the land, but their action hadn't gone unnoticed; there was a rapid growth of lower-class support for the occupation. In the face of this, government efforts to crush the movement weren't successful.

At it's height, this local "revolution" spread itself over an area of 256 square miles. But what was worse from the perspective of the ruling classes was that the movement refused to remain local. As the West Bengal government attacked the insurrection by stepping up its acts of repression (it inaugurated a massive campaign of murder, torture and imprisonment of all suspected militants), word spread to the rest of India that Naxalbari-style uprisings, including a willingness to take up arms, should be the order of the day. This was the beginning of a movement—the Naxalite movement—which, although it never became cohesive nationally, still took root in many different parts of the subcontinent. In some places the unleashed militance assumed awesome, society-shaking proportions.

The most famous of these areas was Srikakulum district in Andhra Pradesh. Here, a liberated base was established which covered 800 square miles and included 300 villages. According to one report, this base was capable of withstanding "large detachments of heavily armed state and federal troops." In response to this, government attempts at repression mounted. In early 1968, government troops raided over 200 villages and arrested approximately 1500 people. But rather than caving in, the Srikakulum rebellion continued, even more fiercely than before. Large groups—sometimes consisting of more than 1000 peasants—waged guerrilla war against the landowners, who were compelled to rely on their only allies, the armed police, for protection. In the course of this open struggle, people continued to take over land and to divide it among themselves. Eventually, though, government power began to take its toll. By the early 1970s, the Srikakulum movement was pretty much defused. But not entirely. The effect of the Srikakulum movement, as well as of the Naxalite movement in general, was still tangible. An unignorable model had emerged for the kinds of guerrilla strategies that might be necessary to bring about social change.

The emergence of this model also had the effect of re-establishing the significance of the peasantry in India's history. Far from being a passive mass, they have frequently shown themselves capable of small and largescale political action. As one writer on India has said:

Peasant revolts have in fact been common both during and since the British period, every state of present day India having experienced several over the past two hundred years. Thus in a recent survey I discovered 77 revolts, the smallest of which probably engaged several thousand peasants in active support or combat. About 30 revolts must have affected several tens of thousands, and about 12, several hundreds of thousands.

One such revolt was the Telengana peasant uprising, which occurred in the state of Hyderbad during the years 1946 through 1950. Although it preceded the Naxalite movement by twenty years, the Telengana movement contained similar patterns, as had many rural upheavals previous to it. For instance, organizing themselves against the feudal ruling class, peasants were eventually compelled to engage in military conflict with government forces.

Although at first the Telegana movement put forward only modest demands—lowering of land rent, an end to arbitrary taxation, cancellation of peasant debts—the resistance with which even such minimal demands were met drove the movement forward towards greater militancy. Subjected to increasing repression, the peasants displayed a tactical and strategic flexibility that transformed their initial activity into a serious revolutionary upsurge. Alliances were formed among all strata of the peasantry, since it was felt that the existence of the whole peasantry was at stake. The need for self-defense was soon translated into a coordinated effort to systematically attack the enemy, to be on the offensive, to forcibly take what was rightfully theirs. The structure of rural life was rocked to the roots. Landlords were chased from their land and driven out of the countryside into the cities. When necessary, especially bullish landowners were executed by detachments of the vast guerrilla army the peasants had formed. In the liberated areas, peasant committees were established for meting out justice and overseeing the redistribution of the land. Soon the peasants' jurisdiction covered an area of 15,000 square miles inhabited by a population of 4 million. What had begun as a set of demands directed toward the official bureaucracy had escalated into a well-disciplined attempt to radically reorganize the whole face of the countryside.

In the end, the Telengana movement began to fade, not so much because of internal weaknesses as because of the absence elsewhere in the country of a parallel movement that could have lent it support. A particular area can only stand up against the power of the central government for so long.

Still, what happened in Telengana—like what happened in Naxalbari and Stikakulum after it—lives on as a provocative image of the potential strength of a united and angry peasantry.

Historically we know that where there's dissatisfaction, there's often rebellion. And where there's rebellion, there's the possibility of revolution. And where there's the possibility of revolution, even the least hint of a possibility, there's government repression. This is true in India today where the reality is that only the most blunt government-initiated terrorism has been able to keep the radical movements stunned into brief periods of relative quiet.

For instance, according to a 1974 Amnesty International report ("Political Prisoners in India"), between 15,000 and 20,000 political prisoners were being held in West Bengal alone. The presence of so many people in jail was a sign of the fullscale nature of the government's campaign to wipe out the Naxalite movement, to extinguish the last sparks of the uprising which had begun in 1967. The Amnesty International report points out, however, that many of those arrested never officially belonged to the Naxalite movement. The West Bengal government used the term "Naxalite" indiscriminately, as a way of rounding up anyone thought to be overly militant. Many of those arrested were never taken to court, yet they were still held in jail for long periods on the basis of vaguely worded charges. This arbitrary use of the Naxalite label, as a way of threatening with imprisonment or physical injury any peasant or worker who even mildly stepped out of line, was a conscious state attempt (through terror) to extinguish the psychological root of insurgency.

The types of torture that Amnesty International lists as being used against prisoners corroborate information that filtered out, via rumor, from Bengal at the time: beatings so bad that they resulted in broken limbs; hanging prisoners upside-down and inserting pins and needles under their nails and into sensitive parts of their bodies like the genitals; electric shock treatments; burning cigarette holes in the skin; and, in the case of women prisoners, inserting iron rulers into their vaginas as a way of forcing them either to "confess" or give information. The report also gives a glimpse into the fascist mentality of those in charge of the mass arrests when it quotes the Jail Minister as saying that all Naxalites are "psychopaths and in need of psychotherapy to get rid of the extremity of mind." This is, of course, the essence of totalitarianism, that it perceives the least deviation from the norm it establishes as a sign of aberration, illness, maladjustment. That the therapy provided for such "extremity of mind" included not only torture but also murder (the report indicates that in the year and a half from December, 1970 through June, 1972, 88 prisoners were killed in 12 jail incidents) clearly indicates the fury behind the government's attempt to restore order at all costs.

But the plight of political prisoners is only one example of repression. There are also others, ones that have to do with the kind of spontaneous, on-the-spot retribution that can flow from the dominant classes when they feel their inferiors have stepped out of line once too often.

Take, as a case in point, the following incident. The place where the incident occured was a small village called Kilvenmani in the Tanjavur district of Tamil Nadu. The village consisted of untouchables who had undergone social transformation into landless agricultural laborers. Already by 1968, when the incident occured, there had been a history of struggle between these workers and the landowners to whom they sold their labor. During the course of these previous disputes, there had been bitterness and anger on both sides. Once a landlord was killed. At a certain point, local landowners decided they had to intimidate the farmworkers through some dramatic and punitive act. According to their logic, this would, hopefully, persuade the laborers to accept existing working conditions.

The landlords, mostly Brahmins, were driven by essentially two motives. First, as employers of labor, they weren't prepared to tolerate any change in their relationship to the farmworkers that might benefit the workers. Secondly, as Brahmins, they had become increasingly irked by what they considered to be an untraditional self-assertiveness on the part of the untouchables.

Having decided to act, one night the landowners organized a gang of thugs and invaded Kilvenmani. They swept through the town, setting houses on fire. By the time they were done, more than twenty of the untouchables' huts were burned to the ground. But this wasn't the only source of grief that night. Before burning the dwellings, the landlords and their assistants herded 42 people (mostly women and children) into a hut and then, after locking them in, ignited it. The next morning all those who had been imprisoned inside the hut were found dead, most of them unrecognizable. There were some details, however, that could be made out. According to the testimony of a man who sat on a commission appointed to investigate the incident: "One woman named Papama had her one-year-old child clutched in her arms; she was holding the child when she met her death. Mother and child. We couldn't separate the two bodies, they were clutching each other so tightly."

A fitting, almost too meaningful symbol: the young and the old soldered together in death, just as in life they were soldered together in their poverty-stricken semi-fuedal existence.

Meanwhile, life in the countryside goes on. Some say, though, that the day is coming when even the dead will rise up to seek their revenge.

ATTACKING THE YELLOW CAR

A major wave of strikes is sweeping across Inida. The government has responded to this unrest as a serious threat to its ability to rule. Workers are "holding the country to ransom" one cabinet minister has been quoted as saying.

An odd flower, the flower of bitterness, is in full bloom.

In December 1977, Ravindra Varma, the Labor Minister, told members of parliament that in the seven-month period from April to October 1977, production losses due to labor unrest came to more than 800 million rupees ($100 million). During this period there were 1,363 strikes and 199 lockouts.

But while the Janata Party is quick to bemoan working class militancy, it has been slow to adopt policies that would transform the economic conditions that compel workers to agitate for change. The fall of the Congress Party and the ascent of the Janata Party have had no significant diminishing effect on the inflation that has wracked the Indian economy for the last decade and a half. Month by month, consumer prices are still on the rise. So, in spite of wage increases, the real wages of the average worker remain stagnant—only increasing by about one percent in the last fifteen years.

In a country that soon after Independence claimed it was going to create a "socialistic pattern of society," the present condition of the working class, as well as much of the rest of the population, is an embarrassment. And this is exactly how those in power respond to them, as a kind of facial blemish to be covered up with a rhetorical clearasil. One of the things this entails is the development of a clear anti-working class ideology.

Moraji Desai, the present Prime Minister, has frequently reiterated that the government won't tolerate illegal expressions of discontent. One such method of expressing discontent is the *gherao*, a unique subcontinent contribution to the arsenal of class struggle. The *gherao* method is simple: a large number of workers surround some important person, a factory manager or politician or whomever, and refuse to let her/him leave until either their demands are met or they're arrested. Because of the physical symbolism of the *gherao*—a mass of workers engulfing, as it were, a single "helpless" individual (or small group of individuals)—both government officials and big industrialists fulminate against it, labeling such tactics an animal-like reliance on physical intimidation. Workers, however, perceive things differently, knowing that the *gherao* frequently provides them with their sole opportunity for confronting those in power. They also know that the *gherao*'s physical intimidation is mild when compared to the physical intimidation they themselves are forced to face.

One recent incident in the Swadeshi Cotton Mills illustrates this fairly well. The company had received state loans to help pay its workers back wages that it had been unable to pay because of financial difficulties. However, after receiving over 280,000 rupees ($35,000) for this purpose, the company still didn't pay the workers. Because of this, in October 1977 the workers *gheraoed* the company's management as a way of trying to force payment of the promised wages. It didn't work. But not only didn't it work, it also angered the civil authorities. Consequently, after the *gherao* a police official made a public statement to the effect that no repetition of the workers' insubordination would be tolerated. Inevitably, however, as time passed and the workers still didn't receive their pay, they decided to once again step up their efforts to get paid. At the beginning of December they once more *gheraoed* the management, but this time the police, fully armed, arrived on the scene and intervened in behalf of those who'd been *gheraoed*. They opened fire. Both workers and onlooking civilians were killed. The official estimate was that only 10 people lost their lives. Unofficial estimates, however, calculated that the number of dead ranged anywhere between 100 and 200. Eyewitness reports described truckloads of corpses being driven away into the night. The area was cordoned off so no one could get in to investigate. Even a week after the incident occurred, it was still almost impossible to penetrate the police lines surrounding the marked-off zone. Every effort was made to minimize the public's access to information about what had happened. Fortunately, these efforts failed and the word spread: ordinary people shot down in cold blood with little, if any, provocation.

Incidents like this inevitably catalyze popular indignation. In response to this, vested interests attempt to publicize their own version of such situations as well as of class relations in general. Frequently, this takes the form of an all-out, no-holds-barred ideological assault on working people's intentions and motives.

As part of the struggle between labor and capital, high government officials as well as a majority of the newspapers attack workers for being irresponsible in their demands, for putting their own petty self-interests ahead of the interests of the country. The picture of the working class that emerges from many daily newspaper reports, for instance, is of a blind, mutinous, avaricious, narrow-minded mass, bent on having its own way, or else. Articles abound with information about well-intentioned employers who are reportedly "forced" into locking out their employees "following...intimidation and violence by some workers." Also, on the back pages of the papers there can often be found little fill-in articles with suggestive headlines like "Murder Case: Union Leader and Seven Workers Arrested." All this supplies the sensationalism necessary for attempting to turn public opinion against workers as a group. This effort to sway popular opinion against workers is a crucial ingredient of government policy. Its purpose is to ideologically remold the general population so that it will be prepared when harsh measures are resorted to for controlling the most militant sections of the working class.

Such harsh measures, of course, already exist. For instance, in Thane district, a heavy industry area outside Bombay that has been the scene of intense labor disputes over the last months, the district magistrate has seen fit to restore "order" to the area. His methods for accomplishing this include police harassment of individuals, denial of democratic freedoms, and repression of workers' organizations. In one two-day period, the houses of 118 workers and certain so-called bad characters were broken into by the police and searched. At the same time, "making public speeches, raising slogans and commiting any other prejudicial act in the municipal limits of Thane" were prohibited. Some of these emergency measures were directed at specific worker groups, like the one that prohibits the assembly of five or more persons near the Mukud Iron and Steel Works. The steelworkers are considered an especially subversive group because of their continuing resentment of the fact that they've been locked out of their jobs for over four months. The justification given by Thane officials for the suspension of civil liberties is that such severe measures are necessary in order to "put down lawlessness and a sense of insecurity in the industrial zone."

Maybe, given the level of discontent and the increase of police-inspired violence in the area, they should have said war zone.

All over India, the struggle goes on. Massive one-day demonstrations in the large cities. Violent battles in the coal-mining areas. Even in Belgaum, which isn't usually known as a center of agitation, there's an increase in tension, a serious wave of worker unrest. This is important. It shows how widespread the discontent is.

Day after day, week after week, Suman and I walk through the city and its outskirts, meet with workers, visit machine shops, factories, mills. If nothing else, one thing is certain: people have a lot on their minds.

As always, you look, you talk, you listen...

Halfway down the alley, on a tall bamboo pole raised higher than the one-story buildings, a red flag is flying. The pole is attached to the cornerpost of a makeshift shed with reed-mat roof, directly outside Privi Industries. A little to the left of the cornerpost, nailed to a six-foot-high stake that has been driven into the ground, there's a white sign with black letters printed on it. The sign announces that the nineteen workers employed at Privi Industries are on strike. Four of the strikers are sitting under the reed-mat roof of the open-front shed, keeping out of the early afternoon light. It's lunchtime, and so most of the other workers have gone to eat. One of the remaining workers, a strongly built, stocky 32-year-old lathe operator, explains some of the reasons behind the strike. First, in a calm, statistic-giving way, he talks about their financial situation—wages that at best provide for a subsistence-level existence. Then, with more emotion, he discusses a series of court battles with the owner, during which the owner promised to rectify certain problems in the shop but then didn't. So now they're on strike. "There won't be any settlement," he angrily says, "until we have the money in our hands."

By this time, most of the workers have returned from lunch. Also, additional workers have strayed over from nearby shops. The dialogue changes from a specific discussion of the situation at Privi Industries to a more general discussion concerning the thinking process workers have to go through when trying to organize themselves. One man says:

It is not enough to have a union and only argue for more money. You also have to ask a bigger question: why is it that we're always in the position of having to beg for a little bit more? It's not just a money problem. It's political. In all the shops around here, you have people working eight, nine, maybe ten hours a day, six days a week. We work; we get sick; somebody else gets rich. There's a question here not just of how much we get paid, but also of control—who controls this, who's controlled by that? I don't know exactly what the answer is, but I can tell this: there are some big fights ahead.

The dialogue continues, different people speaking. Soon the time comes for us to leave. As we walk away, one of the workers shouts at us, "*Iquilab Zinadbad!*" Free India!

The question of how to become free is on many people's minds. Unfortunately, as we've seen more than once so far, the attempt to achieve greater freedom and equality is often met with violent resistance. This is as true in Belgaum as it is elsewhere. One example of this is recent occurrences in the local textile industry.

Until a few weeks ago, the workers from a number of area textile mills were on strike. The mills involved were mostly small, employing from fifteen to thirty people. Altogether, approximately 500 workers were involved in the work stoppage. The main issue was their demand for an annual bonus to help offset the fact that their real wages were continually shrinking due to inflation. Although this was the specific issue at hand, the workers' militance also stemmed from their feeling that they were, in general, being ripped off: low wages, minimal (if any) fringe benefits, bad working conditions.

But striking wasn't easy. Precisely because of their under-paid status, the workers had, at best, meager resources to assist them in getting through the no-work, no-pay period of the strike. Plus, the overall situation didn't look good. As the strike neared the conclusion of its second month, the owners, who had formed a united front against the employees in the different mills, persisted in claiming that the workers' demand for a bonus was irresponsible. It was a war of nerves and, as always in such situations, the main question was who could hold out the longest. The odds favored the owners. A compromise in which they would pay a bonus, but a significantly smaller one than the workers had demanded, was in the air.

By mid-February, the compromise was reached and most of the millhands went back to work. However, in one mill where the strikers' demands had been watered down to almost nothing, the workers refused to return to their jobs. Alone, they persisted in their struggle. As before, every day they picketed the mill.

One day, across the street from their picket, a dedication ceremony was taking place at a recently constructed factory. Attending this function were some of their mill managers. After the dedication ceremony was over, the managers of the textile mill, in a sort of parody of a guerrilla raid, ran across the street and set fire to the workers' red strike flag. In the ensuing skirmish, during which the workers tried to defend their peacefully established position outside the mill, a motor scooter belonging to one of the managers was overturned and (so he said) the workers tried to set it on fire. Whether or not this was so, the fact was that as soon as the managers saw the tide was turning against them, they had the police summoned. Upon arrival, the police immediately took the managers' side and tried to disperse the workers, although they were legally entitled to be outside the mill. The method employed by the police for dispersing the workers was violent: a *lathi* charge (the *lathi*, an Indian version of the billyclub, is made of hard bamboo). Swinging their *lathis*, the police spilled through the crowd of strikers. When those attacked tried to tighten their ranks as a way of protecting themselves, the fury of the police-charge increased. In the end, fourteen workers required medical treatment. The injuries inflicted on both men and women included broken hands, fractured legs, and serious head gashes. According to eyewitness reports, many of the strikers were "soaked with blood." None of the workers, of course, had been armed. Altogether, forty-two of them were arrested and thrown into the Hindalga jail. Nothing, however, was done to the managers who had precipitated the situation by burning the strikers' flag.

Out of such experiences, political consciousness grows. The increasing awareness on the subcontinent that the police arm of the state is subordinate to the interests of the dominant classes isn't an idea arrived at through abstract discussions. Rather, it evolves slowly but organically out of the taste of your own blood in your mouth.

But people don't cringe and disappear. They think. They talk. They act. They move forward. Once more, let's take a look. Up close. Right here in Belgaum.

Mahadev holds out his right hand: one thumb and four fingerless knuckles. He lost the fingers seven years ago while inserting a metal sheet into a die-and-punch hydraulic press. His compensation from the Employment State Insurance Agency was 2000 rupees ($250). After the accident, the company, feeling some responsibility towards its injured worker, transferred him from the shop floor to an office, as a peon. They did this, they said, so he wouldn't have to enter the lists of the unemployed. Now, at the height of his career, he makes 300 rupees ($35) a month. When asked if he thinks he was treated well after his accident, he says: "What can I say? I took what was offered. Of course, 500 rupees ($63) a finger for someone who depended on his hands to operate a machine isn't very much. But what could I do? This is what they gave me, this is what I took." Then another worker from the group of strikers we're talking to breaks in. "That's right," he says sarcastically, "you work for them, the machine eats your fingers, and they give you back a few stinking rupees and a friendly smile. After that, they keep their eyes on you; if they don't think you're showing the proper gratitude, they kick you out."

These striking workers from BEMCO Ltd. (their main line of production is hydraulic presses and jacks) don't mince words when talking about management. They're angry. They're also obsessed with the fact that recently the ownership, in an attempt to break the union, offered fourteen workers raises of approximately 100 rupees ($13) each as a way of drawing them away from the other strikers. It worked. What irks the strikers is that some of the workers who've now disowned the union were once union leaders. Because of this, the strikers are convinced that in order to protect their rights they have to be on guard on two fronts: management on the one hand, self-interested company-appeasing union leadership on the other.

"None of this is a joke," one of the men, a fellow with three missing front teeth, says. Then he continues:

It's a matter of survival. So we hang out here, outside the compound, trying to figure out what to do with these traitors, the ones who sold out. Sometimes it seems the best approach is to leave them alone, forget about them. They've gone over to the other side now, and there's not much that can be done to win them back. In the beginning, we all pretty much felt that way, in spite of our anger. But now we're starting to think that when a small bunch sells out, it's the task of the larger part of the group to force them back into line. Sometimes I say to some of the people here, "Maybe we should really rough up one of those ass-kissers, set an example for the others, make it clear that it's not a good idea to run from your friends when there's a tough situation." Well, there are different responses to that. Some say we'll only end up getting in trouble ourselves. But we all understand that there has to be some kind of harassment, some show of our strength, our seriousness. What's been done to us is wrong. No bribe, no matter how big, can change it.

By this time, we've been here talking for over an hour. When we started there were about twenty workers, all of us crouched together inside the strike shed. Now the number has grown to about sixty, many of them standing immediately outside the shed in the hot sun. The strikers continue to pursue the same question: how militant you have to get in order to win your demands and insure that majority decisions are stuck to by everyone. Anecdotes are related, and a fairly clear picture emerges of how, up until now, they've been handling their situation. One man, with a humorous, folksy talking style, tells a story about nearly being nabbed by the police. It's obvious from the way he speaks and from the positive responses he gets from the other workers that he's a trusted and well-liked rank-and-file leader.

"I almost got arrested for murder," he says with a kind of clownish grin.

All of us followed one of these sell-outs into the street. We were making a nuisance out of ourselves by shouting slogans at him like, "You're a spoon in the boss's mouth—he loves to lick you clean." Some of my friends here, because they were so angry at this fellow, started throwing little stones at him in order to wake him up about the seriousness of what's been going on. Because there were some police around, I said to myself, "Maybe this isn't a good idea, not right now." So I started shouting that rather than throwing stones, we should just crowd around him and yell. Everyone understood this was a good tactic, and so the stone-throwing stopped. Just then, though, the Superintendent of Police drove by in his car. He stopped to see what was going on. Immediately our friend, the company ass-kisser, runs up to this Superintendent and tells him we're a crazy mob, and that we're threatening to kill him. Then what do you think happens? Burman—that's the Superintendent of Police—decides I'm the one who should get tossed in jail. So he tells some of his people to get me. Now do you think this sell-out, who'd just listened to me give a speech telling the other fellows not to throw stones at him, would stick up for me and explain I hadn't been trying to murder him? Not at all. He just stood there, happy to see somebody being dragged away. Luckily, I had a chance to do some quick talking to one of the police who'd been there during the whole thing. I got him to explain to his boss that rather than being a murderer, I was a real peacemaker. The result was that I was finally let off, although the presence of Burman succeeded in breaking up our demonstration.

When he's done talking, it's like the end of a performance. Everybody's smiling and a little riled up.

The conversation continues for another two hours, one topic following another. Everyone throws in their two cents worth. At times the dialogue takes on the quality of a spelling bee in which everybody's spelling different words at the same time. But what's most impressive is that these men are speaking nakedly, out of a great desire to comprehend their individual as well as their class roles in life. They aren't professors for whom intricate discussions, without any concrete solutions in sight, are a pleasurable pastime. There's something awesome about the largeness of their vision; not only are they committed to winnnig the strike, they're also obsessed with changing the world. There's a great deal of give and take—short passionate speeches about the need to go beyond labor unions into the political arena, disagreements about local labor leaders, etc. It's clear they feel part of a large mass of people on the verge of some great, although not entirely definable, move.

Yet they always return to the specifics of their situation. Management's response to them, they say, is predictably stubborn: owners and upper-level company bureaucrats insist the workers economic demands are flighty, without substance. The strikers maintain, though, that their vision of how things should be run is a humane one, whereas the company's is cold, impersonal, exploitative. As an example of what they mean, they talk about the question of a dearness allowance.

Under present guidelines, all workers receive a dearness allowance that amounts to thirty-three percent of their wages. The workers have suggested a substitute system which would allow an employee who has been working with the company only one year a greater (percentage wise) dearness allowance than a worker who has been there ten years. Their rationale for this is simple. In the words of one worker: "The way things are now, a peon who makes a real low wage gets a dearness allowance that doesn't even begin to help him out. Because of this, the percentages should be fixed in such a way that the lowest paid workers would be given better treatment to balance the fact that their pay is so lousy. But the owners say no. The reason they ignore us is because our scheme would entail a slight increase in the total amount now paid for the allowances."

But the workers' analysis doesn't just pertain to economic issues. They're also struggling with management over the question of exactly what kind of workers' organization they should be allowed to have. Management supports the idea of two unions—one for blue-collar workers and the other for office staff. The workers reject this idea, saying it's an inefficient form of self-organization that has the effect of diminishing employee unity and bargaining power. Because of this, they've decided to organize themselves into a single plant-wide union. Management, however, refuses to acknowledge their right to do this— not, anyway, for another two years, until the present contract expires. In response to this, the workers say they're going to get what they want, and soon. "We're the ones who know what's good for us, not them," one worker says.

These are some of the grievances, the sore points.

By now it's four o'clock, and the group's mood has changed, intensified. Almost four hundred workers have arrived for a pre-planned demonstration. Over the last half-hour, they've been straggling in both individually and in small groups. Many of them have ridden here on bicycles. It's the end of the first shift, and the workers want to be at the factory gates as the scabs and company officials come out.

They're just in time. Single file and carrying lunch-tins, scabs begin to exit through the gates. In response, the strikers— who've by this time massed themselves in front of the gates— start shouting slogans, first one then another. "No more union busting!" "We hate those who've become spoons in management's mouth!" The outcoming scabs depart nervously, quickly, but not without having to endure the ordeal of being surrounded and screamed at and threatened. None of them, however, are physically injured or molested. During all this, police hover at the edge of the demonstration, trying to make sure the strikers don't completely block the gates.

A yellow car, belonging to one of the company's top officials is about to leave the compound. As the car comes out, the crowd presses close to it, shouting, "Management shouldn't be afraid to talk to us!" One of the policemen, holding a *lathi* in one hand, stretches out his arms winglike in a futile attempt to single-handedly cordon off the workers from the car that's moving now at a snail's pace. The workers hardly pay any attention to the cop's presence. They swarm around the car shouting slogans at its closed windows. The men, making no attempt to completely stop the vehicle, are content to continue hurling abuse as it creeps slowly forward. Up close, it's possible to get a good glimpse of the official sitting in the back seat of the car, waiting for his driver to make it to the relative serenity of the main road. He sits rigidly, staring straight ahead, as if trying to convince the demonstrators they're of no concern to him. If this is what he's trying to do, it doesn't work. The tense, artificial stiffness of his posture and the sweat drenching his face reveal, only too clearly, his nervousness. The workers can feel it, their sudden unignorable authority. Their voices grow louder as they crowd closer to the car, prolonging the moment of their power.

THE ONLY WAY

Ram Mohan

Second story loft. Dusty wooden floor. At the street end of the loft, a few feet in front of a set of doors that opens onto a small sun-washed balcony, there's a desk piled with books, papers. Behind the desk sits a short man with thinning, grey hair parted on one side. He's in his late 50s, early 60s. He says hello. At first it's difficult to distinguish the outlines of his face, the room is so dark. Also, right behind him is the bright glare of the sunlight on the balcony, which has the effect of throwing the man into even deeper shadow.

This is Ram Mohan, labor organizer for close to forty years.

Mohan is a complex man: militant, progressive, a little cynical. He doesn't like being pigeonholed, boxed into a corner. In talking to us he persists, in a friendly but adamant way, in trying to turn the tables; he's more interested in being the questioner than the questioned. What he wants to discuss is the labor situation in the United States. Even though Suman and I want to talk about India, he keeps switching the dialogue back to the U.S. For instance, when Suman asks about wage differentials within the local working class, Mohan, after supplying a brief answer, immediately attempts to refocus the question on the U.S. labor force. "And what is the situation like in the U.S.?" he asks, pressing for a detailed answer.

Even when his question has been answered, he requests us to expand on our answer first in terms of wage differentials between union and nonunion workers and then in terms of the wage scales of whites and blacks. As it turns out, he's something of a self-taught expert on the West. He's fascinated, and a little depressed, by what he considers to be the implications of life in the U.S. He says:

> I'm curious about what it's like there. Some people say there's an antagonism beween the American working class and the corporations. But it doesn't seem so simple to me. I'm not sure this antagonism exists in America in the same sense Marx said it would in an advanced capitalist country. Although I've never been there, it seems to me from what I've heard and read that labor, along with the capitalist class, has plotted to exploit the consumer. All labor agitation seems concentrated on getting more money, then these higher wages are passed off to the buyer in the form of higher prices. There seems to be no *moral* concern, on the part of either labor or capital, to figure things out, to plan intelligently, to create a fairer market.

He looks at us, confident that he's right, yet bothered by it. He wants to believe people are capable of a higher vision. He then proceeds to go off in another direction: U.S. foreign policy and the attitude of U.S. citizens toward that policy.

> Are there many people there who see American influence on the rest of the world as bad? I mean, does anyone in America describe your country as a colonial power? I understand that America doesn't use her power like the colonializing European nations used to do. When Britain came to India her intentions were impossible to miss. America, of course, isn't so naked in her use of power. It's not always an easy thing to say exactly what's happening. But it's there. If you look close, you can see it.

There's an intensity about him, an energy. You look at him. Although he's knowledgeable, he's not a cosmopolitan man, doesn't have the "I'm familiar with everything" air of many of

India's big-city intellectuals. Yet he digs, pulls things apart. Still, his cynicism, when he expresses it, isn't heavy-handed; instead it has a philosophical edge, no bitterness. It's the foam on the aging wave of his life, something churned up by a relentless subsurface activity. Close to forty years of organizing in a country you'd hoped would somehow, against the odds, turn out to be a real rather than an artificial democracy: this doesn't go by without leaving its mark. So there's this slight cynicism, this fear that the workers of India won't transcend economic issues, that in the long run they'll trade serious social change for a piece, even a small one, of the pie.

This explains the United States' peculiar fascination for him; it's the place where (in his vision) the working class has shown itself to be as greedy and small-minded as the capitalists. But he doesn't seem to really want to believe it. He looks for the loophole in his own argument. He listens closely when we talk. The fact that so much of the U.S. workforce is still unorganized (only about one quarter of the workers are in unions) impresses him, as if these nonunionized people represented a potential force in U.S. society that he hadn't imagined was there. He's also curious about the plight of blacks, the role that they play. "Are there certain sectors of the labor force in which they're concentrated? If so, what does this mean? I mean, what's the effect of their situation on American life in general? Does it help make people more politically conscious?"

The conversation continues, first in this direction, then that. Mohan's hand-gestures are lively when he talks. Finally, under pressure from Suman, he returns to the original topic, India. He says:

> The Naxalites were too dogmatic. They were committed to this idea that there had to be a violent revolution, and then they proceeded to build an organization around that idea. Sure there will be violence to some degree. The problem is they didn't stop, didn't take the time to think it all out. They pushed forward without having a large enough base among the mass of people. Also they were too local, not strong enough nationally.

Of course, on the other hand there's nothing but the
major political parties. I'll tell you something. I
shouldn't say this because I'm the vice-president of the
Janata Party in this district. But I'll tell you anyway. I'm
not very happy with how the party's performing. I'll
put it this way. Yesterday the Janata Party was
claiming that everybody in the Congress Party was
corrupt because they'd supported the Emergency. But
today the Janata Party is welcoming with open arms all
those people who are leaving the Congress Party
because of its internal problems. If you're part of the
oppostion you're corrupt, but if you're with us you're
pure. There's no ideology in this. True, the Janata
Party has ended the worst excesses of the Emergency.
But that's all. Nothing else has changed. The party
hasn't shown even the most minor ability to hold down
prices, to set limits on the industrialists, to stabilize
life, to reduce unemployment. It was important to
remove Indira Gandhi, and so I joined the Janata Party,
but now I'm not sure what to do...

He's leaning back in his chair. He looks to one side. A shaft
of light from the balcony cuts across one of his cheeks. I start to
ask him a question, but before I can he moves his chair forward
and puts his arms on the desktop. His face is taut, thin. He says:

A party, in the traditional sense of a political party,
isn't what's needed now. If that's all we've struggled
for, then we'll end up like you in America: two parties
which are actually the same party, separated only by
certain shallow differences. You can have your Demo-
crats and Republicans; we can have our Congress and
Janata. What we need its something different, a party
that functions efficiently at, and gets its power from,
the grassroots level. Who knows if this will work, if
people can live up to the demands of such a plan? But
it's the only hope. Ideas like this have been put forward
before. But it's time now to make them into more than
ideas. We need action.

People's committees must be set up all over, in every
village and in every district of every city. These

committees must become the new machinery of power. They must be democratic, representative; all sections of the population in each area must be heard. These committees would have to take power; they would have to throw local corrupt politicians out of office. The committees themselves would have to assume the responsibilities of those offices. They would have to become the proper authority for dealing out justice, a new kind of justice, people's justice.

To be honest, I'm not sure if the circumstances are right for the occurrence of such a thing in the future. I don't know. But I can tell you this: it's our only hope.

Vijay Desai

The thick-trunked trees on either side of the road arch toward the center of the street, forming a sun-blocking canopy of branches. Suman and I are walking back into town after spending the afternoon in an industrial area at the city's outskirts. A bright red oil truck speeds past, heading in the other direction, towards the city of Hubli. All day long trucks thunder by on this road, stirring up the reddish orange dust. The trunks of all the trees and the leaves of all the bushes are coated with dust. As a matter of fact, everything along the road has an ochre color from the dust: the wooden walls of the tiny shops, the sign that says THE LIONS CLUB WELCOMES YOU TO BELGAUM, the logs in front of the sawmill, the parked bicycles.

It's about five o'clock. We're walking on the left side of the road. A few feet ahead of us there's a man on his way home from work. He's carrying a small bluish grey shopping bag. Sticking out of the top of the bag is part of his lunch-tin.

Suman asks him if there's a bus stand nearby. "About a mile up the road," he says, waiting for us to catch up to him. He's about 35 years old and looks tired. He has a jaw that gives the odd impression of hanging like a dead weight from the rest of his face.

"I saw you coming out of that factory back there," he says. "What were you doing?" As he talks, he only glances at us briefly, then continues looking straight ahead down the road. It's difficult to tell if he really wants an answer or had just spoken out of a sense of formality. When we tell him we had an appointment there to talk with some workers about job conditions, he livens up a little. "If you're not careful," he says, "the life of a working person can crush you. Something inside snaps. You feel like there's no hope."

We keep walking. His name is Vijay Desai. His shoulders are rounded, slouched, not broad. His shirtsleeves are rolled up to his elbows, a thick film of dark hair on his arms. A lathe operator, he talks about a unionizing effort that took place at his shop. He and a few others were the major pushers. They ended up going out on strike for almost a year, then lost. "But we're still fighting," he says. "There's nothing else to do."

It's getting later. The air is tinged with red. A cool breeze.

Desai begins talking about a political group he belongs to—forty workers, women and men. He says they've read Marx as well as many 20th century radical writers: Lenin, Mao, certain Indian authors, etc. He lets us know, however, that reading isn't the sole purpose of the group. Each member is also committed to doing regular organizing in their respective workplaces and communities. The group also recognizes the necessity of establishing contact with the peasantry. Because of this, every member is required, in their spare time, to go into the villages and do agricultural work with the peasants. Desai says that in this way, by participating in harvesting or in the building of irrigation canals, the rural people learn to trust them, and this provides the foundation for political discussion. "But it's not easy," he says. "For the most part, village life is backward and traditional. It takes a lot of time to convince the people there of the need to organize on a large scale. Still, difficult or not, it's the only way to get anything done, and so we do it."

Vijay Desai. An anonymous lathe operator. A slouch-shouldered nobody.

"It's hard," he says, and keeps walking.

2

CASTE AND SEXUAL RELATIONS

As we've seen, it's possible to look at India and see, all around, the giant paw of the rich beating down—daily, monthly, yearly—those within its reach. On the basis of this, it's also possible to posit that the subcontinent has two basic classes, a rich property-owning ruling class and a laboring class.

But it's not this simple. Even among those who work and are exploited, there are basic divisions and subdivisions. There is the high caste and the low caste, and the non-caste untouchable. In the intricate goings-on of the community, as well as in the suffocating pit of the workplace, these different groups often go at it tooth and nail.

But even that isn't all. There are men and women. In the household, in the backbreaking fields, in the industrial shops, you see it—male dominance over women.

By itself, then, the word "class" isn't enough. We also, at least briefly, have to look at India in terms of (1) caste, and (2) sexual relations.

Caste

To the western mind, one of India's most baffling customs is caste. Caste, for us, is equated with a primitive level of social development. That Indians can perceive some of their own kind as untouchables, as bearers of an inherited spiritual shame that results in total social alienation, this seems to many western observers preposterous, stupid, "unadvanced." When we hear that the untouchable can't drink water from the same well as the Brahmin, or when we read that even the untouchable's shadow is considered polluted, this to many westerners is proof of the hopelessly complicated and taboo-dominated nature of Indian society.

What's absent from such perceptions is a sense of objectivity. Although it's true that social relations on the subcontinent are different from what's we're familiar with in the West, the underlying motives for these relations are often the same. Take, as an example, the Hindu attitude toward untouchables. According to Hindu tradition, untouchables carry, through the many cycles of life and death and rebirth, an interior scourge, a spiritual ineptitude, which condemns them to living out their lives at the lowest economic levels of society. By western standards, such beliefs seem a good example of mind-boggling superstition. What isn't seen, or is purposefully ignored, is how such beliefs in fact parallel many western beliefs. In the U.S., for instance, we have a value system whose ideological roots are traceable to the old Puritan Christian notion of original sin, of the "saved" and "unsaved." The modern form of the myth is this formula: those who are most suited to be the holders of social and economic power inevitably rise to the top; those who aren't so suited sink to their "natural" levels within the social pyramid. But this isn't all. Over the years racist variations of this myth have been used to justify chronic generation-to-generation exploitation of blacks and other people of color in the U.S. Also, it was precisely this myth that emerged during the Vietnam war when the Vietnamese were reduced to being, in the popular venacular, "gooks"—i.e., non-humans. Unless we're capable of recognizing that we, too, have our superstitions and myths, it's impossible to objectively view the Indian caste system.

None of this is meant to excuse the caste system or to obscure its exploitive character. But western feelings of racial or imperialist superiority can have no place in our attempts to look at caste on the subcontinent. Such notions would only produce the obvious result: a continuation of the self-serving western myth of India's backwardness and exotic character.

Caste began as far back as 2000 years before the birth of Christ. It emerged sometime after the invasion of the Indus Valley civilization by so-called arayan nomads from the north. At the time of ths invasion, the Indus valley had a society dominated by two major cities, Mohenjo-daro and Harappa. In Mohenjo-daro, there was an elaborate sewage system, granaries for storing produce, multi-storied buildings, well-planned streets and sophisticated pottery-making techniques.

The invading arayans weren't as developed in terms of social planning. They weren't city-centered people but rather cattle-herding wanderers. In war they used metal weapons and horse-drawn chariots. We can discover some of the group characteristics of these people by exploring, in ancient Hindu texts, their mythology. For instance, one of their gods—Indra— is described as nomad-like, as "a stream resting not but ever active" and as a powerful conqueror-like figure who "destroyed,

with light, black-hued darkness." It is also said about him that
"he brought forth kine with his companions."

Another significant god of the invaders was Agni, god of
fire. One of the arayans' war methods was arson (Mohenjo-daro
was burned to the ground). In the old religious books Agni is
described as being a powerful elemental force—"his flames are
fierce"—as well as being always on the move like the arayans
themselves were. "The never sleeping, never aging rays of Agni,
whose power is light, roll forward like streams across the night."

And so the arayans came, shaking up life on the subcontinent. They penetrated and conquered the Indus Valley civiza-
tion; then they moved further south and east. Over hundreds of
years, the invasion became permanent, irreversible. One of the
consequences of the invasion were social divisions between the
conquerors and the conquered, between arayan and non-arayan.
But eventually such simplicity gave way to greater complexity.
Distinct groups, with specificially ordained social roles to play,
emerged. In this way, over a long period of time the four major
castes came into existence: the warrior caste, the *brahmin* or
priest class, the merchant caste, the *sudra* or laboring caste. A
further elaboration of this system entailed the evolution of a
rock-bottom group, those who performed society's least respected, most alienating work. These were the untouchables, so
low on the social ladder that they were considered "outside" the
caste system.

From this overview we can see how the caste system, in its
original form, was a pre-modern set of class divisions. Only by
understanding this can we overcome the problem of perceiving
caste and class as mutually exclusive categories having nothing to
do with each other. If we make this mistake, we run the risk of
exoticizing Indian social relations, of making them seem
peculiarly unique, odd.

This doesn't mean, though, that when looking at the history
of Indian society, we can understand that society by imposing on
it, mechanically, a western class analysis. This would result in our
neglecting the religious and cultural framework within which
the Indian caste system has in the past, and continues in the
present, to operate. As in all societies, the power of this religious
and cultural framework is vast. Because of this, attitudes and

conceptual systems have been handed on from generation to generation throughout history. People have been taught how to think and how to view themselves and those around them. This is the ideological power of culture.

The Hindu rationale for caste is that it's a social manifestation of people's spiritual status. The higher castes are the spiritual elite, while the lower castes are the spiritually deficient masses. One of the signs of caste and spiritual status is the foods people eat. Theoretically, the highest-ranking castes are vegetarian and the lowest-ranking eat so-called unclean meats like pork. Another elaboration on this food-as-status pattern is that while a lower-caste person can receive food from an upper-caste person, the reverse is taboo. The elite can't run the risk of spiritual contamination.

Another area we have to look at when discussing caste is *jati*. Understanding *jati* will help us understand the caste system as a system characterized by tremendous internal variety. Within the major castes, *jati* is the name given to specific occupational groupings. There is a sheepherding *jati*, a stone-worker *jati*, and so on. *Jati*, then, has to do with people's relations to the means of production—their particular role, or their group's role, in the overall social division of labor. But *jati* is also more than this. Each *jati* has its own history and folk mythology and set of behavior codes. This, once again, returns us to the cultural level. *Jati*, as culture, is never abstract. It's a central, blood-and-flesh ingredient of people's lives. Passed on from generation to generation, *jati* culture provides a complex interior structure for the whole caste system. For instance, there are legends, transmitted both orally and in written form, that supply popular explanations of group or *jati* history. These legends, internalized by people, create a kind of governing system on their consciousnesses, forcing them to perceive the world and themselves in certain ways—ways which, of course, reinforce existing society.

Now let's take a more close-up look at what some of this means. The following story, which has to do with the historical origins of a *jati* of potmakers, is a good place to begin.

There was a well-known warrior. His name was Drona, and his fame included a reputation for being a super-accomplished marksman with bow and arrow. One day a lower-caste man came to him and asked permission to become his student. Although the prospective student was obviously sincere, the famous warrior turned him away because of his low-caste status. The young man was disappointed, and he returned to his dwelling place. He was persistant, however, so he kept thinking about how he could become an outstanding marksman. Finally, he got an idea. He fashioned out of clay an image of Drona and began worshipping it. He thought that if he couldn't obtain actual instruction from Drona, he might at least be able to learn some of the warrior's skill through the act of worshipping him. One day, while the young man was worshipping the clay image, he heard a dog barking in the forest. The noise disturbed him, so he went to find the dog in the woods. At last he came upon the barking animal, which was chasing a hare. With unbelievable precision, he shot arrows at the dog in such a way as to stitch its mouth shut, thereby stopping his barking. His image worship was paying off! Once again, he returned to his dwelling place to pursue his plan. What the young man didn't know, though, was that the dog belonged to Drona. After awhile Drona arrived, trying to discover who it was that had shot arrows at his pet. The young man explained that he was the culprit and that his excellent marksmanship was the result of the fact that he'd been beseeching Drona, through worship of the clay image, to increase his skill. Drona replied by saying, "Since you are my student, you owe me something. Isn't that right?" The young man immediately agreed, whereupon Drona demanded the thumb from his supplicant's right hand. There was no way out of the situation, so the young man cut off his right thumb and gave it to the master. Drona then condemned him to fashioning things from clay. So began a long line of potmakers.

This story has at least two basic elements. First, it shows the low-caste young man in a fairly positive light, depicting him as a clever and resourceful person who managed to become an accomplished marksman even after Drona's refusal to become his official instructor. On the other hand, the story communicates a clear social message: the potential student was dead wrong in thinking he could somehow circumvent the master's refusal to accept him as a student. The level of marksmanship the young man achieved through worship was finally forfeited when the warrior told him to lop off his thumb. This was his punishment for trying to attain what was originally denied to him by a socially recognized upper-caste authority. The story depicts the power of social relations in the world. If you try to mess with them, if you attempt to somehow transcend them, it's like messing with nature itself. Once a taboo has been broken, fate intervenes to correct the rupture. It is in this sense that we have to look at the accident that precipitates the young man's eventual downfall. The barking dog running through the woods apparently has nothing to do with his relationship to Drona. But as the story unfolds, we discover that this incident is far more ominous than it initially appeared, since the dog in fact belongs to Drona. In this way we get the sense that something inevitable has been set in motion, that the young man's downfall was preordained. It is this strong sense of fatalism, of the inviolability of certain social taboos, that is a final key element in the story.

Don't step out of line is the message. Or else.

Such stories create within a society a tremendous psychological pressure towards conservatism. They are internalized; they are accepted either literally or symbolically as containers of ultimate wisdom. The contemporary potmaker may take pride in the cleverness of his ancestor, but the potmaker also knows his place.

In terms of the power of *jati* and caste—in terms of its effect on people—let's look at another example. A living one. Her name is Sharda.

Sharda is an old woman. Through her hut's dark doorway, you can see a grease-stained, soiled-looking blanket on the floor. Sharda squats outside the door in a spot of morning shade. She has a small, impish, shriveled-up face. She responds in a half-friendly, half-cantankerous way to questions. When she gets going, she talks a mile a minute. In terms of caste, she's at the bottom of the ladder. An untouchable. A leatherworker.

There's an event in Sharda's life that I heard about from others. It occurred about two years ago. Her son was employed as a field laborer by a local landlord. When the son didn't receive the exact pay promised to him, he complained to his employer. The very night after he made the complaint, he was assaulted by a group of unknowns and beaten up. Although no bones were broken, his bruises—both physical and psychological—were sufficiently bad for him to remain in bed the whole next day. No one in the hutment colony where Sharda and her son live had any doubt that the unknown assailants were caste Hindus who worked for the landlord.

Sharda didn't take any of this sitting down. With uncharacteristic social aggression, she went to the police station and demanded something be done to the landlord who had arranged to have her son assaulted. They listened to her, then sent her away since she had no evidence to back up her accusations. Over the next few weeks she returned to the station at least one more time, making a nuisance out of herself, but nothing came of her complaints. Finally, she stopped going. Although this is all behind her now, it is still part of her life, her history.

This particular morning, Sharda talks about small, everyday things. She mentions that she has a grandchild who saw some monkeys in a tree and wanted to go live with them. As she tells this story, she rocks back and forth. When she's done, she turns her head to the side and spits tobacco juice in the dust.

So this is Sharda—an old woman who talks and spits and occasionally does out-of-character things like go to the police station and complain. But she is also more than this. She is the residue of a long tradition. Her position in life is reflective of things larger than herself as an individual.

For instance, there is the origin-myth of her group, which is as follows.

There was a Brahmin. His mother and father and before them their parents too had been Brahmins, and so on for generations. All observed the prevelant religious taboos. But in spite of the age-old restriction against eating cow meat, this particular Brahmin desired that meat and his desire mounted and became a passion till he finally got hold of a dead cow and ate its flesh, an unpardonable transgression. Subsequently he was punished as the gods stripped him of privilege and drove him out of the Brahmin caste. But the punishment wasn't directed solely at him. It was to affect all generations that would flow from his seed. They would eat cow meat and then work with the hides of dead cows. They would make sandals and things of leather. Their contamination and spiritual defilement would be forever visible.

This story is part of Sharda's *personal* history.

When you've internalized such a myth, when you've accepted its literal or symbolic truth, when you recognize it as a summing-up of your group's status, then you are gripped in a giant social vise. Both culturally and psychologically, the possibility of a positive self-image has been seriously diminished. The powerful have described you, and you, at least in part, have accepted their description. Your consciousness, in other words, has allied itself with the enemy. In an odd, socially schizophrenic way, you have joined forces with those who would oppress you, and you assist them.

But nothing is ever so simple. Sharda, for instance, isn't exactly like the above analysis would indicate. As shown by her willingness to confront the police two years ago, a struggle goes on within her. If she is held back by the old society, it is also true that, at the same time, there is something within her that desires to beat its way forward into a different kind of world.

This morning, in her little spot of shade, Sharda talks. As she relates a particular incident that happened to her awhile back a kind of cackling laughter erupts from her skinny throat. As with many people, there is something inscrutable about her. She is, in fact, a person whose life is, and has been, determined by the cultural and economic power of caste. Yet there is also something else, just beyond the onlooker's reach: a refusal to knuckle under, a desire to live on her own terms.

It is important to point out that the caste system, as it once was, is being shaken up.

Take Meeda Mamma, the basket weaver in Vijaynagar, as an example. Meeda Mamma comes from a tradition of basket weavers. One of the signs of his group's social as well as spiritual lowness is that the members of the group are pork-eaters. Because they are stigmatized as bottom-of-the-barrel people, they have been historically required to live at the edges of the villages they inhabit, removed from the mainstream of life.

Meeda Mamma's existence in Vijaynagar, however, is different than one might expect, if the only thing we knew about him was his caste affiliation. Meeda Mamma lives in the midst of the village, feels free to go into the hut of the higher-caste peasant next door, fraternizes with people on pretty much an equal level and can be seen sharing food with neighbors from higher and supposedly cleaner castes.

Meeda Mamma's mobility, when compared to the mobility of his parents' generation, is greater. This isn't due, however, to any sudden economic advancement or attainment of an important village-level political position. Meeda Mamma is poor, and he ekes out, at best, a subsistence-level existence. The reason Meeda Mamma isn't as trapped by caste as he might have been a generation ago has nothing to do with him as an individual. It is part, instead, of a general trend: the gradual transformation of caste distinctions.

There are reasons, of course, for this transformation.

Across the subcontinent, as the old feudally-organized agricultural society is being disrupted by the emergence of capitalism and neocolonial exploitation, the caste system, which in the past provided a neat framework for people's occupational and religious lives, is also being disturbed. In the countryside, for instance, the polarization of those with and without land increases creating an environment in which preoccupation with caste becomes less useful. Similarly, another set of anti-caste pressures are created by India's migration patterns. Movement from the rural areas to the cities results from poverty in the countryside. But once in the cities, people from diverse caste backgrounds are compelled to work together on construction crews, assembly lines, and in government offices, etc. Caste barriers are, as a result, weakened. As a low caste factory worker expressed during a strike:

> There are all these differences, even among ourselves. Working inside, there's Muslims, Hindus from different castes, untouchables. Sometimes we argue and yell, but we've found out that if we want anything, the only way we're going to get it is by sticking together. We can't afford to be squabbling all the time in terms of who's higher caste.

Slowly, then, the caste system is undergoing transformation. But if the trend is toward change, it is also true that this change isn't occuring either smoothly or nonviolently. Almost in direct proportion to the mounting pressures against caste, both economic and social, there's a powerful, semi-hysterical backlash attempt to preserve the caste system. This is why today India is going through a period of extreme caste violence.

The major example of this is the relationship between caste Hindus and non-caste untouchables. As the dominant castes/

classes attempt to hold onto the reigns of power in the midst of a rapidly transforming India, they do whatever they can to reinforce caste divisions, since such divisions ensure a fragmented, powerless workforce. In doing this, they all too frequently can rely on the caste prejudices of laboring people. There's no doubt that in the contemporary period, the continuation of caste divisions serves a specific class purpose: the preservation of power for those who already have it.

So, there is violence. Sudden. Earth-scorching.

One incident, which occurred in Villupurum in the southeastern state of Tamil Nadu, began when a caste Hindu tried to grab the breast of an untouchable woman in the town vegetable market. There was a brief skirmish, but she got away. When later she returned to the hutment colony where she lived—and where 3000 other untouchables lived also—she narrated the story of what had happened to her. That evening, in response to her harassment, a small group of untouchable men went to the home of the man who had taken advantage of the woman and beat him up. This act set in motion a chain of events that was to culminate in mass violence and twelve brutal deaths.

The untouchables' assault against a caste Hindu was considered a major transgression by many townspeople. Subsequently, the next morning the local Vegetable Merchants Association closed down their shops in protest over the incident. Large numbers of caste Hindus began milling around in the streets and soon an anti-untouchable procession was organized. It marched toward the hutment colony. When the rioters arrived, they used flamable materials and explosives to attack the untouchables' living area. The attack continued through the night and through most of the next day. Large sections of the colony were set on fire. Of the 800 dwellings, about 100 were destroyed. Even when the large-scale rioting finally subsided, the violence itself didn't end. Anti-untouchable gangs roamed the streets, looking for victims to harass. For the twelve known dead, the murder techniques employed were various: strangulation, crushed skulls, lethal beatings. Local police were noticeably ineffectual in trying to put a stop to what was going on. For the most part, they stood back and watched.

But the description given so far is only part of the picture. The facts, as we've seen them, don't fully explain the occurrence of mass violence in Villupurum. We have to dig deeper. As it says in the report on which the previous information was based:

At the root of the tension was a growing conflict between the town's dominant economic interests— traders and merchants—and Harijan laborers who have become emboldened and more conscious of their rights and organized strength. The most wrenching elements of the tragedy lay in the success of the former in mobilizing a large number of laboring people who are in most respects as oppressed as the Harijans they attacked.

Not surprisingly, then, the violence in Villupurum was at least partially the result not just of caste values but also of a changing economic climate. Untouchables, beginning to see themselves as exploited workers and as a consequence organizing themselves against oppression, had become "emboldened" and in so doing were rejecting the age-old notion that it was their duty to resign themselves to silent servitude. Traders and merchants responded to this threat to their traditional privileges by instigating, the moment an opportunity arose, mass rioting. In the process of doing this, they were able to manipulate the prejudices of caste Hindus who were in fact "as oppressed as the Harijans they attacked."

What happened in Villupurum is indicative of a pattern of caste violence in contemporary India. It's a single image riding on a tidalwave of grassroots upheavals. Change doesn't come easy, not ever.

So: as India's growing capitalist system develops and sets in motion the need for new forms of social organization, there is a distinct backlash from the most powerful beneficiaries of the caste system. When untouchable agricultural laborers organize in the countryside, for instance, caste Hindu landlords do everything within their power to mobilize the local population along caste lines, hoping, through the stirring-up of mass violence and religious hysteria, to shatter the strength of the newly-organized farmworkers. From all over India, reports come of caste-related conflict and tension. In one instance, an untouchable man is castrated by an angry mob. In another, seven untouchables, women and men, are killed as a result of a district quarrel over land rights. In a third situation, rioting breaks out when a public institution is renamed after a pre-Independence untouchable militant. The list goes on. The incidents pile up. Even in the midst of a growing tendency on the part of working people to perceive themselves along class (as opposed to caste) lines, caste remains an explosive, potentially chaotic cutting edge. Untouchables who represent between 13 and 15% of the population, remain the most exploited sector of the workforce. Because of this, any revolutionary movement which aims at the meaningful transformation of Indian society must confront head-on the emotional, economic and cultural inequities of the whole caste system and its special oppression of non-caste people.

Increasingly, untouchables are taking the struggle into their own hands. They are projecting a picture of a different, freer kind of world. They are willing to fight for this world. They are willing to put their lives on the line.

In the words of one untouchable poet:

like the elephant leading the charge
on the pike-studded doors of the fort,
let us die laughing.

Sexual Relations

Just as when looking at caste, when looking at the position of the Indian woman within society, we have to be extremely careful. We run the risk of making a false comparison between women of the West and women of the East and their treatment within the different societies. For instance, when we hear of the old Indian custom of *sati* (a widow burns herself on the funeral pyre of her dead husband), we think of such self-immolation as "barbaric," horrible. It is another one of those apparently foolproof signs of India's backwardness. We say to ourselves, women would never be expected to act in such a way *here*. But, somehow, when looking at the contemporary degradation of western women in pornographic cinema and Madison Avenue advertising or at the high incidence of rape in the U.S., we tend not to use the same kind of derogatory descriptions. The point here is the obvious one: we once again stand in need of guarding ourselves against cultural preconceptions. If we self-indulgently excuse our own culture's sexism, it will be impossible to achieve an accurate view of what life is like for women in India. We'll only see our own self-serving projections: *that's* bad, and *we're* good.

But the problem is even more multi-layered than this. In trying to overcome our cultural biases and in attempting to apply a sensitive feminist analysis to the Indian situation, we also have to avoid the risk of assuming that western feminist analysis is universally applicable and can be imposed, whole hog, on another culture. Even in our own country we have this problem. Women from different classes and racial groupings often articulate their sense of sexual oppression in distinct ways, revealing that there is no single, airtight feminist analysis. But if this is true right here in the United States, it means we have to be especially careful when trying to comprehend the problem of sexism in another culture. If we aren't, we'll be involved in a self-defeating act of cultural aggression.

Look: in the early morning light, on the Vengrula Road at the bottom of Vijaynagar's hill, peasants stream towards the city from the surrounding countryside. In straw baskets balanced on their heads, groups of women carry vegetables and grains. Some walk silently, others talk and laugh. Their posture is perfect: straight-backed, erect. There are also men—on bicycles, driving bullock-carts, walking. In this crowded road scene there is something you notice when you look closely. In general, the women and men are gathered into separate, mutually-exclusive groups. There are, of course, exceptions—that woman there, gesticulating with her hands while she talks to the man walking alongside her. Yet the exceptions don't, can't, destroy the general impression: two worlds, male and female.

Here's another scene. There are two women. They are standing next to a hole in the ground; a well is being dug. Inside the hole, there's a clanging sound as a man bangs an iron spike against solid rock. Another man tosses up shovel-loads of dirt and broken stone. The women, after a brief two-minute rest, begin working again. With their hands, they scoop up soil and rock fragments and drop them into basket-shaped metal containers. When the containers are filled up, they carry them to a spot about twenty-five yards away and empty them onto a growing earthpile. Then they return and repeat the process— once, twice, again and again. Sometimes when they're scooping stones into their containers, they'll duck and angrily shout "watch out!" as a shovelful of dirt comes flying up out of the hole, landing too close to them. For the work they're doing, the women get paid less than half what the men receive.

Here, in this briefly summarized scene, we see the typical Indian working woman. She is carter. She is doer of the dirty work. She is low paid. She is also (when she wants to be) tough, or charming, or timid, or beautiful or foul-mouthed. Frequently she's tired—and maybe, also, on edge. If she is, she doesn't like to be pushed around.

But, like it or not, sometimes she is. It's not, after all, *her* world. It's built into the social system, the assumption that men "naturally" predominate over women. This means that for the subcontinent woman there's no smooth road to the place of dignity and solid self-esteem.

As with caste, anti-women attitudes can't exist without reinforcement. The power of culture must be relied upon to continually recreate the psychological conditions necessary for preserving a male-oriented society. Old ideas, rooted in the past, must be allowed to swim forward into the present, inhabiting people's minds and influencing their vision of what's natural or preordained, and what isn't.

At the same time that this is true, it's also true that the subcontinent's attitudes toward women aren't of a single fiber. There are layer upon layer of intertwined meanings, implications. In the ancient Laws of Manu, it says, "Where women are honored, there the gods are pleased." But it also says, in the same text, "Day and night women must be kept in dependence by the males of their families, and, if they attach themselves to sensual enjoyments, they must be kept under one's control." So, on the one hand there is adulation, while on the other there are philosophical statements concerning men's regulatory powers over women. Such attitudes, woven irrevocably into the texture of Indian consciousness, exist even today. But the carry-over from past to present doesn't occur without modification. There are new contexts to which the old ideas must be adapted. For instance, in the bookstalls there are rows of western-style magazines with the faces of Indian movie starlets splashed in bright colors on their covers. This is, in a sense, a neocolonialized reinterpretation of one of the maxims previously quoted— "Where women are honored, there the gods are pleased." Similarly the idea that "day and night women must be kept in dependence by the males of their families" must also be given a new content in keeping with the conditions of the times. It can't be allowed to mean, for instance, that a woman can't work independently of her husband on a roadcrew or in the fields or somewhere else. Present-day economic pressures dictate that this must be allowed, and so the old attitude is adjusted accordingly. This isn't really, however, such a new phenomenon. There have always been in India these variations on apparently absolute behavior codes. Laboring-class women were never, for instance, mere prisoners of the household. Still, we have to acknowledge that built into the culture there is a clear imperative: female is subordinate to male.

There are also other examples of the cultural reinforcement of the philosophy of male dominance. Some of these provide an interesting picture of how, throughout Indian history, conflicting attitudes concerning women have collided as the male vision struggled to gain pre-eminence. In order to get a closer look at such an example, we can once again, as with caste, turn to mythology.

There is a goddess, Yellamma. Not far from Vijaynagar, less than a sixty mile journey into the hills, is her temple. Near this temple, there's a rock from which an underground spring erupts. According to local religious tradition, this water has healing properties. Washing with the water supposedly can cure leprosy and syphillis. Yellamma is viewed as a powerful goddess hidden away among the ancient rocks. Her festival days fall on full moon nights. The full moon is a symbol of female strength.

The Yellamma myth is an old one, probably stretching back into pre-history. It's interesting to look at the myth's development, to see how the contemporary Yellamma story in all likelihood reflects a previous and different story. What we will notice about the present-day (accepted) version of the story is that it reflects male values. But by reading between the lines of this story, we can catch glimpses of a far older version that probably originated in a matriarchal or more women-oriented period. In this original story, female, as opposed to male, power is celebrated.

First, however, let's look at the present-day version.

Yellamma was the wife of an extremely religious man, a devotee of the god Shiva. She was the perfect wife. She was self-disciplined, she served her husband with unwavering obedience, her mind was free of impure thoughts. Everything she did had an air of worshipfulness and high-mindedness about it. Because of her, their house was filled with an aura of holiness. They lived in a state of near human perfection.

One of Yellamma's household duties was to go every day to a nearby brook and fetch water. As with everything else she did, her performance of this small task was characterized by a humble sense of service. But one day when she was at the stream, she noticed something. The king of the celestial musicians was playing in the stream with some water-nymphs. There was something sexually suggestive about their activity. Seeing this, for a split second Yellamma desired to be part of this game. At the very moment that this thought passed through her mind, the clay water-vessel on top of her head broke and the water poured out. As a result of this, she regained her composure, driving away, through an act of will, her bad thought. Then she returned home. Once again she had achieved her previous state of holiness.

Her husband, however, noticed that there was something different in her demeanor, and he interpreted this to mean that her purity had somehow been undermined. It seemed to him that he had only one course of action. He and Yellamma had five sons, and he went to each of them, beginning with the oldest, and related to them his suspicions. After informing each son, he asked them individually if they would be willing to slay their mother because of her new, contaminated state. The four oldest said no. Finally, however, the youngest one agreed to the plan, so he took an ax and lopped off his mother's head.

When the son had completed his task, the father said to him, "Because you are the only son who would do what I requested, I will grant you any wish you want." To this the son replied, "I want you to bring my mother back to life." The father kept his word and immediately restored Yellamma's health. She was once again pure. She lived the rest of her life with a mind free of all negative thoughts. She was the living symbol of service and obedience.

The Yellamma myth, as just told, is what we would call a patriarchal or male-created myth. That is, it assumes as one of the bases of reality the dominance of men over women. But in this same myth, as well as in the contemporary rituals surrounding Yellamma's worship, we can find glimpses of an earlier non-patriarchal myth. For instance, Yellamma's association with the full moon and the fact that there are special festivals in her honor at harvest time, indicate that Yellamma, in her original historical form, was probably a fertility goddess. The sexual overtones of early fertility cults are well documented. Vestiges of sexual consciousness are still present, although in distorted form, in contemporary Yellamma worship. One example of this would be that the waters flowing from the rock near her temple are said to be endowed with a magical capacity to cure syphillis, a disease popularly believed to be the result of sexual excess. Another example was cited earlier in the book— the priests' pattern of securing virgins who will devote their lives to the goddess, then funneling these same young women into the world of prostitution.

For our purposes, what's interesting is that none of the Yellamma myth's connections to ancient fertility rites are directly stated in the myth's present form. The clues are there, but they have to be pieced together, puzzle-like. This is because as Indian society developed, moving away from more matriarchal forms of social organization, the old myths were rewritten in such a way as to reinforce the emergence of a new, male-dominated world view. This is what apparently happened, a long time ago, to the Yellamma story.

Looking at the myth from this perspective, we're able to see some interesting things. It becomes significant that Yellamma's "crime" is a momentary desire to participate in the sexual playfulness of the king of the celestial musicians and the water-nymphs. This is the precise part of the story in which she is reconnected to the story's original matriarchal form, with its emphasis on female power and fertility. For this she must be punished, since the original story is being rewritten by a male consciousness that wants to obliterate all memory of Yellamma's—or women's—past power. So, Yellamma's punishment is dramatic and symbolic all at once. She isn't only decapitated; she is, in fact, lobotomized. Her memory of her sexual lapse is destroyed, since according to the patriarchal view, female sexuality cannot be allowed to exist independent of women's designated role as mother. She must be passive, subordinate, non-self-activating. Only after her lobotomization is Yellamma allowed to come back to life—a beaten-down and properly chastised woman who will certainly, from this point on, be perfectly obedient. The myth's older form has been defeated, and a newer form has taken its place.

The Yellamma myth is only one of hundreds, yet it offers us an opportunity to look at the long historical process which stands behind contemporary attitudes about female roles in India. Even today the Yellamma story has a powerful effect on people from the Belgaum area. This effect isn't just religious, it's also cultural in a larger sense; Yellamma, subdued and unquestioning, is a role model for all women.

As in all societies, in India woman is perceived (romanticized) to be fundamentally nurturer and mother. She is a childbearing vessel. She is the protective wing. Her basic purpose within the family is to "belong" to the husband so that with her and through her he can produce children.

This meaning of womanhood has been handed down through the generations. Women accept it, believe it, judge themselves on the basis of it. They look at themselves through the eyes of male authority.

But, predictably, there is tension between what actually is and what is supposed to be, between day-to-day life and tradition. Not all women are content to be judged on the basis of the conventional codes.

Minakshi is the wife of a tailor. She and her husband have been married for seven years. In her mid-20s she is lively and, by existing standards, attractive. The one sorrow in her life is that she has not yet had a child. Not only is she worried, so is her husband. He has arranged for her to go to a number of different doctors in order to find out if something's wrong with her

physically. Another related pressure on Minakshi is that she's
certain she's being gossiped about by people in the area. She
thinks they're saying, "Poor Arun (her husband), he's stuck with
the barren Minakshi."

Minakshi chastises herself for being infertile, and yet, at the
same time, she's angry at herself for being so self-lacerating. In
an emotional moment she blurts out, "Maybe it's not me; maybe
it's him. Why does everybody have to assume I'm the one to
blame?" Yet she's caught. Her mind swings back and forth
between judging herself over-harshly for "failing" to be a
mother and resenting the fact that she's been singled out, both by
others and herself, as the deficient one.

The days go on and Minakshi's torment doesn't end. Only a
child will bring relief. Or a nonconformist refusal to accept the
prevailing criteria for what it means to be a woman.

There are also other, different stories. Other woman-lives.

Unlike Minakshi, Kamlavah is a mother, but nonetheless
she also has her pain, her tragedy. This pain, as in Minakshi's
case, is related to the equation of woman with motherhood.
Kamlavah is a young, working-class woman whose 28-year-old
husband has a factory job. Originally they had two children, a girl
and boy. After much hesitation, two years ago Kamlavah allowed
herself to be persuaded by the local family planning association
to get sterilized. Initially she resisted the idea because it seemed
to her that the operation would be an assault on the very basis of
her existence: her fertility. But if she resisted on the one hand, on
the other she was attracted to the idea of insuring that she and
her husband would have a small, easily manageable family. So,
after at first saying no to the suggestions of the family planning
people, she finally gave in. No other forms of birth control had
been mentioned.

After the birth of her third child, a boy, Kamlavah was
sterilized. A year later a tragedy occurred; Kamlavah's one
daughter died in the middle of the night. After the child's death,
she and her husband wanted desparately to have another
daughter. Only then did Kamlavah find out the operation wasn't
reversible. For approximately a year after this she lived at the
edge of a nervous breakdown. She cried continually and got upset
over the least little thing. She couldn't control her moods. She

sank into despair and felt that life was meaningless. Her daughter's death had precipitated a crisis in which she had to confront her new reality—that she had sacrificed her access to the traditional meaning of womanhood, the power to reproduce. Although today Kamlavah has regained some of her emotional composure, she is still a sad, bitter woman.

Two women, two lives. But it isn't just the equation between woman and motherhood that oppresses. There is more.

At the center of sexual relations in India, we also find the idea of property ownership. This is evidenced in many ways. "In childhood," the words of tradition say, "the female must be subject to her father, in youth to her husband, when her lord is dead to her sons; a woman must never be independent." Subject, here, is the key word; a woman lives only as an owned object, to be manipulated by male hands. All around, this idea can be seen, not just as *idea*, but as a physical reality. For instance, when we look at the local Muslim woman with the veil on her face, we must interpret the symbolism correctly. The veil is a protective covering over the husband's "property." This property is for him to treasure and hoard; no one else must look at it. The veil on the face is like a fence marking off a plot of land. It means: what you see here is owned, no trespassing, stay away.

But once this is said, we run into another problem. When trying to understand the significance of the Muslim woman's veil, it's easy to oversimplify, to make quick hit-and-run judgements and then proceed to another topic without fully understanding what we've seen. The reality is that in the Belgaum area we can't grasp the meaning of the veil without knowing that most Muslim women here are working class and *don't regularly wear* veils. Veil wearing is reserved for the better-off, who preserve the tradition for the reason that it is the foundation of their sense of social superiority. So, in terms of veil wearing, we aren't confronted with a simple, clear-cut example of sexism. There's a class context that also has to be understood. Often this is the case.

Class and sexual relations—let's pursue some of the interconnections.

A man tells me about his place of origin, further to the north. He has a way with words. He creates a living picture. Part of this picture is a portrait of the power of local landowners. In doing this, he goes beyond economics, entering the more shadowy areas of power relations. As he talks, there emerges a picture of quiet, moonlit fields in the middle of nowhere. There's a house. The landlord waits in his bedroom. His wife is pregnant and he needs someone to "substitute" for her in the conjugal darkness. Finally a young, low caste village woman enters. Tonight she belongs to him. She is one of the possessions that goes along with his fields.

Such things happen. You can hear about them from individuals or read about them in certain reports. The powerful landowner has feudal jurisdiction over his domain. The wives and daughters and sisters of local working men are part of that domain. This is sexism, then, but within a strictly defined set of class relations. The landlord wouldn't dream of compelling the wife of someone of his own class to enter his bedroom. He wouldn't treat such a woman as his rightful sexual property, as his due. He would still, of course, perceive her as an essentially subordinate being, obligated by tradition and the laws of nature to spend her life in service to her husband, father, brother. If she fails in this service, the landlord knows (because it says so in the texts) that she "is disgraced...after death she enters the womb of a jackel, and is tormented by diseases, the punishment for her sin." But knowing and feeling all this, the landlord will nonetheless treat the women of his own class differently than those lower than himself in the social pyramid. In the end, it is the laboring class woman who bears the brunt of the landlord's sexual arrogance. It is she that he can abuse with total abandon and without remorse. She is always the potential target and victim, the most likely recipient of his power-hungry assaults.

So: even when looking at sexual oppression, we have to view it through more than one lens. On the one hand, sexual oppression exists as a general trend within the whole of Indian society, and, therefore, affects all women regardless of class or caste. On the other hand, many forms of sexual oppression exist within the framework of particular class/caste relationships and can't, therefore, be understood independently of these relationships.

This helps explain certain female attitudes that might otherwise, on the surface, appear contradictory.

For instance, in Vijaynagar, both Holika and Shamabai see themselves as exploited women. Holika, who regularly works both outside and in the home, complains of double labor. Besides the predictable domestic chores, Holika digs wells, builds the foundations for houses, cuts hay, etc. She takes pride in her work and in her contribution to the family's economic well-being. Yet it grates on her that she gets no special praise for what she does. When this frustration builds to the breaking point, Holika lashes out at her husband, cuts him with sarcastic salvos, puts him down. Holika, then, is an example of a woman responding to sexual oppression.

Shamabai's problem, however, is different from Holika's. It's not double labor she complains about, but actual sexual contact. She feels that, with the exception of using her to satisfy his sexual needs, her husband, Ram, doesn't notice her. Shamabai takes this problem seriously and is looking for a solution. She wonders if maybe after the birth of her next child she should be sterilized. Such an operation, she thinks, would limit the need for sexual contact with her husband. Anything that will limit this need seems to her like a good idea.

Because both these women are intelligent and capable of generalizing on the basis of what they see around them, they perceive their personal experiences (in Shamabai's words) "as like what happens to lots of women." But because this understanding doesn't exist abstractly or in isolated form, it is mediated by other concerns. If on the one hand the two women find their men, in different ways, unappreciative, on the other they identify with their husbands' plights and see them as exploited part-broken people. Holika, for instance, perceives Laxshman's drinking problem and erratic behavior as related to his inability to rise above the pressures of daily life—the sunup to sundown workday, the social immobility, the smashed dreams. Similarly, Shamabai has, in spite of her anger, a spontaneous sympathy for her husband, Ram. She sees him as beaten down, overworked, exhausted. "He's not a bad man," she says.

These women don't defend their husbands because, as women, they're ignorant or undereducated and therefore have been brainwashed into denying their own needs while excusing their husbands' faults. They defend them out of a sense of social class and out of a sense of mutual bondage to those in power. The women perceive their men as brutalized. They know first-hand how as part of the scheme of things this brutalization is then passed off onto them, as women and wives. Neither Holika nor Shamabai passively allows this to occur. They struggle, they go at it tooth and nail with their husbands, they brood and fight. But still, in the end, the women perceive "society"—and by implication the upper classes—as the major culprit in their inability to achieve stability and happiness. This perception is the core of their identification with, and defense of, their husbands.

In Holika's words, while most people work and suffer, there are others "who run things and get rich."

So, as with caste, when looking at the role of women in India we find a variety of different but interlocking facets: economic, cultural, etc. What, then, is the correct way to perceive the problem? What does all this mean in terms of the subcontinent's overall situation?

One woman—her name is Seta—supplies a possible answer.

Seta, the daughter of a successful editor, is in her mid-20s. She says:

Only a few people will admit it, but I think one of the major crises India now faces is the difference between women, men. The view that women are not as good as men has a harmful effect on our country. Because Indira Gandhi was in office for awhile doesn't mean that women are treated well here. Most women don't have any chance to get power, except maybe over their children. For the country to take advantage of its potential, it's going to have to allow more women to become doctors, lawyers, judges, movie directors, business people. Many things will have to change. They will have to stop doing all those things that make us look funny or useless. As time goes on, you can expect to see the struggle for more equality growing. The time has come for India to move away from the past.

Seta isn't a typical Indian woman. She is characterized by what she calls a modern sense of the world. There are other women like her, mostly in the cities, but not many. Anyone who talks with Seta will certainly be impressed by her grasp of the different ways in which women are degraded: in the household, in the media, in arranged marriages, etc. But there's something else that one also notices. She wears bell-bottom jeans and a beautifully embroidered western-style blouse. This is significant. The more Seta talks, the more it becomes clear that her feminism and clothing style are linked; both, in a sense, are neocolonial imports. This doesn't mean Seta's insights are without value or superficial. It does mean, however, that her insights are limited, especially if we expect them to provide us with an understanding of how most Indian women perceive their problems.

There are, of course, reasons for this.

Seta's social class has a lot to do with how she envisions the world. Traditionally the Indian middle class woman has been trapped in the house and protected whenever possible from doing actual labor; the servants do it. In general, such a woman is seen as a nice decoration—maybe she can sing or play the sitar—whose fundamental occupation is to oversee the house and bear children. Obviously such an existence can be stifling. When women from this background, like Seta, fight against the traditional women-limiting values of their class, their struggle is frequently dosed with strong elements of career preoccupation. They want activity, moving room, recognition, full access to the public sector's male domains. Therefore, Seta's emphasis on professionals: doctors, lawyers, judges, etc. Therefore, too, the absense of any statement having to do with the lower classes. Such a response is determined by what she is rebelling *against*, not by intentional arrogance or disdain.

As we have seen, for women of the lower classes life is dramatically different. Although they are also viewed as child-bearing possessions of their husbands and are in general oppressed by a male-oriented culture, the similarity stops there. With no servants to rely on, they have hard physical labor to perform in the house. But they also work outside the home, performing a wide variety of jobs—road and construction work, grass cutting, farming, etc. Inevitably, when these women work for pay, there are wage differentials along sexual lines as well as a sexual division of labor. The women are forced down into the

lowest paid, most unskilled work levels. But working women
tend not to stress such things as examples of sexual oppression.
The reason for this isn't hard to find. Even though the men have
the more skilled and higher-paying jobs, their wages are barely
sufficient to cover the costs of the most meager, rock-bottom
existence. The women, therefore, have nothing concrete, in
terms of day-to-day economic survival, to envy the men for.
Instead, they're inclined to see themselves, along with the men,
as oppressively trapped in society's lowest regions. Although
many of these women don't use the formal vocabulary of class
analysis, they nonetheless tend to see their situation in class
terms.

So: in India, as in other countries, the problem of sexual
oppression is a complicated one. On the one hand, sexism affects
all women, regardless of caste or class affiliation. In other words,
all women are oppressed by male values and institutions and
social relations. Yet, if we look at the majority of women—
working women—we find that their sense of sexual exploitation, which is often keen, is mediated by an equally keen sense of
class exploitation. It should go without saying that if there's
going to be revolutionary change in India, these women, the
ones from the laboring sectors, are going to have to play a
crucial part in deciding the kind of analysis and strategies most
suitable for attacking male dominance within the Indian framework. If this doesn't happen and women from the more
privileged sectors gain hegemony over Indian feminism, then
the needs of the majority of women are bound to be only weakly
articulated.

3
INDIA SINCE 1947
A BRIEF POLITICAL HISTORY

1.

In 1949, Jawaharlal Nehru, Prime Minister of India, visited the U.S. According to one Indian historian:

India was in the throes of famine, and he hoped to obtain from the United States wheat and capital for economic development....Those were the days when the cold war was at its peak and the ruling American cliche was: "If you are not with us, you are against us." To the ardent advocate of non-alignment that Nehru chose to be, the supreme virtue lay in being with everyone and being against no one. Despite the reprobation of disapproving American senators and congressmen, Nehru stood firm against receiving "aid with strings attached"....

The half blunder and half braggadocio of American businessmen also distressed Nehru. At a dinner given in his honor, one of them boasted to him: "Mr. Prime Minister, just around this table are presidents of corporations worth twenty billion dollars!" Nehru's socialist sensibilities were deeply offended and he exploded later in private that India was not for sale.

In this brief description of Nehru's first visit to the U.S., there are certain key points that should be highlighted: for instance, the theme that India, just recently rid of its colonial shackles, wasn't "for sale"; and also the suggestion that India's leadership had strong socialist, as opposed to capitalist, leanings.

At the time, this picture was broadly accepted, especially in the West. Even today, some commentators persist in this vision, a sure sign that the original Indian post-Independence propaganda scheme was successful in determining how India would be viewed internationally. The only problem with accepting this portrait of India as a "socialist" country "not for sale" is that it can only be believed if one consciously chooses to ignore the actual political and social dynamics of Indian life.

2.

Immediately after Independence in 1947, the dominant classes in India had reached a consensus on government policy:

India had to move toward a "socialistic pattern of society" if it wanted to achieve stability and take care of the needs of its vast population. Social planning would entail an economy guided and directed by the state. This meant that the state would adopt a program of achieving, over a period of time, exclusive control of certain key industries: arms and munitions production, railway transport, communications, atomic energy, etc. Because of the prevalent western belief that such a strong state presence in the economic sphere does indeed display a socialistic rather than a capitalistic vision of economic growth, many people assumed India had opted for socialism. The actual nature of what was going on, however, was different from this.

The development of a strong state or public sector was never, in reality, intended to foster socialism. Its purpose was to create an opportunity for the Indian bourgeoisie—industrialists, bankers, etc.—to pursue a course of independent (not controlled by the western economies) capitalist development.

The thinking behind this strategy was simple. The Indian capitalist class, although it was the strongest in Asia other than the Japanese, wasn't fully mature. Its development under British colonialism had been stunted by the self-serving imperial policy. This put the Indian capitalists in a difficult position after Independence. Not having sufficient resources to single-handedly, as a group, lead India into the future, they had to secure assistance. One alternative for getting such assistance was collaboration with the advanced capitalist classes of the West. Pursuing this alternative, however, would have endangered the very thing that had driven them to push the Independence movement forward: their desire to secure the country's wealth "for Indians," that is, for themselves. They knew that collaboration with the West would inevitably, because of the West's superiority in technological know-how and productive capacity, lead to western domination, at their expense.

The other alternative was to get support from within the country itself, but from "outside" the bourgeoisie. This would entail setting up a large state-sponsored public sector which would take responsibility for the development of industries that the capitalists felt, for the moment, inadequately prepared to deal with (like arms and munitions production). This would take some responsibility off the capitalists' shoulders and at the same time allow them to flex their newly-freed muscles in the areas they felt more confident in. In this way, the capitalist class would be given a certain protected space in which to develop without being burdened by responsibility for the whole economy. This was the alternative that was chosen.

But the bourgeoisie's problems still weren't solved. Far from it.

Having laid the groundwork for their own development, there was still a major problem to contend with: the rest of the population. Since rural and urban poverty were so extraordinary in India, somehow the masses had to be convinced that steps were being taken to alleviate their situation. If they weren't convinced, it seemed certain they would soon withdraw their support from the present leadership and start agitating for radical change. Part of the solution to this problem, the capitalists hoped, was in the propaganda campaign they were launching in support of the development of a large public sector. The message of this propaganda was clear: the state, neutral and uncontaminated by class bias, will oversee industrial development and insure the fairest possible distribution of the wealth that is produced. If enough people could be persuaded of the truth of this, the capitalists knew, there would be a waiting period of relative calm. And this was just what the wealthy needed: time.

But the capitalists also knew that propaganda, by itself, wouldn't be sufficient to defuse all problems. There were certain areas that required immediate action; for instance, the agrarian sector. Since it was in the countryside that the greatest absolute poverty was found, people there had to be addressed specifically, had to be given some reassuring message, some proof of better times to come. The peasants had to be promised land reform. A method for giving the majority of the peasantry enough land to live on had to be initiated.

But in putting forward a program of land reform, there were serious dangers for the capitalist class. The main problem was that any serious land reform scheme would drive a wedge between it and the dominant rural classes: landlords, rich peasants, moneylenders. This couldn't be allowed to happen, since the capitalists felt they would have to rely on the support of precisely those classes if there were ever an eruption of popular discontent with the government. Mass peasant land occupations that had occurred during the 1940s were still fresh in the capitalists' minds; the power of an organized peasantry was frightening. Also there was the reality of the Chinese Revolution, which had taken the greatest precautions against allowing the development of an all-powerful capitalist class. What would happen if the Chinese communists became a model for the Indian people and a movement was initiated for the radical reorganization of subcontinent society? In such a case, the wealthy rural elite would have to be relied upon to help control the masses.

The result of all these considerations was an ambivalence about how to approach poverty in the countryside. On the one hand, feeling ran high among government officials that the rural poor had to be placated in order to defuse their anger. On the other hand, however, they were intimidated by the possibility of alienating the vested interests in the countryside, whose support they needed. This vacillation amounted to nothing less than a sort of continual flirtation, on the part of those in power, with political suicide. How long they could keep the lid on the bottle was anybody's guess.

During the period from the beginning of the 50s to the early 60s, it became evident that while the capitalist class was growing stronger, the economic condition of the average Indian was getting worse. No annual or decade-long rise in the Gross National Product could hide the fact that an increase in productive capacity wasn't eliminating poverty as had been envisioned. For instance, to the capitalists' advantage, profits were rising at a far greater pace in the private sector than in the public sector, and yet these profits weren't at all distributed to the workers. While worker productivity increased, real wages remained the same from year to year or at best increased only minimally. On top of this, the growing Gross National Product didn't, as had been projected, diminish unemployment; in fact, the total number of the unemployed grew. All talk about socialist planning aside, the country that was supposedly bravely steering a middle course between capitalism and communism was in trouble. And it wasn't steering a middle course, either. It was pursuing, without a doubt, the capitalist road of development. The prevailing philosophy was that growth in and of itself, without any additional attempt to transform society as a whole, would solve society's problems. But it wasn't working.

One way to get an idea of what the situation was like at the time is to take a brief look at the rural areas.

Poverty was everywhere. The number of people who had to resort to agricultural labor, either as their sole source of income or to supplement the meager livelihood they made off their small landholdings, was increasing. At the same time, the percentage of agricultural laborers without any land at all was increasing. Complicating the situation was the fact that more than sixty percent of the rural population was in debt to local moneylenders, who were either themselves landlords or who had close social/political connections with the landlords. The rates of interest charged on loans were usurious, ranging as high as fifty percent. Once in debt, the peasant was often in debt for the rest of his life. This was fine with the moneylender, who could make more from regular partial payments over many years than he could from quick repayment in one lump sum. It's an indication of the extent of poverty in the countryside that most borrowing wasn't for improving farming methods, but was merely a way of trying to cover basic household expenses. While the majority of the peasantry ate their bitter bread, the landlords looked on, satisfied that the government's public statements about progressively dispersing the national wealth weren't anything to worry about.

By the end of the 50s, the time had come for a change. It didn't take much intelligence to see that if there weren't some general economic improvement, the people might flare up and bourgeois power be jeopardized. The question was: how to secure such an improvement? Gradually the answer became clear: economic growth had to be speeded up through the presence of foreign capital and technological know-how. The old fear of being dominated by the western economies had to be laid aside. It was time to collaborate with the advanced capitalist countries in order to insure the continuation of "democracy" on the Indian subcontinent.

This, anyway, was the thinking of those in power.

In 1957, the number of government-approved schemes for foreign investment and/or technical collaboration was only 24. By 1960, the number had increased 16 times to 388. Eventually a pattern would emerge in which the rate of such approved schemes would be in the vicinity of 300-400 per year. At the same time, a pattern of increasing reliance on foreign aid was emerging. Whereas at the beginning of the 50s an average of 5 million rupees per year was going toward the repayment of foreign debt, by the early 70s this would soar to an annual 370 million rupees.

It's also necessary to note exactly who these foreign investors and givers of aid were. In 1948, the year after Independence, Britain's share of the foreign investment in the Indian economy was 80%, whereas the U.S. share was a measly 2%. By 1967 the gap had narrowed, Britain now controlling only 48% of the foreign investment while the U.S. share had risen to at least 25%. In terms of foreign aid, the U.S. emerged as the undisputed leading contributor. In the two decades from 1950-1970, total U.S. aid to India exceeded the total amount from all other sources. This was a more than accurate reflection of the changing world situation; the U.S. had emerged as the dominant international capitalist power.

But it isn't enough to say that India, after a brief intermission, was being reabsorbed into the western capitalist orbit. Nobody was making a secret of this. It was being argued that precisely such a scheme would stimulate the subcontinent economy, pushing it forward toward a healthier future. In order, then, to understand the effect this new reliance on foreign capital had on India, it's necessary not just to say that there was an increase of outside influence on India, but to study the quality of that influence.

To do this, let's look at the relationship between India and the U.S.

3.

One of the first major U.S. breakthroughs into the Indian economy was initiated in the early 50s when the Indian government opened its doors to Burmah Shell, Caltex and

Standard Vacuum for the purpose of setting up oil refineries. Not only did this entail a dramatic concession on the part of India's government in terms of encouraging a large foreign investment without a controlling Indian share in that investment, but there were also special inducements involved: for instance, tax exemptions and a guarantee to the incoming companies that they wouldn't be nationalized for at least twenty-five years. The oil refineries were set up and the project swung into action.

The real indicator of the nature of this business relationship, however, only emerged slowly over the next decade. During that time, a controversy arose between the Indian government and the U.S. multinationals concerning at what price and from whom the crude oil for the refineries should be purchased. The companies were buying their crude from the Persian Gulf area where there were other U.S.-related interests. The fact that the prices were higher than could be obtained elsewhere on the international market didn't inhibit the companies, since they could guarantee their own profits by selling the final product within India at inflated prices. In response to this situation, strong opinion developed within India that the foreign investors should be required to purchase their crude oil from another seller, at lower prices. The companies, however, resisted this proposal and eventually, at the beginning of the 60s, the Indian government capitulated to the companies' conditions under pressure from the U.S.-dominated World Bank. The power of U.S. business interests in influencing India's economic policies had been established.

Another example will highlight the cynicism that often characterizes the attitude of the multinationals toward a country like India. In 1966, there was a disagreement between Standard Oil of Indiana and the Indian government. The source of the disagreement was India's established policy of distributing and setting prices for all fertilizers made by foreign companies. Although Standard Oil at first willingly submitted itself to this policy, once it had its foot inside the door of the Indian economy it began to bite at the bridle. It laid down the law: it wanted the fertilizers marketed at a price that it (Standard Oil) thought was appropriate (i.e., higher than what the Indian government thought was appropriate).

The pressure that was brought to bear on the Indian government to change its policy, in spite of the mutually agreed upon nature of the original contract, was enormous. At the time of the dispute, India was plagued by a famine resulting from insufficient rainfall. At precisely this moment, when millions of Indians were literally starving and suffering from malnutrition, the oil interests, using to the hilt their influence within the U.S. government, managed to have the U.S. hold up food shipments that were destined for India under the auspices of the Agency of International Development (AID). The tactic of denying food to the starving as a way of forcing India to submit to the dictates of U.S. business interests was a stroke of "pragmatic" genius. It worked. The indigenous government surrendered and permission was given to Standard Oil of Indiana to market its fertilizers within India at prices it thought fit.

By far the area of greatest U.S. involvement in the Indian economy was agriculture. This was in keeping with the Indian government's assessment that the limping pace of agricultural development was having a serious retarding effect on the economy as a whole. It was this consideration that lay behind India's willingness to accept U.S. leadership in trying to develop the agrarian sector. The result was the two-phase Green Revolution, beginning with the Intensive Agricultural Development Program (early 60s) and followed by a program for introducing high-yield-variety seeds into the countryside (mid-60s).

Enough has been said previously about the deprived living conditions of the majority of the rural population to indicate that the attempt to stimulate agricultural growth occurred in a profoundly human context. It is an interesting fact of the U.S.-designed Green Revolution, however, that it did little, if anything, to confront head-on and to therefore try to diminish the existing economic disparities that left much of the rural population in the worst imaginable circumstances. The reason for this was simple: in keeping with the general U.S. vision that economic growth in and of itself is the solution to social problems, India's new agrarian programs were designed to raise agricultural productivity *without tampering with* rural class relations. This meant that the primary beneficiaries of the new programs were the already socially powerful landowners, who were the only ones with sufficient wealth to buy the tractors, pesticides, fertilizers, seeds, etc., that were a necessary part of the so-called revolution that was occurring in agriculture. If their available capital had to be supplemented by loans, the government made this possible by setting up special credit-giving agencies for such "good risks." For the most part, everyone else was left out in the cold.

Some of the negative consequences of trying to transform agriculture without eradicating long-established class inequities became apparent when the rich farmers, during the two major famines in 1966-67 and 1971-72, insisted on marketing their produce at high prices in spite of the fact that millions of the poor were starving. Having benefited from U.S. assistance, the rich farmers had apparently also adopted their tutor's unsentimental pragmatism: emotions of the moment shouldn't stand in the way of maintaining price stability (i.e., high profits). Also, it's a telling fact that during the key years of the Green Revolution (1960-1968), the percentage of the Indian population living below poverty level increased from 38% to 52%, with these percentages higher for the rural than the urban areas. The equation was clear, if distasteful: as the alliance between U.S. agribusiness and the well-off Indian landowners grew stronger, the situation of the average Indian deteriorated.

Another (related) area of U.S. involvement in the subcontinent was foreign aid in the form of food shipments. Because such aid made up the bulk of U.S. assistance to India, it's necessary to take a closer look at this aspect of Indo-American relations.

The legal foundation for sending food shipments to India was laid in 1956 with the passage of U.S. Public Law 480. The law's central purpose was to set up a situation in which U.S. agricultural surplus could be channeled into India "to the benefit of both parties." Because of the U.S.'s immense agricultural resources, by the early 60s it had become India's major food supplier, and, in the process, the U.S. farming community reaped substantial profits.

The method by which U.S. agricultural surplus was to be transferred to the subcontinent was as follows. India would purchase the desired commodities on the U.S. market. It would pay for the purchases with loans received from the U.S. government. Repayment of these loans would be in rupees, not dollars, and annual repayment installments would be deposited in a U.S. account in the Reserve Bank of India. Then, out of this account, the U.S. would make the Indian government new loans (also some outright grants) for previously decided-upon projects ranging from the creation of educational facilities to the development of an adequate power supply.

On the surface, everything seemed clear and mutually beneficial, draped as the program was in the smooth-sounding rhetoric of the financial experts, both U.S. and Indian. But the reality was that slowly but surely the U.S. was gaining an unbelievable, for a foreign power, position of strength within the Indian economy. By 1968, through its account in the Reserve Bank, the U.S. had secured control of approximately half the Indian currency in circulation. There was nothing ambiguous about what this meant; it meant the U.S. was in a position of near-dictatorial power in terms of being able to "advise" the Indian government on issues having to do with the correct (i.e., pro-U.S.) path of economic development, as well as on certain noneconomic political questions. For instance: the U.S. had gained enough power to force India, through World Bank pressure, to devalue the rupee in 1966; at the political level, it was able to force the Indian government into changing its trade relations with North Vietnam. Needless to say, as all this was going on, India continued to buy U.S. agricultural surpluses at prices substantially higher than they would have been able to get on the international market, if they had been free to shop around. But since India didn't have sufficient purchasing power without U.S. loans, and since U.S. loan agreements stipulated that India must buy from the U.S. at U.S.-determined prices (often 30-50% higher than world market prices), there was nothing much India could do but comply with the wishes of its more powerful partner.

In the words of an old proverb: if you let a giant sleep in you house, don't expect there to be much room left for yourself.

4.
India was in trouble.

By the end of the second half of the 60s, it was no longer possible to obscure the fact that the situation in India wasn't improving. Independent economic growth was a dead dream. In order to bail itself out of economic trouble and to firm up its position vis-a-vis the Indian masses, the bourgeoisie had formed an alliance with foreign capital. There was also the fact that both the industrial and the agrarian sectors were unstable. In industry, for instance, as the result of the introduction of advanced technology, productivity went up; but the advantages stemming from this weren't extended to the workers, whose wage levels remained static. Then there was the countryside where the trend, in spite of the government's new programs, was toward the increase rather than the decrease of poverty. The reason for this was that the old set of feudal relations, only slightly modified, had been allowed to remain. If, on the one hand, U.S. influence facilitated the emergence of a few big capitalist farmers with high productivity rates, on the other hand many peasants with small landholdings ended up losing their land because they found it impossible to compete with the large farms. The power of the rural elite had grown.

All this resulted in a predictable phenomenon: increasing political unrest.

One sign of this unrest was that the Congress Party, which had dominated the Independence movement and then, in the post-Independence period, secured control of India's political life for twenty years, was in trouble. Massive public disenchantment was shaking the foundations of Congress rule.

In the 1967 elections, the Congress, under the leadership of their new Prime Minister Indira Gandhi, suffered a major setback. Although the Congress managed to preserve a skimpy national majority (after twenty years of a large majority), at the local state level it didn't fare so well. In state after state coalitions made up of opposition parties assumed power. But this wasn't all. Labor unrest had reached new heights and prolonged strikes were creating the impression of imminent industrial chaos. Then, in Naxalbari a peasant revolt broke out, and the militance of this revolt, spreading to other areas, catalyzed an increasingly radical approach to the problem of continuing upper-class dominance in the countryside. On top of all this, there was the emergence of a communist-led United Front government in West Bengal, the leading industrial state of India.

Things weren't going well for the entrenched elite. The fact of public disillusionment had its effect: a major debate was unleashed within the ruling classes concerning exactly how the country should be run and their power preserved. Invariably, this debate took the form of mounting tension between the most conservative and the most "progressive" elements of the ruling classes.

The so-called progressive position was based on a projected strategy for stepping up the pace of industrialization and concentrating more power in the hands of the state so that it would be able more effectively to oversee economic and social development. By and large, this position had the support of the capitalists as well as their adjutant classes: managers, planners, technological experts, etc. The conservative position, on the other hand, was against what it considered to be an over-emphasis on industrialization and increased centralization of power in the state. It favored a looser, more decentralized form of government. Although on the surface this position may appear to have contained an element of populist resistance to growing state authoritarianism, the fact is that it was merely an attempt on the part of the rural elite—landlords, rich peasants, moneylenders—to put a ceiling on the growing power of the bourgeoisie. In this way, by minimizing state interference, they would be able to retain, they hoped, power at the local level.

A good example of this division within the ruling classes over the question of how to run the country was the 1969 split in the Congress Party. Trying to recover from its setback in the '67 elections, bickering within the party had been intensifying. A great deal of hostility, emanating especially from the older and more conservative party bureaucrats, was directed against Indira Gandhi. According to them, she was a "weak, ineffectual leader," and her ministry was sarcastically referred to as the "Kitchen Cabinet." The question of who was to lead the party crystalized around the need to appoint a new president of India. In opposition to the official party candidate, Gandhi put up her own candidate, who won. The result was that the major conservative leaders within the party claimed that Gandhi's faction wasn't the "real" Congress—their faction was. This meant that in essence there were now two Congress Parties: the old Congress of the conservatives and the new Ruling Congress of Indira Gandhi.

Once Indira Gandhi had achieved power within the Congress Party, she moved forward quickly and with a great deal of skill in her attempt to insinuate herself into the public consciousness as the leader of the country's progressive forces and the first friend of the poor. In her speeches, she continually stressed the plight of the downtrodden, and maintained that the federal government must be transformed into an instrument for serving the have-nots. Simultaneously, she attacked dependence on foreign capital, made hostile remarks about rich nations that were only too willing to exploit the poor and spoke, in strong nationalistic terms, about the need to develop economic self-reliance.

She also made two moves that seemed to symbolize the seriousness of her socialistic/populist intentions: she nationalized the banks and abolished the privy purses of the old feudal princes. The nationalization of the banks (1969) seemed proof of her willingness to use the state as an apparatus for taking profits out of the hands of private financiers and putting them at the disposal of the people in the form of a "planned" economy. The abolition of the princes' privy purses was popularized by the government as a dramatic move against the rural elite. The purses were originally established, in the period following Independence, as compensation for the princes' loss, by government decree, of their fiefdoms. The decision to cut off this compensation seemed to imply that the government was no longer willing to cater to the idea of privilege if that idea got in the way of mobilizing all available resources for the country's march toward self-reliance. Better that the princes' money should be taken away from them and used to help the people.

It could only be beneficial to the Prime Minister—and it was—that sections of the bourgeoisie and much of the rural landed gentry were nervous about what she was going to do next. The public impression being created was that the Prime Minister was willing to stand up to and accept the wrath of the most powerful vested interests, and all in the name of ordinary people. As one Indian writer, looking back on that period, described it. "Anyone listening to her powerful speeches and seeing the responsiveness of the crowds would have the impression of someone in between an Earth Mother and a fiery feminist revolutionary." Gandhi's popularity soared. When, at the beginning of the 70s, she put forward the slogan "Garibi Hatao" ("Remove Poverty"), many Indians honestly felt her goal was to liberate India from the oppression of the privileged classes.

But social disparities remained and, at best, the economy moved forward slowly and snail-like. In the years 1964-1973, for instance, the country's real per capita net national product increased only 2%. No amount of rhetoric could change the fact that society wasn't being transformed, that the numbers of the destitute and the near-destitute were growing. And yet, the Gandhi government had at its disposal a key strength in terms of being able to ward off political disaster: brute power.

Over the years, federal monies alloted for special police and security forces had increased. Whereas in 1951 such monies amounted to only .78% of the total revenue disbursements of the central government, by 1972 the percentage had increased to 2.89%. Between the years 1969 and 1974, the amount alloted to central police budgets rose from 726 million rupees ($91 million) to over 1500 million rupees ($188 million). One of the agencies funded with these monies was the Central Reserve Police, whose numbers had grown by more than three times in the decade ending in 1974. It could be called upon, when necessary, to quell civil disorder (i.e., public expressions of discontent). Another agency was the Central Industrial Security Force, whose function was controlling workers during labor disputes. As government spokespersons increasingly made paranoid Nixon-like reference to "asocial forces" that were supposedly obsessed with sabotaging the government's ability to lead the country in a healthy direction, the message became clear: we have the power to crush dissent, and we'll use it.

And they did.

Examples.

In West Bengal, where the Communist Party of India (Marxist) played a crucial role in the escalation of worker and peasant militancy, the central government sent in federal troops. It also arranged to have the Youth Congress, a supposedly innocuous wing of the Congress Party, organize terror squads made up of petty criminal types. The task of these squads was the harassment of people suspected of antigovernment sentiments. Repression occured on a massive scale. In the end, over a thousand communists or communist-leaning organizers were killed.

Likewise, in the Srikakulum district of Andhra Pradesh in 1968, the Central Reserve Police played a crucial role in crushing rebelling Girijan tribal people, who were in the process of demanding land reform and the end of the usurious practices of local moneylenders. Gradually, with the onset of such military-style suppression, the Prime Minister's repeated statements about her interest in "the genuine needs of ordinary people" were being put into a clear context. Verbal niceties on the one hand, bloodletting reigns of terror on the other.

Another example of government repression was its handling of the general railway strike in May 1974. Close to two million workers were out on strike, agitating for industrial worker status, an eight-hour workday and a need-based minimum wage. The strike

> was met with a reported 20,000 arrests, both under the preventive detention regulations...and others; with 25,000 dismissals; with the intervention of the territorial army, the regular army, the Central Reserve Police, and even the navy at Cochin. It was met as well with assaults on railway workers' families, and eviction of railway workers from their homes in the railway colonies.

The form of government intervention in the railway strike is indicative. But it was willing to go even further than that when confronted with opposition. Under Indira Gandhi, the government was developing more sophisticated skills, was learning the methods of the religious inquisition and the political purge. The Maintenance of Internal Security Act, for instance, empowered the state to use arbitrary arrest as a device for curbing open discontent. The possibility of imprisonment and of police brutality inside the jails, then, was a reality to be considered by anyone—worker, peasant, woman, man—who contemplated voicing even minimal dissent. The government consciously cultivated an attitude of paranoia in the population. What better way to get the people to think twice before speaking out or, through the adoption of other methods, demonstrating their discontent?

None of this was an idle threat. Arrest as a tactic for terrorizing the population became an unignorable political phenomenon. Two specific examples should give at least a beginning picture of what the situation was like.

Case of Sandip Kumar Dey (in his own words):
I used to work in Jamshedpur and lived there with my wife and child. Next door to us lived a young man whose friends used to visit him often. We had normal neighborly relations with him, and his friends often came to my house. Suddenly one day my room was packed with policemen, and I and three young men were arrested. At first the police beat us up and then tied all four of us with a rope. Later, they untied two, one after the other, and murdered them in cold blood, hacking them to pieces with a sharp weapon. A number of police officers witnessed the incident. Afterwards the police fabricated the story that two Naxalites were killed and three injured in an open confrontation. For some reason we two were spared our lives that day and are still rotting in jail....The police did not find any weapon or bomb in my house; they only found some Naxalite literature next door. When the police were beating us up, my wife somehow managed to escape with our child. Nobody knows to this day what has happened to them. In this letter I have tried to describe briefly everything that happened. I was kept in police lock-up for a week and transferred to Jamshedpur jail. To this day I have not been taken before a magistrate even once.

Description of the case of Sipra Roy, mother of two, age 28 or 29 at the time of arrest:
She was taken to Lalbazar lock-up and put through "interrogation"....The police were not satisfied with her answers. They had her hung from the ceiling by the wrists and whipped mercilessly. Her sari was torn to

shreds, her body lacerated, tatters of her sari sticking to her bloody wounds. She lost consciousness. She was revived by a doctor and subjected to further questioning. Still not being able to get anything from her, the police put her in ice for about half an hour. She again lost consciousness. And again she was revived. Again there was "interrogation." Still there was no information. Again she was whipped. Failing still to get any information from Sipra, one of the officers raped her. She lost consciousness....

Later, charged with a fabricated case, Sipra was sent to Burdwan Jail, her left side paralyzed by the beating and torture. She was unable to take anything but liquids. After six months in Burdwan she was brought to Presidency for treatment. Even during her bouts of excruciating pain, other political prisoners were unable to reach any doctor for her. And when a doctor came all he gave her was pain-killer.

After three months of this, Sipra became completely insane and the police released her. Sipra is still insane. Her health being what it is, she will probably not live long.

5.

Repression increased for a simple reason: no other method was sufficient for controlling the population. The disease of instability, caused by drastic class inequities, had thoroughly eaten into the fabric of Indian life. People were despairing, nervous, angry. Economically, in spite of innumerable uplift programs, the nation seemed on its deathbed. In terms of rectifying the deprived condition of the majority, nothing was working.

Item. In the decade 1960 through 1970, foodgrain availability per capita didn't rise, despite the hopes raised by the Green Revolution. In 1971-72, foodgrain availability per capita fell by 1%. In 1972-73, it fell again, this time by 5.2%.

Item. In the decade 1960 through 1970, consumer prices rose at an annual rate of 6.2%. Although in 1971-72, consumer

152 NOTES ON INDIA

prices only rose by 3.2%, in 1972-73 they rose substantially again, by 7.8%.

Item. In the early 70s, according to conservative government estimates, the total number of the unemployed was on its way to exceeding 20 million. Non-government estimates indicated that the actual figures were much higher.

Item. In terms of economic self-reliance, the 70s, in spite of the bouyant anti-neocolonialistic tone of the administration, were proving to be a failure. The increasing foreign debt was approaching 820,000 million rupees ($103,000 million).

Predictably, people wanted change. No amount of government rhetoric or repression could alter this.

It was in this context that in the period (1974) immediately prior to the Emergency, a mass anticorruption movement arose, led by an old follower of Mohandas Gandhi, J.P. Narayan. The movement was called the J.P. Movement. As a form of popular resistance to the entrenched Congress Party, it was only partially successful. If, on the one hand, the movement came to represent, for many people, an inspiring and moving symbol of the actuality of mass resistance to the existing regime, on the other hand it ultimately showed itself to be ideologically unequipped to provide any workable alternative to the very system it so emotionally opposed.

Precisely for these reasons it's important to understand the J.P. Movement and its leader, Narayan. In the West, Narayan was depicted as a well-credentialed moral voice organically linked to the pulse of the people. He was written about as a leader who "has abruptly, almost unwittingly, emerged to challenge the Congress Party leadership, which he terms corrupt and out of touch with the needs of the poor and the students." In other words, it was implied that he was a somewhat politically innocent populist savior.

The distortion in such a view lay in the notion that Narayan had emerged "almost unwittingly" as an opposition leader. The reality was that although Narayan had officially given up political life after Independence (during the Independence struggle he had been an active Gandhian leader), he had periodically re-emerged as an old-guard Gandhian spokesperson who offered his advice on issues ranging from land reform to

Bangladesh. If there was anything true about Narayan, it was that he never did anything "unwittingly." Overall, his political positions were characterized by three main ingredients: Gandhian nonviolence, a pro-U.S. ideology and distinct anticommunism.

From the beginning, J.P.'s role within the anticorruption campaign was to restrain it, to transform it into a rhetorically powerful, but ultimately unorganized, utopian movement. The language of the movement, of course, had a popular grassroots ring: freedom was pitted against dictatorship, government corruption was harangued, the idea of a people's "total revolution" was put forward along with the demand that all state brutality against the populace be immediately stopped. But if the movement had the evangelical air of the inevitability of the triumph of good over evil, and if on the surface the campaign seemed to have accumulated mass support throughout 1974 and into 1975, a closer look shows that the movement was far more complicated and contradictory than it at first appeared.

Although Narayan's leadership might have seemed to symbolize the still-existing power of the Gandhian vision to stir up the people, the fact is that an analysis of "the people" shows that many of those most responsive to his message were middle class intellectual types: social workers, scholars, journalists, economists, students. This was a strong indicator of the specific class interests that dominated the movement's interior life. Students, especially, played a key role, being susceptible to the moral idealism and semi-apocalyptic fervor that characterized Narayan's language.

The role that students played in the movement is particularly important. According to one report "the movement started with 12 demands. Eight of them related wholly to student issues." Narayan himself never tired of insisting on the crucial significance of student participation: "I want to tell you...that this movement is of the youth, of students, of people." And also: "Nobody...can stop this movement. It has been born because the system of education is rotten and the students don't see a ray of hope. It was born because the people are being crushed under high prices." In such quotes, when Narayan mentions youth and students before acknowledging "the people," it's a significant indication of how the movement prioritized the relevant social forces. To Narayan, the students were an appealing sector because they hadn't yet been compromised by the world: they were, in his eyes, politically pure.

The implications of this aspect of Narayan's approach can best be seen by looking at how the anticorruption campaign operated in the state of Bihar, where it originated. Two excerpts from a pertinent article will provide insight into what the situation there was like. The first excerpt gives some background information on the state itself. The second draws a clear portrait of the consequences of Narayan's preoccupation with students. Background:

> Bihar, with its poverty, its high tribal and Untouchable population, its unresolved rural feudalism in many areas, its growing and militant working class in the south...offered natural potential for the next explosion in India.

Then, on student participation:

> In terms of the social forces in the state the Bihar movement could have developed as a class-based movement under working-class leadership. But J.P., who was the only political leader with an independent mass-based organization, told the untutored youth of a state where the working class wherever it had the opportunity was in fact taking the most militant leadership, that the working class could not lead. Youth must be the leaders, youth must go to the villages. But the educated youth who joined his movement and went to the villages were, in the Bihar context, drawn from the semi-feudal ruling strata of those very villages and the kind of leadership they would give on their own was quite clear.

Such an approach had the effect of creating serious obstacles to the Bihar movement's development. A potential source of momentum was dampened, as peasant and working class militants remained crucially isolated from the campaign's nerve-center of decision-making. In their place, the children of the rural privileged sectors dominated. So the movement continued, superficially strong but ideologically blurred and, in terms of clear political goals, directionless.

Not everyone, however, was blind to these things. The movement was criticized, even by some of its supporters, for being weak and for not being organized around any meaningful strategy for bringing about radical social change (land reform, measures for stabilizing the inflation-ridden economy, etc.). But such criticism wasn't received open-mindedly. It was countered with responses like: "The fact is that such a requirement has no meaning. It is a movement of the people, started by students. It should not become a party." In other words, the absence of ideological and goal-oriented clarity was justified on the grounds that the anticorruption campaign was a "movement of the people," as if the phrase "movement of the people" was a magical incantation that would inevitably produce, spontaneously and when the proper time came, clear direction. But this was, unfortunately, far from true. As time would tell, this persistence in remaining ideologically independent was a fatal crack in the movement's armor, a crack through which organized right-wing forces infiltrated the movement. This was especially noticeable in the movement at the national level

Because of the serious level of subcontinent discontent and because of the crowd-capturing nature of the J.P. Movement's populist slogans ("Listen, Queen of Delhi, no longer will you be allowed to do what you like"and "Exploiters will go. The new era will come."), the movement, for all its contradictions, became the nucleus and articulator of the disenchantment of many of India's 600 millions. Furthermore, the movement's powerful position attracted two normally antagonistic groups: the right-wing rural elite parties, who were opposed to the Indira Gandhi regime because of its pro-industrialization policy and its adamant attempts to concentrate all political power in the central government in Delhi; and various left-leaning worker and peasant groups, like the Naxalites.

One of the leaders of the right was Moraji Desai. For Desai and the people he represented—the landowning and money-lending classes in the countryside—the new mass upsurge led by Narayan offered the possibility of re-emergence into power, if only they could somehow get hold of it and use it as their own instrument. Desai himself had once been Deputy Prime Minister of India. (This was the Desai about whom a Narayan supporter stated: "I remember even in the early 50s in Pandit Nehru's reign, Moraji Desai, who called himself a Gandhian and a votary of nonviolence, as Chief Minister of Gujrat ordered firing on unarmed crowds of people demonstrating against some unpopular action of the government. This he did dozens of times.")

For different reasons than the right's, left-wing groups were also attracted to the anticorruption campaign. For them, the J.P. Movement offered the possibility of broadening their base among the people and also the second possibility of providing them with protection against an increasingly repressive anticommunist state apparatus.

So, with a membership leaning in different ideological directions, the Narayan-led opposition cruised toward some kind of final showdown with the Congress government. But, not surprisingly, as the movement became superficially stronger, expanding in terms of its national numbers, internally it grew weaker, riddled by contradictions stemming from the different interests of its member groups. Eventually, because of the leadership's dreamy ideological attitude, the right-wing faction led by Desai maneuvered itself into power within the movement. Toward the end, immediately before the declaration of the Emergency period, Narayan and Desai weren't speaking. Ultimately, the right's opportunistic persistance would pay off: in the post-Emergency period, they would have a firm policy-making grip on the Janata Party, and Moraji Desai himself would be appointed Prime Minister.

But that comes later. First we must look at Indira Gandhi's response to the growing sentiment against her government.

6.

If, in early 1975, it looked as if the mass opposition movement might in fact drive Indira Gandhi to resign, by June she was to show that

the most powerful woman in the world was able to manage her own affairs. On June 27, a state of

Emergency was declared which gave the president full
power to handle what was said to be a "right wing
conspiracy" that included calls to the military to revolt
and which aimed at preventing the democratically
elected government from functioning. Arrests of all
top opposition leaders, including Jayprakash Narayan
himself and a number of his supporters within the
Congress Party, were made. Public meetings and
demonstrations were banned in most places throughout the country; those attempting to organize such
meetings in protest against the Emergency were
arrested and total press censorship was instituted.

All this was the prelude to the full consolidation of power in
Indira Gandhi's hands. The government tried to publicize the
Emergency as a measure taken in the name of the people to
protect their (the people's) government from the growth of
destabilizing forces. In the language-factory of those in power,
expressions of popular discontent were automatically translated
into signs of right-wing reaction and fascism. According to
Gandhi, the Emergency was an unfortunate but necessary step,
dictated by the need to preserve the nation from chaos: "It was
not an easy decision for me to take, because I am by nature a
person who does not believe in restricting people." She certainly,
anyway, didn't believe in restricting herself or that section of the
ruling classes she represented. The fact was that under her
guidance, the state was equipped with extra-constitutional
powers for the purpose of eliminating any and all dissent.

But surprisingly, given that the Emergency was being
described by the opposition as the suppression of "the last
vestiges" of democracy in India, the government's tactic of trying
to shift the blame for the Emergency onto the right was partially
successful. The reason for this, however, wasn't hard to find: as
we have already seen, there *had been* a noticeable shift to the
right within the J.P. Movement. The public was confused. On the
one hand government repression, on the other right-wing
agitations—which force was actually responsible for India's
economic and social backwardness?

There was little immediate public reaction against the
Emergency. By and large workers, peasants and middle

classes saw it as an attack on rightists, not on them; they showed almost no inclination to go to the defense of the arrested leaders; and they seemed inclined to wait to see whether the slight initial downturn in prices and the promised new measures would really indicate a fundamental change.

The fact was that for many Indians, especially those from the chronically exploited sectors—poor peasants and agricultural laborers in the countryside, key sectors of the working class in the urban areas—the opposition's talk about the obliteration of democracy had the air of a meaningless, hairsplitting abstraction. For them, their lives characterized by continuous social and economic deprivation, the question seemed to be, "Can something (i.e., democracy) that has never existed be destroyed?" From their perspective democracy was, and always had been, a non-entity. At most it had been a word in the mouths of powerful politicians (and also, although many of them didn't know it, a word in the mouths of U.S. leaders who, trying to diminish the significance of the communist revolution in China, referred laudingly to India as "the world's largest democracy," as a way of attempting to establish that post-Independence India had the moral edge over "red" China).

And so, many people were willing to wait, to feel the situation out. Maybe Indira Gandhi had been right when, metaphorically describing the relationship of the Emergency to the health of the nation, she had said, "This bitter medicine is necessary to cure the patient of his serious illness."

But as the first year of the Emergency dragged on, it began to become obvious to people that if the Emergency hadn't destroyed democracy (which hadn't existed), it was nonetheless a dramatic departure from the old mode of political life: the constitutional facade had been toppled; the ruling hand had become more nakedly authoritarian; and repression, rather than diminishing, increased. It was clear that, under the guise of moving to destabilize the right, the government was launching a series of brutal assaults, not just against particular opposition factions, but against the people in general.

For instance, the Emergency entailed a systematic and escalating attack on workers. Within a few months after the

Emergency was declared, federal law reduced workers' bonuses from 8.33% to 4%. Although the Gandhi government attempted to achieve an air of impartiality by publicly posturing as a neutral overseer of labor-capital relations (if strikes were officially frowned upon, so were the weapons of capital: layoffs and lockouts), the reality underlying this posture was slightly different. After the initial arrest of 2000 labor leaders and the methodical creation of a political climate in which workers were expected to raise production levels without receiving any portion of the profits (according to the Prime Minister, the workers were supposed to "put heart and souls into increasing production without asking any rewards at the present moment"), capital felt free to flex its muscles, to take advantage of the unignorable anti-labor atmosphere. Speed-ups were initiated, workplace grievances were flagrantly ignored, and by the time the Emergency was a half year old, 480,000 workers had been laid off their jobs as a way of trying to minimize labor costs. The pressure was on.

Worse than this, however, was the fact that workers, faced with arrest and/or physical intimidation by the police if they agitated against unfair labor practices, were for all practical purposes stripped of their right of self-protection. Consequently there arose situations like that at the Chas Nala colliery in Bihar, where in December 1975 there occured one of the worst mining tragedies in Indian history.

The night before the disaster the workers attempted to organize a strike against unsafe mine conditions, but, because of the political climate created by the Emergency, their effort failed. So the next day they went to work. It was then that the tragedy happened: over 400 killed, "engulfed by 110 million gallons of water in a pit known beforehand and declared to be perilous, and where even during normal conditions the mine was knee-deep in water."

But the condition of workers was only one aspect of the government's new severity. Another example of government repression was the adoption of a policy of forced sterilization.

Overnight, during the Emergency, India's family-planning program was turned into a massive attack against the lower sections of society, an attempt to achieve state control over the actual biological functioning of millions of bodies. The basic philosophy behind the family-planning program was that the subcontinent's large population was the cause of Indian poverty. The government, rather than pursuing a policy of structural reform that would have aided the poor in their struggle for survival, instead chose to pinpoint them as the problem. It was *their* children (both those living and those yet to be born) who, through their "excessive" numbers, stood in the way of national economic coherence. Such an attitude was a dramatic state attempt to sidestep an obvious truth, that widespread poverty in India was an integral part of the unequal social structure and wasn't, therefore, automatically traceable to population size.

A typical peasant in his dusty village, for instance, wasn't poor because he had five children. He was poor because, in the absence of private capital, he couldn't get a loan from a bank to help make ends meet and so had *to take a loan, instead,* from a moneylender, which he had to pay back annually at an interest rate that was as high, maybe, as 50%. He was also poor because his small plot of land wasn't sufficient to survive on (in terms of crop yields) and consequently he had to hire himself out seasonally to a local landlord who paid him less than a subsistence-level wage. These were the shackles, not family size, that strangled the peasant's life.

But even this doesn't exhaust the problem's complexity. Let's look at another peasant, one in a slightly different situation.

This peasant was also confronted with the dilemma of how to survive with only a little bit of land. But he was stubborn in his commitment to somehow make a go of it. Because of his bad economic situation, however, putting money out for new technology (tractor, chaffing machine, etc.) either wasn't worth it or was impossible, since he'd soon find himself either in debt to the moneylender or losing money anyway because he didn't have enough land to produce sufficient crops to cover his outlay. Not investing in the new technology, though, increased his need for physical farm labor, but here also he was in a bind, since he didn't have the necessary funds for hiring labor. Consequently, he had only one alternative: to look within his family for the labor that was needed. The reality was clear: for him a larger, as opposed to smaller, family was a source of economic stability. The implication of such an example should be obvious. Only by creating a new context, in which it made *sense* for the poor to have smaller families, would the government be able to initiate a successful and non-oppressive family-planning program.

This, unfortunately, wasn't the direction the government chose to go in. And the government, of course, would have its way. And it did.

A massive sterilization campaign was launched. People were going to be sterilized, and that was that. Both nationwide and local quotas were set; job-hunters were refused state positions if they couldn't verify that they'd been operated on; women and men were dragged out of their homes or rounded up on the streets, then marched off toward the place of surgery—a police van transformed into an ambulance, or a makeshift wooden roadside "hospital," or even, sometimes (but not often), an actual medical clinic. There were reports of people being "accidentally" sterilized more than once, of newly-married childless couples falling victim to the surgeon's science, of old widowed men being hauled off and given vasectomies because there was a government quota to be met and no one else was around except them.

Another, only flimsily disguised form of aggression against the people was the new "city planning" vision that grew to full bloom during the Emergency period. In the major urban areas, slum clearance and landscape renewal became the order of the day. This entailed police-protected work squads, armed with pickaxes and sledgehammers, going into slum colonies and leveling them as rapidly as possible, in spite of the protests of area residents. To facilitate the speed of the job and to heighten the demolitions' physical drama as well as to symbolize the state's power over the population, bulldozers were used. In this way, whole communities that had just the day before housed hundreds or maybe thousands of people were crudely transformed into rubble, which was in turn crushed into the dust. Although, according to one myth, the victims were mostly beggars and lumpen types who'd migrated to the cities from the sun-seared countryside hunting for jobs, this wasn't so in fact. Also caught in the crackdown of state-directed city renewal were the lower-level employed—unskilled industrial workers, sweepers and sanitation people, petty shopkeepers, etc.—who, because of the economy's constrictedness and the resulting meager wages, had been forced, even though employed, to integrate themselves permanently into the slum landscapes of the cities.

By April 1976, 500,000 people in Delhi alone had been "relocated." It's impossible to give an exact estimate of the total numbers affected by such projects nationwide; hundreds and hundreds of thousands were affected. Behind the benign poetry-like slogans of the government ("we are prettifying the cities"), lay the actual data: the destruction of people's homes; groups of people dumped miles outside the cities in near uninhabitable wasteland areas; forced enlistment into below-minimum-wage government jobs; feelings of panic and hysteria.

Although these are probably the most dramatic examples (the oppression of workers, forced sterilization, slum demolitions) of government repression during the period, there are also others. Press censorship was inaugurated; non-Congress opposition governments were toppled in Tamil Nadu and Gujrat and replaced by pro-Emergency forces; the policy of arbitrary arrests, if anything, was pursued more vigorously than before. A new amendment to the Maintenance of Internal Security Act allowed the government to imprison people for up to a year without the introduction of formal charges. It's estimated that during the Emergency, 150,000 persons were jailed.

But in order to truly understand the situation, it's necessary to go beyond a narrow discussion of the living hell that was being inflicted on people. It would be misleading to merely draw a picture of repression's hand molding a will-less population-mass into whatever convenient shape it (the state) desired. The fact was that, in spite of the severity of the repression, people—workers, poor peasants, prisoners, teachers, students, men, women—fought back. That the hush of censorship was like an acid of artificial silence eating into the plains and mountains and villages and jungle areas of the subcontinent shouldn't be allowed to distort or obscure the factual story of people's resistance. Although the jaws of the officially sanctioned newspapers were chained shut (or had happily acquiesced to the government's dictum that "nothing should be allowed to be printed which is likely to convey the impression of a protest or disapproval of the government's measures"), still, in spite of this, information concerning public resistance began to surface in different ways: via word of mouth, in illegal underground journals and newspapers, through secretly-given interviews with foreign journalists. And the implications of the information were clear: the "numb millions" (Indira Gandhi's phrase) who were supposedly being serviced by the Emergency were in fact fighting that very Emergency tooth and nail.

Increasingly, there were incidents of resistance. One example is the number of jailbreaks that occurred. Those involved were militant peasants and workers and left-wing communists. In early 1976, for instance, prisoners escaped from the Tihar jail in Delhi after digging a 100-foot-long secret tunnel. Also in early 1976, there was a flamboyant liberation of prisoners from the Presidency jail in Calcutta, a maximum security prison reputed to be inescapeable. The escape was the product of superior coordination between outside sympathizers and approximately fifty incarcerated "antisocial elements." A band of armed guerrillas made a head-on assault against the jail, hand grenading those in their way and finally dynamiting open the gates. Close to fifty prisoners escaped. Not only was the break successful, but the timing was perfect, almost symbolic, occurring as it did on a day when Indira Gandhi was touring Calcutta. It was becoming obvious that the heavy shadow cast by her dictatorial presence wasn't enough to black out continuing discontent.

There was also resistance in the countryside. For instance, at the beginning of October 1976 "a five-hour gun battle between the police and a group of extremists took place" in the Siligini district of West Bengal. The confrontation occurred at night, after the police had attempted to break up a meeting in the home of one of the "extremists." This is only a small example, but indicative. The countryside was becoming a maze of quick hit-and-run confrontations.

But rural conflicts with the authorities weren't limited to military-style gun battles. There were also incidents of collective mass action, as peasants tried to liberate themselves, through the forcible siezure of land, from continuing poverty. In one area of Andhra Pradesh, the lower-strata peasants of six villages collectively occupied over fifty acres of land that had been held, in defiance of the law, by local landlords. In spite of landlord-inspired police harassment, the peasants remained committed to sowing and harvesting the crops. Likewise in the Kapurthala district of the Punjab. There, in response to government plans to publicly auction 1100 acres of land at prices that would have effectively eliminated the poorer peasants' chances of getting any of the acreage, the peasants decided to take matters into their own hands. Uniting collectively, the peasantry of four local villages staged a mass occupation of the 1100 acres, taking it over as their own. In the process they armed themselves, considering this a minimal precaution for self-defense.

Another story, from the period immediately preceding the cessation of the Emergency, simultaneously shows the homo-cidal dimension of police repression and the ambition of ordinary people to achieve justice even in the face of such repression. The case in point is that of Gucharn Singh of the Faridkot district of the Punjab.

Gucharn Singh's native village was Manuke, a rural center of radical activism. At the beginning of the Emergency, his brother Bant Singh, a vocal peasant leader, was proclaimed an outlaw. Police attempts to locate and jail Bant Singh entailed not only pursuit of the so-called criminal, but also systematic terrorization of his family, including the arrest of relations and the confiscation of household goods. Toward the end of the Emergency, at the beginning of March 1977, the police staged an early-morning raid on Bant Singh's house. The result of this raid was the arrest of Bant's younger brother, Gucharn, also a peasant militant, and two others. After two days in police custody, Gucharn Singh was dead. Police attempts to "convince" Gucharn to give them information had included, among other things, fracturing his skull and kicking him in the face in such a way as to break his jaw.

By word of mouth, news of Gucharn's death spread among the local villagers. Soon a large crowd of a few thousand people marched on the police station and *gheraoed* it, demanding that the corpse of the martyred militant be put into their care and also that all political prisoners be immediately released. Over the next two days, with the police attempting to downplay their role in the murder, peasant militance escalated. A complete work stoppage halted activity in the markets for a day. Meanwhile, the crowd outside the police station swelled to over 20,000. They cut off the station's water supply and refused to let those trapped inside leave their offices. Finally, confronted with this dangerously mounting (and organized) anger of the peasants, the police capitulated and gave over the body of Gucharn Singh to the waiting demonstrators.

This was on March 10th. Three days later, on March 13th, there was a huge funeral procession, its size estimated at between 20,000 and 25,000 people. At the end of the procession, Gucharn Singh's ashes were immersed in the Sutlej, a holy river. The peasants' message was clear: regardless of what the officials say, this man was a hero, *our* kind of hero, standing up to the powers-that-be and refusing to flinch even when faced with death.

Another example of group resistance (this time urban) to the state's totalitarian measures, is an incident that occurred near the Turkman Gate area of Delhi in mid-April 1976. In broad outline, the incident was a mass upsurge of unarmed slum dwellers that culminated in open street-fighting with Central Reserve Police who were equipped with guns and tear gas. The source of the slum population's anger was a three-pronged assault on the very fabric of their lives: demolition of their homes, forced relocation by truck to the countryside and compulsory sterilization.

The slum-housing demolition project near Turkman Gate began on April 14th. By April 18th, building-wrecking bulldozers and police-protected demolition squads were accompanied by a new force: roving sterilization teams that roamed the streets hunting potential "patients," sterilization having been made a prerequisite for relocation. Victims were aggressively and indiscriminately (regardless of age, marital status, etc.) hauled off to sterilization clinics that had been set up on the spot. There, they were operated on. With such state-of-siege conditions prevailing, predictably the slum population exploded. When it happened, it happened quickly; an initial resistance-group of a few hundred soon expanded into the thousands, and the network of narrow streets and alleys became an inner-city battlefield.

According to an Associated Press report the following day:

Slum dwellers fought a bloody conflict with police in the Indian capital yesterday...to prevent the razing of their shacks and forced resettlement. As many as thirty policemen and ten slum dwellers were reported killed and dozens more injured. According to witnesses, some slum dwellers refused to leave their dilapidated urban village, and the violent protest was touched off when police manhandled women and children.

Unfortunately, bricks, stones and makeshift clubs (the rioters' weapons) comprise a limited arsenal when confronted with the rifles and machine guns of the regular army, the Central Reserve Police and the Border Security Force, all of whom were called in to quell the disturbance. In the end, the A.P. death-estimates proved conservative; the testimony of eyewitnesses established a minimum figure of at least 100 slum inhabitants dead and far more injured. Ultimately, state power prevailed; 10,000 troop-guarded people were "suburbanized," forcibly uprooted from their urban dwelling places and relocated in the countryside.

Still, the point was that there had been dramatic resistance. In the midst of momentary defeat—the glowing embers of revolt. The state's attempts to manhandle certain sections of the population, to reduce them to a passive, moldable mass, were having an unintended effect: an against-the-odds daring on the part of the people was being inspired. This could only, in the end, bode ill for those in power.

The event at Turkman Gate wasn't an isolated or unique phenomenon. Increasingly, reports of violent collisions between state authorities and the population surfaced. For instance, in a single one-week period in the autumn of 1976, there were four occurrences of public resistance to the sterilization program in the state of Uttar Pradesh. In one of these occurrences, in a place called Gorakhpur, during a confrontation over sterilization six policemen were injured and several demonstrators killed. In another place (Basti), a government official associated with the sterilization campaign was assassinated. In a third location (Sultanpur), there was rioting in the streets. And in Muzzafarnagar, thousands of unarmed protesters were shot at when police attempted to disperse a demonstration. On-the-spot witnesses reported the death total to be near 150.

Spontaneous warzone-like situations were erupting, sometimes briefly, sometimes for longer duration, in different parts of the country. The only drawback to this form of resistance was that many of its episodes were characterized by minimal organization and a sort of strategyless impulsiveness. Often, no concrete, long-term goals were envisioned; there was only the bitter, undying, almost apocalyptic hatred of the people for the authorities. Still, if the resistance was structurally—i.e., organizationally—limited, it was nonetheless true that struggle and hardship were producing growing political consciousness. "Some lives are not taken too seriously," one poem stated, and then went on to add:

> but those they slay and slay again
> will bloom many million times
> from the flesh of our sisters;
> guns cannot move the moon of those who know what
> wood they are made of—ask any Vietnamese.

Popular resistance to government authority was also present in another crucial area: the workplace. As indicated earlier, a major aspect of state policy during the Emergency was the attempt to radically raise production levels without giving workers anything in return. Inevitably, the adoption of such a federal position entailed the inauguration of subsidiary policies that were anti-labor in content: reduced bonus rates, minimization of wages, no-strike programs, destabilization of workers' groups, official encouragement of non-negotiable speedups, etc. All this was done in the name of strengthening the nation. Yet in spite of regular police harassment of workers and the imprisonment of unsubmissive pro-rank-and-file labor leaders, workers still resorted to the major weapon at their disposal: the withholding of their labor, the strike.

> There were for example strikes in Hyderabad on 4 and 5 October 1975 of pharmaceutical workers; in Bombay on 15 and 16 October, and from 9 to 16 November 1975, of woolen workers; and a general strike in Tamil

Nadu on 24 October 1975...of textile, engineering, sugar, cement, plantation, leather processing, rubber, tobacco, sterilizer and foundary workers. In November 1975 there was a strike of power workers in Uttar Pradesh; in Bombay in January 1976 of journalists and newspaper and printing workers; and of plantation workers...on 28 January 1976 in Kerala, and for thirty-nine days, there was a strike of 12,000 shoe workers in Calcutta and in other centres of India; we know of workers striking at the Steel and Allied Products plant in Calcutta in February 1976, protesting against closure. We know that on 17 March 1976, 800 workers were on strike at the Madras cycle factory, besieging the plant, and bringing armed police to its gates threatening to open fire; we know that on 26 March 1976, tannery workers in Calcutta, also protesting at closure, were tear-gassed and arrested. We know that from 18 to 25 April 1976, Birla Mill textile workers in Delhi...struck against arbitrarily increased workloads, while 600 garment workers struck in Delhi on 1 May in protest against the compulsion to work on May Day. These were only some of the strikes—which continued to the Emergency's last moments, and included textile workers, engineering workers and dockers, among many others—against the bonus ordinance, strikes against arbitrary violence, strikes against the increase of workloads, strikes and protests against industrial closures. And despite the great toll taken on all forms of resistance to the license of power, they represented the continuation of such resistance.

7.

So, beneath the brittle veneer of the more stable India that was suppossedly coming into being during the Emergency period, there was tense, often violent, confrontation between the population and the state. Inflation hadn't been successfully curbed, no significant diminishment of social (class) inequities had occurred, countryside and inner city still seethed with the dispossessed and half-starved. It wasn't surprising, then, that the ice of political hatred was firmly lodged in the minds of the millions.

Under this pressure, the Congress Party began to feel its once solidly constructed platform of power shaking in the wind. It was time for one final effort, one last-ditch attempt to hold together the political scaffolding. And so, in January 1977, Indira Gandhi announced that national elections (postponed during the Emergency because of the "crisis of security" that was facing the nation) would be held in mid-March.

The gamble—this government gambit to appear liberal and flexible—was destined to be lost. The network of alliances that had held the Congress Party together since the split in 1969 had at last come apart. By pursuing an anti-working class industrial policy intended to create a climate conducive to the rapid accumulation of capital and higher rates of investment, the Congress had seriously strained its relationship to the working class. Also, the federal emphasis on industry as the key to India's salvation, and its coincident inclination to cater to the needs of the capitalist class, were experienced negatively by the dominant rural classes: more and more, they felt, their interests were being sacrificed to the interests of heavy industry.

But this wasn't the only phenomenon that antagonized the rural elite. Under Congress/capitalist leadership, there was an increasing centralization of power in the federal government, this being the only method of insuring the implementation of the ruling faction's policies. Rich peasants, moneylenders and landlords in the countryside experienced this process of increasing centralization as a direct blow to their power, since traditionally their hegemony had been expressed through the local state governments which were now being shoved into the background. On top of this, in order to sustain the pattern of "more power to the center," Indira Gandhi had studiously developed a policy of replacing local Congress leaders with her own agents, hand-chosen from Delhi. This also had the effect of disenfranchising some of the oldtime rural elite.

Another crucial area where there was a powerbase breakdown for the Congress Party was its relationship to the petty bourgeoisie and the Indian middle classes (professionals, managerial types, technicians, middle-level government bureaucrats and civil servants, small shopkeepers, etc.). Initially, in the late 60s, when the Congress/capitalist alliance was consolidating its strength, it had gone out of its way to offer concrete allurments to these sectors in order to win them over to its side. This attempt at political seduction grew out of the leadership's understanding that, as the state apparatus was enlarged and its ability to intervene in all aspects of the nation's life was increased, members of the educated sectors would be needed to oversee and manage this intervention. More jobs and more power for the middle classes was the message. The logic of this approach was persuasive, and crucial support was garnered for the ruling alliance.

But the triangular relationship between the Congress Party, the capitalist class and the petty bourgeoisie/middle class wasn't destined to remain stable. This was because the relationship only flimsily camoflaged the fact that real power was in the hands of the capitalist class and higher-level government bureaucrats. With the re-emergence of economic instability in the period (1973-74) immediately prior to the Emergency, this became more clear than ever. Unfavorable weather conditions resulted in bad harvests, inflation was up, layoffs increased. Along with the lower sectors, the middle sectors were also hit hard. At best, the petty bourgeoisie/middle class became an unstable and vacillating government ally; at worst, its confidence in the government began to completely disintegrate.

It was no surprise, then, when precisely this grouping (especially professionals, social workers, teachers and upwardly mobile students) came to play such an instrumental leadership role in the previously mentioned J.P. Movement. Sources of anger for this sector were rising prices, the growing unemployment rate among the educated and government corruption. During the Emergency, the petty bourgeois/middle class alienation from the Congress Party wasn't healed. Not only was the Emergency characterized by government attempts to forcibly restrain and even assault broad sections of the laboring classes, it was also characterized by government efforts to cut into and curb freedoms traditionally relished by the educated sectors. Press censorship and the jailing of liberal (as well as radical) opposition leaders are examples of government tactics that cut into the already disgruntled collective heart of the petty bourgeoisie and the middle classes. Not surprisingly, then, the disenchantment of these more educated sectors played a major role in overthrowing Indira Gandhi in the March 1977 elections.

For the Congress Party, the elections, when they came, were a catastrophe, the final denouement in its long fall from power. According to the opposition, its victory symbolized the full restoration of democracy and freedom in India; fascism was dead and a new post-Emergency period had been inaugurated. A sigh of relief swept across the country.

But this feeling of relief, unfortunately, has been shortlived.

It's now almost the end of the first year (1977-78) of the post-Emergency period and already serious doubts have begun to emerge, especially among the laboring classes, concerning the quality of the new government. Steadily the attitude is growing that once more ordinary working people have been manipulated, then left out in the cold. Without their support, without the popular upsurge of discontent prior to the elections, the new ruling Janata Party wouldn't have come into power. But now that the party is federally entrenched, its previously proclaimed sensitivity to the needs of the average person is noticeably on the wane. Regardless of the apparent diversity within the Janata coalition, effective power is held by right-wing forces, as was indicated in the selection of feudal-supported, anticommunist, pro-American Moraji Desai as Prime Minister. The restoration of democracy in India has come to mean not actual democracy, but merely the re-inauguration of certain privileges traditionally enjoyed by the educated sectors—i.e., freedom of the press, endless open debate on public issues, etc. Meanwhile, behind the face of western-style democracy, the Janata Party has been methodically pursuing a policy of curbing the freedom of the working classes, both urban and rural. Often this has been done through outright terror. As shown elsewhere in these notes, state-supported police violence against workers didn't stop after the cessation of the Emergency; it continued.

As each day passes and the government displays 1) its continuing inability to stabilize the economy or eradicate class inequities, and 2) its willingness to resort to violent methods for repressing people, the outlines for a picture of the near future become clearer. The days of Janata Party power are numbered. What will happen as the Janata Party declines bears watching. This will require some reading between the lines. The maneuverings of the officially recognized power blocs, including the Congress Party and Indira Gandhi, will probably be fairly well reported here in the West. But such coverage of traditional politics runs the risk of obscuring the real pulse of subcontinent life: the people themselves, especially in the form of the workers' and peasants' movements. These movements, unfortunately, aren't likely to be overly emphasized by our press. The reason this is problematic is because, on the subcontinent, occurrences at the top of the political pyramid—at the so-called official level—don't necessarily accurately reflect the moods being generated at its base, among the millions. At the top, famous faces will fade and reappear, depending on the political winds of the moment. At the bottom, often independently of traditional political life, there will be the emotional creation of dreams and plans for a radically different subcontinent future.

Inevitably, there will be detours and setbacks. Still, it is true: the day of the final confrontation is approaching.

8.

Before concluding this section, some additional notes are necessary on the period immediately prior to the Emergency, as well as on the Emergency itself. These will shed some important light, I think, on the nature of Indian attempts at economic reconstruction and self-reliance during the 70s and also on the subcontinent's continuing dependence on foreign powers.

Supposedly, the early 70s represented a major turning point in India's relationship to the West. Indira Gandhi's speeches were characterized by a strident anti-imperialist tone. At a conference of non-aligned nations in 1970, she made it clear that from the neocolonial powers of the West "it would be unrealistic to expect miracles of magnanimity....We must determine to help ourselves." This was only one of a series of blows directed at the U.S.-dominated capitalist world. The timing of such an attack was perfect, coming as it did at a moment when, internationally, U.S. prestige was at a low ebb because of its involvement in Indochina. The shift away from submission to capitalist neo-colonialism and toward, instead, anti-imperialist socialism was apparently symbolized in 1971 by the signing of the Indo Soviet Treaty, which represented an official tilting toward the Soviet-led international bloc.

The strain in India-U.S. relations was well covered by the North American media. Initial, relatively mild comments about the diminishment of U.S. business investments in India eventually gave way to sarcastic editorial remarks that derided Indira Gandhi, personally, for her "arrogance" and the fact that she was "biting the hands that feed India" (a January 5, 1975 *New York Times'* comment on Gandhi's supposed lack of proper gratitude for U.S. food shipments). After the declaration of the Emergency, U.S. press coverage was almost universal in its disdain for the erosion of democracy on the subcontinent and for India's continuing "irrational" hostility toward the U.S.

Reading the papers or listening to the evening news at that time, one got the distinct impression that relations between the two countries had been permanently paralyzed. A palpable and mutual distaste was in the air.

Yet the situation wasn't as severe as it seemed on the surface. Gradually, as the pre-Emergency period faded into the Emergency period, the slow arduous work of rehabilitating relations was undertaken. Public detestation of the birth of totalitarianism in India notwithstanding, the U.S. government put out feelers in an attempt to strengthen its position on the subcontinent. India played its part too, making it clear that it was open to offers that might symbolize the beginning of a "new" economic relationship. An interesting aspect of this process is that India's censorship apparatus was occasionally employed to eliminate unfavorable reference to the U.S. in the press. It was necessary that there be no unnecessary obstacles to a rapprochement between the two countries.

By summer/autumn 1976, both Orville Freeman, chair-person of the Indo-U.S. Businessmen's Advisory Council, and William Saxbe, U.S. ambassador to India, were confident that the U.S. and India had entered a new phase of mutual cooperation.

Also there was a World Bank report that spoke highly of the "vigorous measures" employed by the Indian government to stabilize the economy. In all this, the United States' pragmatic, business-like approach to deepening its ties with India conveniently overlooked the death and torture statistics piled up by the Emergency government. The whole question of human rights was secondary to the real problem of keeping India addicted to financial and political inputs from the West. Stressing human rights made sense only when beneficial, not otherwise. The important thing, according to a February 1976 issue of the U.S. magazine *Business Week,* was that the business atmosphere in India had undergone a positive transformation because "the emergency has resulted in labor peace." What this meant to prospective U.S. investors was that the subcontinent had a government-controlled army of cheap labor that could potentially be used to create profits for U.S. multinationals. Such was the backbone of the new attitude of many western India-watchers.

In reality, of course, there was nothing new about this attitude. We've already seen what the buildup of U.S. capital in India was like during the 60s. That pattern, in spite of Indira Gandhi's rough anticolonial language, was never completely broken. For instance, in 1975—the year the Emergency was initiated and one of the supposed low points in Indo-U.S. relations—U.S. economic aid to the subcontinent represented 37.1% of the total foreign assistance received by the country. Although on the surface the U.S. carefully cultivated an air of being disenchanted with India, its actual economic behavior displayed a continuing desire to keep India subordinate to western influences.

The new "self-reliant" India had never really left the warm embrace of U.S. capital. At best it had limped off a few steps, and then returned.

In the spring of 1976, a food-grain deal was made between the two countries that accurately summed up the persistent leader/led nature of their relationship.

At the time, India was supposedly experiencing the stability of a good harvest year, which meant that for the moment at least it had liberated itself from its chronic dependence on foreign food shipments. Still, an agreement was reached with the U.S. that included, among other things, India's commitment to purchase 100,000 tons of surplus rice. What was interesting about the rice part of the deal was that it came in the middle of a crisis for U.S. rice growers. Prior to the withdrawal of U.S. forces from South Vietnam in 1975, surplus rice was sold to that country at U.S.-determined prices. With the disappearance of the Vietnamese market, however, U.S. farmers found themselves in a bind. Because of overproduction, by March 1976 the market price per 100 lb. bag of rice had dropped to $5.86, almost $3 less than the government support price of $8.52.

This was the economic background of the agreement the U.S. proceeded to reach with India, an agreement which had India purchasing the equivalent of a million 100 lb. bags of rice at the above-market price of $8.52 per bag. Having lost one neocolonial market (Vietnam), the U.S. proceeded to find another (India). The Indian government, knowing what was expected of it by its western partner, described the agreement as a "gesture of friendship and cooperation" on the part of the U.S. government. But this wasn't all. The fact that U.S. farmers were bailed out of their predicament by a predictably pliable India was only one aspect of the deal misleadingly called "Food for Peace."

A second aspect was that in order to pay for the rice (as well as the wheat that was included in the transaction) India had to secure an $85 million loan from the U.S., thereby increasing its foreign debt and making the country more vulnerable to unsolicited political "advice" from the loaning nation. Given this reality, it was no surprise when, within two months of the deal's finalization, India stood solidly behind the U.S. at a Nairobi meeting of UNCTAD during which a tension-ridden debate took place over recommendations presented by Henry Kissinger concerning the relationship between developing and developed nations. The tight neocolonial ties between India and the U.S. were further expressed at this same conference by the fact that "while India was extending its support for the proposals of Kissinger many spokesmen from the Third World countries said they saw few signs that the industrial powers are ready to compromise on key issues that would help prevent a deepening crisis between the rich and the poor nations." India, economically connected to the U.S., was alienated from her own natural allies.

9.

As we have seen, U.S. relations with India during the Emergency period weren't as bad as certain state department remarks or newspaper editorials might have indicated. Still, India's apparent tilting away from the western capitalist orbit and toward the Soviet bloc in the early 70s shouldn't be viewed as a merely superficial phenomenon. The fact was that Soviet influence within India did increase. This also raised a set of problems, and these problems were at least partly analogous to those characteristic of the India-U.S. relationship.

Although it can be said "that the financial terms of Soviet assistance have been much better than western aid," and it can also be said "that for nearly every Third World country some form of economic relations with the U.S.S.R. is incomparably more advantageous than exclusive reliance on the western imperialist group of nations"—still, such statements shouldn't be allowed to obscure the fact that the Soviet Union's economic-political relations with such countries are damaged by a pattern of big power/small power contradictions.

Its relationship to India is a case in point.

Soviet influence in India started slowly, only mounting to serious proportions in the late 60s, early 70s. By 1971 (the year of the signing of the Indo-Soviet Treaty), the two countries were displaying their new closeness regularly, as in their joint attempt to control, to both their advantages, the outcome of the conflict between West and East Pakistan, a conflict which finally resulted in the separation of East Pakistan from West Pakistan and its transformation into the new nation of Bangladesh.

1971 was a crucial turning point. U.S. outrage over India's public desertion from the U.S. sphere of influence resulted in a sudden cancellation of all aid projects to the subcontinent. The smell of a desperate enmity was in the air. U.S. technical assistance to ongoing projects in India diminished. The Indian government decapitated the Indo-U.S. agreement which had allowed the U.S. to employ Indian rupees (which it had gotten hold of through the PL-480 arrangement) to finance U.S.

programs in Nepal. No love was being lost between the ex-partners.

That all this was indicative of a radical altering of India's position, not just in regard to the U.S., but also in terms of its relationship to the Soviet Union, is amply shown by the following excerpt from a well-documented report:

> The changed position...in India was dramatically reflected in changes in the direction of trade. There was a drastic fall in imports from the U.S.A.—from 30 percent of India's imports in 1968-69 to just 12.6 percent in 1972-73 (of course, this went up to 16.9 percent in 1974-75, proving that U.S. imperialism still has a considerable base in India)....At the same time the total turnover of Indo-Soviet trade rose rapidly. In 1973 the turnover was Rs 612 crores—an increase of Rs 105 crores from 1972....In that year, the Soviet Union became India's largest trading partner, for the first time displacing U.S. imperialism from the position it has held continuously from the Second World War onwards.

The question is: what were the consequences of this new relationship? Whereas with the U.S. the major portion of financial assistance given to India was designated specifically for agricultural development, Soviet assistance was predominantly geared toward the public sector: armaments and munitions, the bureaucracy, heavy industry. Once it had its foot in the door, the Soviet Union didn't hesitate to fling the door wide open. Increasingly, Indian economic development hinged on Soviet assistance. This was true in heavy machinery, heavy electrical equipment, steel, crude oil output, petroleum products and metallurgical equipment. Also there was India's escalating military dependence on the U.S.S.R. By 1976, Soviet military aid to India was close to six times more than the U.S.'s. India's military-supplies production within India was, for all practical purposes, supervised by the Soviet Union. At the same time, its need for bigger, more sophisticated equipment was satisfied by imports from the Soviet Union.

Once more, the pattern of India's dependence on foreign powers was being perpetuated.

One example of the negative consequences of India's economic relations with the U.S.S.R. was switch-trading. This was a process whereby the Soviet Union (or the eastern European countries within its range of influence) would purchase products from India and then resell them at higher prices to other countries, thereby making a profit and limiting India's accumulation of foreign exchange. For instance, in 1974 the Soviet Union purchased 62,800 tons of pig iron from India at a cost of 30.5 rubles per ton. At the same time it exported 65,700 tons of pig iron to other Third World countries at an average price of 137.8 rubles per ton. Even if the pig iron sold to the other Third World countries wasn't the same pig iron imported by the Soviet Union from India, the fact still remains that India's chances for foreign exchange were hindered by the overall Soviet strategy. The practical effect of this strategy was that it steered 62,800 tons of subcontinent pig iron into the Soviet Union and away from a higher priced market, which the Soviet Union itself had access to and did business with.

Other examples of switch-trading primary Indian products like jute, tea and cashews could also be given. But we don't have to go further. The point is that Soviet trade relations with India haven't necessarily proved to be in the ultimate best interests of India.

One of the domestic political consequences of improved Indo-Soviet relations was the peculiar role that the pro-Soviet Communist Party of India (the most conservative of the subcontinent's three major communist formations) played during the Emergency. Accepting the Congress Party line that the Emergency was essentially a move against right-wing forces, the CPI aggressively supported the new measures. Behind this position lay a stunted Soviet vision of what was occurring within India at the time.

According to Soviet analysis, the Emergency was a progressive step in the context of Indian development because it supported a policy of maximum industrialization. Such industrialization, said Soviet thinkers, would have the ultimate effect of enlarging, and increasing the political consciousness of, the working class, the only class capable of creating socialism on the subcontinent. Therefore, the Emergency was good. The CPI accepted this view and so developed its strategy accordingly. It stood behind Indira Gandhi, offering her support and attempting to steady her political boat whenever it began to rock. Spitting forth a dizzying series of rationalizations for the government's behavior, the CPI stubbornly failed to perceive (or admit) that the primary victims of state and police violence were ordinary people increasingly on the verge of mass revolt. That there is evidence to the effect that CPI support of the Emergency diminished during the latter part of the period, and that some cadre within the CPI even began to courageously speak out against the Emergency's employment of large-scale terror, doesn't absolve the CPI of its willful, tragic compromise at a key moment in Indian history.

4
THE EXOTIC
METAPHYSICAL CONTINENT

CALINGUTE BEACH, IN GOA

It's almost paradise. The kind of place Gaugin needed to find before the "primitive" part of his genius could emerge. In the morning the fishermen return in their mangowood fishing boats from a night on the Arabian Sea. Every muscle flexed with the effort, they come in rowing hard and in unison on the backs of the whitecapped breakers. When the boat's finally grounded, they get out and push it up onto the beach. Within a half hour, the night's haul of fish has been unloaded and carried off in large baskets balanced on the tops of women's heads. The bold primary colors of their saris—bright reds, yellows, greens, purples—ignite the beach as they walk off toward the nearby villages. After the fish have been unloaded and carried off, the men, heads protected from the hot sun by different-shaped straw hats, sit down in the sand next to their boats and sew up the holes in their red fishing nets. Behind them, where the beach ends, the land is thick with coconut, palm, banana and jackfruit trees.

The life-rhythm here seems as natural and inalterable as the rhythm of the incoming and outgoing tides. It's like entering a different, uncontaminated world. In their crazy high-speed way, sandcrabs dart across small sections of beach, then plunge down into little dark holes. This is the one sign of a fast pace. Everything else is relaxed. Clocks, it seems, aren't needed. The rising and setting of the sun and the night sky—a vast navigator's map of stars—are sufficient to survive by, to know when and when not to do something, to decide what course to steer. And drumming behind everything is the infinite, steady beat of the surf. A sound that gets into the blood, calming the body. A sensation something like the fetus in the uterus must feel, rocked by the regular beating of the mother's heart.

This is the picture, the dream. It's a real place, and yet it has the slight out-of-focus blur of fantasy. It speaks to something deep within the western observer, an age-old fascination with images that suggest the "natural life." This is the secret pull that has brought here—to the village of Calingute in Goa—a second, but alien, population that lives side by side with, but always psychologically apart from, the first, indigenous population

The strangers are westerners, many from the U.S.

Some of these foreigners, having come to India to study meditation or yoga at certain ashrams, end up here in Calingute in order to take a brief break from their ascetic curriculums. Others are here as a week or two-week respite from the foundation-funded research they're doing on the subcontinent. Still others are just wanderers, seekers in search either of their own personal destiny or some kind of exotic amnesia. Some of these stay camped on the beach here for months at a time. And then there are the merchant seamen, temporarily on leave, hunting excitement. But whoever they are, and however they get here, the local inhabitants have the same name for them all: hippies. A word often pronounced with noticeable disdain, as if the speaker were spitting in somebody's face.

In Calingute village you notice them everywhere, these aliens: hanging out in front of the fresh fruit-drink stalls, wandering idyllically down winding dirt paths, browsing in the clothing shops. These clothing shops have a special flare, like psychedelic crossroads on the far side of the planet Pluto. It is in these shops that members of the foreign community crowd together, picking up the decorations they feel they need in order to fit neatly into the dream. The prevailing assumption is that in order to properly inhabit the we're-returning-to-earth atmosphere, they have to look right. And so, coming out of the shops are the young women and men (ranging in age from the late teens to the late 30s) wearing *lungis* and dyed pyjama bottoms and Indian undershirts. The clothes are intentionally worn in haphazard unIndian ways that make the wearers look like totally-adrift, footloose gypsies. What attracts them to the *lungis* and dyed pyjama bottoms is obvious: the bold primary colors and the exotic printed patterns of the material. The colors somehow symbolize a key psychological element in this crossing over from one culture to another: undiluted "primitive" colors, suggestive of a world somehow less complex, more basic, than what you find in the West.

But it's only on the beach that you get a sense of the full extent of the foreign invasion. Here, in both directions among the fishing boats lined up in the sand, you can see the ragamuffin tourists sunbathing naked, rubbing themselves with oil, reading books, talking, smoking joints. A steady parade of Indians, pushed by an uncontrollable curiousity, marches down the beach looking at these indecipherable people from another world. Why are they here? Who, in god's name, *are* they? Out of all this, another interesting question arises: whose beach, actually, is this? Unfortunately, the answer isn't as clear as it might seem it should be.

Example. Two American women sit naked in the sand at the edge of the foamy surf, cleaning tin pans. As some local inhabitants walk by, sneaking looks at the two strangers, the women don't even look up; they keep cleaning, unperturbed by the walking Indians. In a weird way, the Indians are transformed into sightseers in their own country. It's as if they're visitors, and the foreigners are the native inhabitants. If there's such a thing as a psychological upper hand, these two women have it. They dominate precisely because of their assumption that it's the most natural thing in the world for them to be there, precisely where they are. In this assumption, they don't budge an inch. The ultimate sign of their power is how the fisher-people walk by, wanting to look, but a little afraid to.

Another example. A hut on the beach, simply structured, made of straw matting and bamboo poles. A small sign, white with red letters, hangs from a hook on a bamboo pole to the left of the entrance. It says: BOBBY'S DRINKS. Inside you can get cold fruit drinks mixed in an old-fashioned 1950s-model electric blender. The drinks available are bananna, chicoo, jackfruit, guava, and mango. There's room for about twenty people. The furniture is simple: old, dirty, weather-beaten wooden tables and rickety benches whose legs are slightly sunk into the sand. At the end of the hut opposite the entrance, there's a makeshift counter behind which sits a Goanese man ready to take orders.

Besides Suman and myself and the two children, there are nine other people, seven westerners and two Goanese, in the hut. One of the two Goanese is dressed like the westerners. He has a red bandanna tied gypsy-like around his head, and he's wearing beads. He's sitting alone in a corner, smoking a cigarette. He's young, about sixteen, and has the air of a hanger-on, someone delicately balancing himself on the shifting, cobweb-thin line where two distinctly different cultures meet. The other Goanese gives an opposite impression. Dressed in neatly pressed pants and a bright seablue silk shirt, he has a bold, flamboyant air as he walks from table to table asking each customer individually, "Wanna smoke?" As he asks this question, he shows each person a bone pipe in order to make sure they know exactly what he's talking about: dope. There's something unignorably "international" about this man: the decked-out dude eking out a marginal existence at the edge of petty criminality. One gets the distinct feeling he'd be entirely at home as a subway-riding junkie suddenly disembarking at 42nd Street, or as a smalltime Brooklyn pimp. He's learned his lessons well.

When the three French people sitting next to us say they want a hit, the Goanese man's face lights up with the kind of salesman's smile that says, I knew you wouldn't be able to resist my charming soft sell. He tells them to wait a minute and then goes into a back room to the left of the counter. Just inside the doorway, he reaches up and takes a small plastic pouch off a shelf piled with fruits for fruit drinks. He loads the pipebowl and then comes out, lights the pipe for his customers and then sits down next to them while they smoke. Soon three other westerners (Americans), sitting at another table, signal to him that they also want some. When the French people are done, he goes into the back room again, reloads the bowl, comes back out and, sitting down next to the Americans, lights the pipe for them and hands it to the man sitting nearest him. Dylan's "Like a Rolling Stone" is blaring over two loudspeakers whose wires lead into the back room, where there's either a phonograph or tape recorder. For a minute, it's difficult to tell exactly where one is, Calingute or California.

Suman and the kids and I go outside. The sun's glare, its reflection on sea and sand, is a dramatic contrast to the hut's shaded interior. But that isn't the only contrast. Not twenty-five yards from Bobby's Drinks, there's another, different world. A man's sitting next to his whitish-grey boat mending a fishing net. Near him, two women walk by with big baskets of fish balanced on their heads. And away from the beach, through the trees, you can see a man and a woman chopping wood with long-handled axes, while close to them another woman is washing clothes by rinsing them in a bucket and then banging them against a flat stone. People, ordinary people, working.

Then we're down by the surf, still walking away from the hut. We're in paradise, it seems. We're the strollers on the beach in the tourist ad that invites people to "vacation in lush Goa." There's only one omission in the travel ad: the confusion, the anger with which the local fisher-people view the odd foreigners who, obsessed with living "the natural life," have invaded the coast.

That these things are on local people's minds is evidenced by their almost compulsive willingness to talk about the situation. Anyone who's a sympathetic listener is guaranteed a good earful.

One man, the proprietor of a small store in Calingute, broaches the subject with Suman, at first hesitantly, but then when he sees she's supportive, more openly.

> The question is no longer whether we *like* having them here. The fact is that the government has said we're supposed to go out of our way to make them want to stay. When the people here said they didn't like this idea, that they couldn't stand the way the ones who came acted, the government finally established a fine for walking naked on a certain part of the beach. It didn't do any good. The fine's about 200 rupees ($25) but all these hippies have money, and so they pay the fine and then do the same thing again the next day. And if they don't have the money, or if they've been taking drugs and aren't in the mood to care, they go to jail for three days and it doesn't bother them at all. For us, 200 rupees would be a lot of money, fifteen days' or maybe a month's pay. But for them, coming from a rich country, money's no problem. And yet there's another side of this too, especially for people like me. The fact is that my business has picked up since these people came. But money isn't everything. I'll tell you, I just don't like the way they behave. It doesn't fit here.

That's a mild response. Another man, a fisherman approached casually on the beach in the early morning, tells us: "Look, I don't know why you're interested, but there's only one thing you have to know: they should all be thrown off the beach. That's all, just thrown off."

A woman, a schoolteacher, tells Suman:

The area's totally ruined now. Everything's geared towards making these foreigners feel good. About a year ago the fisherwomen here got very upset and decided to demonstrate. They dressed up in their prettiest saris. They put on their jewelry and fixed themselves up with flowers. Then, each of them carrying a black flag of protest, they marched on the state house in the capital demanding that the government put a stop to all this nakedness and other behavior on the beaches. But nobody paid attention. The only thing that happened was that a few meaningless signs were posted on the beaches saying nudity was prohibited. Of course, this had no effect. People also protested at local meetings right here in Calingute, but the hippies merely responded by saying the beach belonged to them as well as to anyone, and so they had a right to stay. But, we said, this is our country. They didn't pay attention, however, and so they're still here. Can you imagine that?

What's also bad is that our young people have started to copy this way of life. The use of drugs has never been bad in the area, but now it is. The children growing up think that if they don't adopt these ways of behaving they'll get laughed at for being afraid. It's all because of these people from Europe and America.

The hippies say they want to live close to nature, but if that's what they want why don't they go live in the jungle where we won't have to deal with them. I don't think they could get away with this in their own countries, and that's why they come here. Why is it that we have to get this garbage? What they're really doing is running away from reality. They talk about freedom, but what about our freedom, the people who live here? They show almost no respect for us, for our way of living, for our sense of what's right and what's wrong.

You know, some foreign company built a fertilizer plant near here, and some stuff got into the sea and killed the fish. Since fishermen can't live off dead fish, the people from the area protested and got the plant

closed down. But now there's something else foreign
poisoning the area, and we haven't found a way to get
rid of it yet...

Voices. Some milder, some more strident. But in all of them,
the anger runs deep

Meanwhile, the drama of a strange cultural colonialism
continues, act after act.

Two people, a man and a woman, walk toward the surf. As
they pass by us, I can hear their voices: Americans. He has on a
white t-shirt and dungaree shorts. She's wearing an orange *lungi*
wrapped around her in such a way that she looks like a slavegirl
in a grade-b Cecil DeMille movie about the fall of ancient Rome.
When they get near the surf, they both step out of their clothing
and stuff it into the man's knapsack. She takes a small bottle out
of the knapsack and pours some of its contents into her friend's
open hand and then pours some into her own. They start
applying the liquid (probably coconut oil) to each other's bodies:
shoulders, arms, back, neck.

About fifty yards behind them, an Indian man who has been
walking on the beach with his wife approaches another Indian
man, a fisherman, and pointing to the two Americans, says
something. His excitement is evident from the way he keeps
pointing to the two westerners, jabbing the air with one
extended finger. The fisherman nods in agreement and, having
received this support, the one who has been talking starts
marching straight toward the two Americans. When he reaches
them, he points back at the sign that says nudity is prohibited and
people breaking the law will be prosecuted. The Indian first talks
to the man, then to the woman. While he talks to the man, the
woman, looking away from them both, stares out at the sea,
having adopted an oh-my-god-how-long-is-this-going-to-go-on
attitude. When the Indian starts addressing her, her male
companion returns to nonchalantly annointing his already
tanned skin with oil.

Eventually, shaking his head in obvious disgust, the Indian
walks away. When he rejoins his wife, they wander off to another
part of the beach. The two Americans are still down by the surf.
The man has gone out up to his knees in the water: he's stooped
over cleaning some small object in the foamy waves. The woman
is rubbing oil on her thighs.

This is it: the daily confrontation.

But it would be wrong to assume that all westerners at Calingute have consciously chosen to degrade the area. Some of them, having adopted romantic anti-technological ideologies, have traveled half way around the world in what they consider to be an honest quest for greater simplicity. The tragedy is that they don't see how their countercultural explanations for why they've come to the subcontinent are, at best, frail wrapping-paper packagings for the same old imperialist attitudes. In this way, misled by their own fancy rationales, they're blind to the brutal interface that occurs here between two cultures.

A case in point. He's from California. He dropped out of college when he was a junior because "what's the use, they just train you there to be one more speedster in the rat race." After quitting school, he lived for two years from hand to mouth, doing odd jobs, drifting around. During that time he started studying eastern religions, as a way of "learning to know myself in a new way, of discovering new potentials."

Then he decided to come to India. After flying to Paris, he traveled to the subcontinent overland through southern Europe, around the Mediterranean, then through Pakistan. "After leaving Greece," he says, "you could feel yourself entering a new world, Istanbul, Tehran, all those mosques with the sun glittering on them, while below in the streets there were big biblical-like crowds. What got to me was that the nearer I got to India, the more my sense grew that I was getting closer to something ancient we've lost in the West. You know, an emphasis on inner orientation, on being centered within."

And so things come full circle. The new India-lover, disgruntled with life in the West, peers at India through the same lens that the original ideologues of western colonialism used.

India: that nest of metaphysics, that bizarre cauldron of gurus, that crazy spiritual place.

We don't have to wonder what the people of Calingute think of this.

The anger burns deep.

NOTES ON COLONIAL ATTITUDES

1.

Always, there has been a strange semi-mythological quality
to the United States' relationship to India. From the first
exploratory European contact with the North American continent, the "discovery" of that continent was linked to a search
for a western route to materially rich, exotic India. The discovery
of the so-called New World was the furthest thing from
Columbus' mind:

> Out of nowhere
> over the calm sunlit waters
> the Santa Maria came
> looking
> for India,
> gold
>
> & by mistake it bumped
> against
> a gigantic rock
>
> an accidental continent
>
> a steppingstone
> to dreamland.

As a matter of fact, when Columbus first landed in the
Americas he thought he'd found the oriental location of the place
the Bible referred to as Ophir, from which the Queen of Sheba
brought the gold, almug trees, and jewels she presented to
Solomon, king of the Jews.

Columbus's search for the orient's material wealth was the
basis for a later western myth in which India was seen as a source
of "spiritual" wealth. This myth grew up slowly but regularly
over the centuries. In this myth, India's material wealth—spices,
grains, textiles—became, not an end in itself, but an analogy for
the transcendental riches it was hoped would be found there, in
this the supposedly most metaphysical of all countries. This
transformation—from a search for material wealth to a search
for spiritual wealth—was limited, of course, to the myth. In the

real world of cross-cultural interactions, as part of a process of colonialization, India's natural resources were plundered and its population reduced to a nation of slave-laborers.

A good example of the emergence of the myth of India's spiritual riches can be found in Emerson, the 19th century U.S. essayist.

For Emerson, Indian thinking was associated with purely mental liberation. For him, Hindu philosophy was "as sublime as heat and night and a breathless ocean. It contains every religious sentiment, all the grand ethics visit in turn each noble and poetic mind."

Here, Hindu philosophy, which supposedly represents a certain perfection of thought, is compared to a still, hot, windless night, to the immense silences of ocean and space. What's interesting about this description is that there's nothing *human* in it. Mere humanity is drowned out in the vastnesses of Eternal Thought; mind seems to have split off from body and become free, having entered a zone of pure thinking. With the naive confidence of a man half a planet away, Emerson said, "The orient has always tended to this (metaphysical) largeness."

But while Emerson was writing such descriptions of what he considered to be the definitive nature of Indian thinking throughout the ages, the Indian economy, as a result of being colonialized, was undergoing gigantic upheavals. India's manufacturing industries based on handicraft production were destroyed, and the subcontinent was transformed from a net exporter of its own goods to a net importer of foreign goods, as well as being converted into a supplier of raw materials for British industry. Yet Emerson, unsnagging himself from the rocks of history and floating like a balloon into the sky, could say, "The East is grand and makes Europe seem like the land of trifles."

It goes without saying that the this-world realism of much Indian thinking, that part of Indian philosophy which is unesoteric and down-to-earth, was totally ignored by Emerson. Lines from the Upanishads like:

> If, when looking at this, you see that,
> And if, when looking at that, you see this,
> Then
> You will never be saved

went unmentioned. As did bold statements like this, from the 13th-century South Indian woman poet, Adyakki Lakkamma:

> Is it charity
> when devotees hand out food
> supposedly for free
> but get a profit
> and then say
> this is their duty?

Such statements were ignored by Emerson because his relationship to the subcontinent was basically a colonialistic one; he scanned the history of Indian thinking opportunistically, merely to find verification for his own philosophical preconceptions. Just as the colonializing nation objectifies the colonialized nation by reducing it to a "thing" that can be used for the self-aggrandisement of the home country, so the liberal, supposedly sympathetic western philosopher reduces the colonialized's philosopohy to a "thing" that can be exploited along the lines of his/her own cultural biases and needs. This was Emerson's situation. In other words, subcontinent philosophy was there for him to do with as he willed, for him to decide what was and what wasn't worthwhile in it. This typifies the colonializing philosopher's power, his "freedom." In the instance at hand, India was nothing more than an intellectual trinket, or a sort of pill for stimulating fantastic dreams, for the man who has been referred to as the seer of Concord. Whether intentionally or not, Emerson's emphasis on Hindu metaphysics, at the expense of all other Indian social relations, indirectly supported a picture of India as a continent filled with thin-chested men sitting in the lotus position and chanting the single word "Om." One of the consequences of this was that Emerson created an image of the subcontinent that fitted neatly into the western worldview of his time: that the orient was inhabited by lethargic other-worldly populations incapable of entering the modern world without guidance.

2.

Over the years, the West's preoccupation with India's apparent psychological remoteness from western modes of existence has resulted in some predictably distorted (and self-

serving) views. One such view—that exemplified, in part, by
Emerson—pits the empirical West against the spiritual, sub-
jective East. The special form this attitude has taken in the U.S.
mind is that the U.S., pinnacle of western empirical/techno-
logical development, is the counter-image of India, the metaphysical continent *par excellence* with a population prone to
meditativeness and quests for transcendence. Coming from
North America, where some of the prime exponents of Indian
culture are western-born Hari Krishna devotees who bald-
headedly parade the streets in saffron robes, it should be easy to
understand how widespread this myth is in the popular
imagination.

In order to understand the implications of such attitudes,
it's necessary to view them historically, in the context of their
original cultural/political development. In an essay by the
historian Romila Thapur, precisely this problem is dealt with.

Increasingly trade contacts between Europe and Asia
from the fifteenth century led to a gradual interest on
the part of various European scholars and missionaries
in the culture of Asia. In the case of India the interest
began with a study of languages, particularly Sanscrit
and Persian. These studies gained momentum at the
end of the eighteenth century with the founding of the
Royal Asiatic Society and the systematic recording of
work on what was regarded as the classical tradition of
India. Most of the work was done by scholars who came
to be called Indologists. Those of them who studied
Sanscrit became great enthusiasts of the culture of the
Aryan speaking peoples.

The basic point is that increasing economic contact with the
subcontinent created the material basis for an acceleration of
western interest in Indian culture. Scholars rather than merchants oversaw this part of the West-East confrontation. The
question is: what were the historical motives that involved these
Orientalists in the methodical distortion of Indian culture? A
primary reason was that

many of the Orientalists were persons who were
alienated from their own society and were extremely
suspicious of the historical changes which Europe was

undergoing, particularly as a result of industrialization. Thus they searched for utopias elsewhere, and for many these lay in the ancient cultures of the Orient.

The fact that many Indologists operated at least partially out of a strong feeling of alienation from their own society explains the element of mystification in their approach to the subcontinent. But it didn't stop there. The interpretation of India that glorified its past—the so-called ancientry of its wisdom—didn't remain a harmless plaything in the hands of academic intellectuals. It resulted in the build-up of a set of assumptions about the Indian population that were to become an integral part of the colonial rationalization for occupying India.

The implicit faith in the spirituality of Indian culture is one such assumption. The theory that Indians were always concerned with metaphysics and philosophical speculation and not with the mundane things of everyday living has now become an accepted idea.

One can immediately see the practical usefulness (for the colonializing power) of such an attitude. In the western vision concrete realities like Indian industrial underdevelopment could be conveniently attributed to the transcendental and otherworldly psychological bias of the population. The logical conclusion was that down-to-earth western pragmatism was the missing ingredient on the subcontinent, the potential catalyst for "full" development. The West was only too willing to offer what it had, to help out, to provide a pragmatic guiding light. In this way colonialism was rationalized, transformed in the western mind from an exploitive act into an act of pure generosity.

But the idea of Indian spirituality wasn't just used in the West to rationalize colonialism. It was also used in India to facilitate the development of a colonial consciousness in the people, especially those of the educated sectors. The myth that Indians were prone to metaphysics and philosophical speculation was propounded by apparently disinterested western ideologues, who secretly believed this might be

an effective way of keeping the minds of Indians away from such mundane but essential things as...freedom from foreign rule. The notion was eagerly taken up by

Indian scholars who found in it an ideal counterpoise
to their humiliation at being subservient to a foreign
power.

In this way, one aspect—the ideological aspect—of the colonialization process was brought to fruition. It was forgotten that

Indian culture did not have a monopoly on spiritual
content. The same characteristics as are associated
with Indian spirituality can be found in many other
ancient cultures and are frequently recognizable in
traditional societies. Not surprisingly, the ancient
Indians never saw themselves as more spiritual than
their neighbors in adjoining or far-away lands. Nor did
visitors from other equally significant cultures, such as
the Greeks, the Chinese and the Arabs notice any
markedly distinctive spiritual characteristics.

3.

The attitudes we've discussed so far in this section aren't, of
course, without their modern parallels.

The 1960s were a momentous time in the U.S., characterized by social and psychological upheavals. One aspect of this
was that India was rediscovered by masses of North Americans.
It was as if the Santa Maria had finally sailed into the Bay of
Bengal, its crew on their knees, sniffing flowers and dropping
acid and proclaiming the discovery of new zones of
consciousness.

At the beginning of the 60s, Timothy Leary and Richard
Alpert were setting the tone of a "new" emergent culture with
statements like:

We have become more aware of the undiscovered
universe within, of the unchartered regions of consciousness....But what are the stimuli necessary and
sufficient...to open up the "potential forms of consciousness?" There are many. Indian philosophers
have described hundreds of ways.

Certain parts of the counterculture, searching for methods
of liberating themselves from the overly materialistic, con-
sumer-oriented U.S. society, made India their own. Indian

classical music, yoga, the *Bhagavad Gita*, imported gurus, all were essential ingredients of this new movement. Somehow the idea of the lone *saddhu* (an Indian holy man) wandering in search of spiritual enlightenment got fused with a western prototype: the hip, footloose drifter. For many of the wandering disenchanted, India became a symbol of an alternative way of life, of transcendence. Some actually circled the world and went to the subcontinent, to study music or meditation or just to get close to "something ancient that we've lost in the west." For many others who didn't leave the U.S., the journey still occurred, but in an inner psychological way. India symbolized freedom, escape.

In the 60s, the McCarthy-era lobotomization of U.S. consciousness ended. Repressed dissent surfaced, and for many of the young it seemed as if the raw gut of life in the U.S. was being exposed for the first time. Many developed a vision of the U.S. as a bizarre futuristic nightmare, as, in the words of Allen Ginsberg, "a sphinx of cement and aluminum that bashed open their skulls and ate their brains and imagination." In this context, the reason for fascination with India was clear: culturally it still contained many elements that were pre-modern and pre-technological. Third World underdevelopment had romantic precedence over western overdevelopment. The feeling ran high that there was nowhere to go in the States, no way to be free. Moving outward from the inner cities you entered the ugly industrial fringes of the major metropolitan centers, and beyond that, there was suburbia...and the quickest way out of suburbia was nirvana. In a strange way, for many of the young time and history had become something to be "overcome." In the words of the poet Gary Snyder:

> Arms shielding my face
> Knees drawn up
> Falling through flicker
> Of womb after womb,
>   through worlds,
> Only begging, Mother
>   must I be born again?

But the flower children weren't just foolish rejectors of U.S. society. They were a sociological phenomenon born out of a major disturbance in the national consciousness. The U.S. was supposedly the most technologically advanced and economically stable country in the world, yet what this meant in fact was that people were reduced to the daily performance of alienating and tedious tasks. In the factory and in the office it was becoming increasingly impossible to have any kind of meaningful relationship to one's work. Related to this was the additonal factor that human value was determined by property ownership and its adjunct, the capacity to consume. What's more, the fairly high rate of employment during the 60s was a direct result of the well-groomed war industry; involvement in Vietnam was the pin holding together the disintegrating cloth of the U.S. economy. On top of this, it was obvious that large numbers of Third World people in the U.S. suffered a form of domestic colonialization analogous to what was being done to their counterparts in underdeveloped nations, where whole populations were exploited as cheap labor by U.S. multinationals and as markets for surplus U.S. goods. And in the background, there was always the gothic music of napalm cannisters exploding in Vietnam. There was nothing in all this to excite young people to patriotism, to stimulate any blind "yeses" to the indigenous culture.

One consequence of these material conditions was the flourishing of a rebellious romanticism that signified the need to transcend the "fallen" capitalist world. Young people were in search of something pure, uncontaminated: a new innocence. One of the options was far flight, either into the inner worlds of the spirit, or outward into exotic cultures and rituals....This was the background against which the old distorted picture of India re-emerged, ripe for new exploitation.

Underdeveloped and with still tangible traces of a culture that flowed back thousands of years into the remote primitive past, India became, in the hands of certain sections of the counterculture, the perfect medicine for white western alienation, for this feeling of being imprisoned in "this awful stone moment/in the streams/of change." Obsession with India was a baroque occurrence that could only have happened in a capitalist country (where everything, at one time or another, is transformed into a commodity) during a period of major disillusionment. To the dispossessed, India represented a less complex, more colorful, more stable world. India became pure "idea," a compulsive thought stuck in the mind of a generation that felt itself on the brink of either extinction or liberation. India: where women wore jasmine in their hair, where coconuts were broken open before gods, where goats and water buffalo roamed the streets, where there was a still-living tradition of herbal medicine that appealed to the need of young westerners to "return to the natural, to the things of the earth."

But just as important as these things, there was also a prevalent Indian philosophy (popularized by western writers who hadn't tried to grasp the dialectical relationship between Indian thinking and Indian social relations) that said the world was *maya*, illusion. True freedom resided in the interior struggle to free oneself from ego-domination, and in so doing to penetrate the world of illusion in which everything appeared isolated from eveything else and to discover instead the mystical interconnectedness of everything. For people unwilling to accept any of the existing political revolutionary traditions, such a philosophy seemed to offer the only possibility of release from insecurity, anxiety. The word revolution changed meanings; it came to mean inner psychic transformation, rather than social transformation. And so, a pseudo-Indian vision of consciousness became god. Each individual was seen as the potential incarnation of the ultimate cosmic power: pure mind. But the new notion of transcendence also included the idea of fidelity to the earth, to nature. This aspect of transcendence was articulated in the philosophy of flower-power, which was conceived of as a spiritual getting-back-to-the-earth power. The new philosophy was depicted as a sort of fist, smelling of lilies, in the face of U.S. capitalism. It had the quality of being different and invigorating. Or so those promoting the new attitudes liked to think.

But beneath the surface of this modern, supposedly open-to-life primitivism, there were specific neocolonialistic thought and behavior patterns. Theoretically, the counterculture represented a rejection of U.S. capitalism/imperialism. For instance, Standard Oil of Indiana's holding up (through government influence in the 60s) of food shipments to India during a time of famine and mass starvation, as a way of coercing the Indian government to open its doors to Standard Oil's economic expansion on the subcontinent, was typical of the kind of economic aggression the counterculture repudiated as inhumane. But on the other hand, the counterculture was inadequate in detecting within itself a more subtle, though still concretely neocolonialistic, attitude. Having discarded the factual India of actual social relations, it had created instead a fantasy India, based on the old western myth that the Indian people were metaphysical and non-empirical. This exotic package was developed and marketed as the supreme escape valve. One can see Emerson here lurking in the shadows, smiling and pointing the way to: LIBERATION.

Those involved in India-obsession displayed, on the whole, a self-protecting innocence with regard to their actions. It was as if they'd gouged out their eyes with lotus stems. A secret utopian assumption that young white U.S. citizens could "become" Indian in the same way that one could become an engineer or schoolteacher indicated the culturally schizophrenic nature of this modern East-West confrontation. People simply didn't grasp the symbolic sigificance of what they were doing. For instance, in the 60s, studying yoga became a mass fad because physical discipline and meditation were perceived as necessary aspects of the process of simplifying, even dewesternizing, the self. But implicit in a westerner's studying yoga is a rejection of one's own cultural background, whereas, for an Indian, studying yoga is an act of becoming connected to her/his cultural-religious roots. This difference, of course, makes them fundamentally distinct and nonequivalent experiences. Another example of the kind of confusion that characterized the new relationship between West and East was that for those who went to India on some sort of spiritual quest, the freedom to travel half way around the world to satisfy a fantasy—one of the advantages of being brought up at the center of an economic empire—wasn't scrutinized in terms of its being a privilege that inevitably (if ignored) contaminated one's relationship to the very society one wanted to experience.

In summation, it can be said that such cross-cultural escapades were limited precisely where they should have been strongest: the counterculture couldn't comprehend how nothing "Indian" was being done at all, whereas something quite

"North American" was. Such innocence, of course, was actually the mask behind which hid the power of international class privilege.

To the extent that India has come to represent an exotic place of self-discovery for westerners, it is being treated neocolonialistically. India is still there to satisfy the needs of westerners; its doors are expected to remain open so that each western whim can enter undisturbed. In this countercultural neocolonialism, India's reality is determined by western fantasy. The actual India—a semi-feudal, semi-capitalist country in which workers, both urban and agrarian, are oppressed by a ruling elite—is entirely left out. Union struggles, women's demonstrations against high prices, bands of guerrillas fighting in the countryside to expropriate land from the largest landlords—all these are missing. What we have instead is a series of images ripped out of context: a swami sitting crosslegged on a straw mat, an Indian god with flowers in his hair, lyrical-looking women carrying water-vessels on their heads, etc. The raw materials being plundered in this narrow picture of the subcontinent are no longer material but "spiritual."

This is the children's version of the older generation's more blunt form of economic aggression.

MOHANDAS GANDHI

The colonial myth of Indian spirituality has persisted into the present era in many different forms, some of which we've already seen. Another example of such persistance is that, according to certain contemporary historians and India-watchers, India's most ancient traditons have put on a modern face, and transcended the materialism of the West, in Mohandas Gandhi's philosophy of nonviolence. If we accept this vision— that Gandhian nonviolence was an organic outgrowth of India's finest centuries-old traditions, and that Gandhi's genius lay in his ability to organize a mass anti-imperialist movement on the basis of an indigenous spiritual world-vision as opposed to a western materialist one—then we will be compelled to accept the possibility that India is somehow unique among modern nations. Such a view, if adopted, would have some significant consequences: for instance, that social change, if it comes to India, is likely to be initiated by some gentle-eyed guru type rather than, as we have increasingly seen happening in various Third World countries, through militant alliances between peasants and workers.

In reality, however, there's no historical basis for accepting the notion that Gandhi's politics were either uniquely pure or especially successful.

The fact is that Gandhi's vision was, from the beginning, a limited one. It would be unhistorical to suggest that people accepted his leadership because they felt a deep cultural attachment to his notions of nonviolence. There were many other, just as important, reasons. The most dramatic of these was his famous willingness, after winning people's trust, to employ a unique form of psychological blackmail in order to diminish resistance to his leadership. He would throw in the face of those who challenged him a threat to fast until death unless his organizational and philosophical directives were adhered to. Such tactics reveal a fundamental flaw in that perspective on Gandhian nonviolence which claims that, as an organizing tool, it was a highly egalitarian process. In reality, Gandhi's vision was basically authoritarian: it was always expressed as a power "over the people" as opposed to springing from them and taking direction from them.

This is precisely why the period of Gandhi's leadershp was so dramatic. Not only was he struggling against British rule, he was also struggling against his own people, using every device at his disposal to get them to accept his version of the meaning of freedom. So, on occasions when the nationalist movement erupted spontaneously into truly revolutionary forms—for instance, the setting up of a people's "parallel government" in Satara district in 1942—he did everything within his power to crush such militancy. Behind all his talk about truth with a capital T, there was a glaring disrespect for the people's—the peasants' and workers'—vision of what form the Independence movement should take. There's no doubt that Gandhi pictured himself as the nationalist movement's spiritual center, as a sort of transcendent ego whose job it was to control the masses, who were like a continually upsurging and undisciplined id.

Such arrogance had serious political side-effects. A close-up view of these side-effects can be garnered by examining the way in which Gandhi handled a labor dispute in Ahmedebad in 1918.

The source of the Ahmedebad labor troubles was a disagreement between millhands and millowners over a wage increase. In the ensuing struggle, Gandhi intervened on behalf of the workers, assisting them in their efforts to get a 35% wage raise. But Gandhi demanded payment for his participation: the exploited must submit to his moral authority. *His* view, therefore, on how the battle against the owners should be fought, would have to prevail. One of the consequences of this was that at the beginning of the conflict, Gandhi insisted the workers put aside their militancy and instead trust in an arbitration process. Those arbitrating on their behalf with the owners would be Shankerlal Banker, an upper-class disciple of Gandhi's, a local lawyer named Patil, and Gandhi, also a lawyer (a fact sometimes obscured by those who romanticize him). It isn't surprising that the workers, feeling to different degrees alienated from these procedures, went on strike against Gandhi's counsel. Gandhi, who was out of town at the time, immediately returned and, according to one report, "scolded the workers" and "apologised to the owners." Gandhi was too late, however; the strike had been turned into a lock-out. The owners wouldn't budge.

To Gandhi, there was nothing contradictory in his patronizing attitude toward the workers. It was part of his policy of bringing "no harm to either party in a dispute." In his vision, the workers' going on strike had been an act of premature aggression against the owners. As such, it wasn't to be tolerated. His goal was to impose on the workers' class anger, as a sort of restraining force, a highly abstract concept of justice. This concept included the notion that even if capital was guilty of exploiting labor, this didn't give workers the right to "unfairly" take advantage of their employers. Gandhi's puritanism never failed to flinch when confronted with the kinds of sudden anger-bursts that inevitably accompany serious class conflict. Given this, it isn't difficult to see how Gandhi must have appeared in a confusing light to many of these millhands, as when, for instance, he offered to personally escort scabs into the mills if the occasion arose. To say the least, what Gandhi required of the workers was severe: that, in the middle of their labor struggle, they put aside their "lower worldly" instincts and submit themselves to the "highest" principles of justice. Any tendency on their part toward action of a so-called lower nature had to be, in Gandhi's view, curtailed by the spiritually advanced leadership. This was in keeping with his practice of continually transforming questions of social struggle into questions of personal spiritual struggle. ("What I want to achieve—what I have been striving and pining to achieve these thirty years—is self-realization, to see God face to face, to attain *Moksha*.") For Gandhi, the world was merely a testing ground, the religious arena in which the individual quested for transcendence. Even collective social struggle drew its basic meaning from the fact that it was a useful discipline for facilitating individual spiritual growth.

Gandhi applied this perspective to the owners as well as to the workers. He felt the owners' major problem wasn't inherent in the inordinate power they held over their workers, but rather had to do with the fact that they had abdicated their socially ordained responsibilities towards those workers—i.e., to guide them, to set a good example, to be fair with them, etc. Gandhi believed the owners could be converted to the right path without jeopardizing the paternalistic structure of their relationship to their employees. It was a question of getting them to understand their *karma*, their pre-ordained role in life. As one student of Gandhi's thinking has pointed out: "Gandhi affirmed not only that it was *not possible* to abolish class distinctions but also that it was *not desirable* to do so....According to his interpretation of trusteeship...wealth belonged to society as a whole, and it just happened that some persons were in charge of the use of that wealth for the whole society—i.e., they were trustees."

The fact that Gandhi accepted such a vision is key to understanding his own self-view as an activist: he was the instrument of moral edification for *all* the Indian classes. The problem wasn't between this class and that class, but was rather a question of an individual moral sluggishness, on the part of many people from different classes, that had to be overcome. He would be the match that would ignite the dried firewood of future redemption in the hearts of the people.

All this was evident at Ahmedebad. On the one hand, Gandhi was persistently trying to persuade the millowners (some of whom were his personal friends) to be more generous when it came to setting wage scales. When simple discussion proved unsuccessful, his methods of persuasion became more militant; he got the workers to take a pledge that they wouldn't return to work, under any circumstances, until a 35% wage increase was established. But this didn't mean Gandhi's allegiance was onesidedly in favor of the workers. In a series of pamphlets issued by Gandhi during the dispute, the top-down, leader-led nature of his relationship to the millhands was amply revealed, as was the fact that the workers were under an obligation to prove themselves "worthy" if they wanted him and his people to keep defending their rights.

The pamphlets contained moral instructions that ranged from advising the workers "to harbor no grudge" against the owners to telling them that one of the goals of their leaders was to raise their (the workers') "moral level." They were also told that because the leaders had an impartial, objective interest in justice for everyone, they (the leaders) would put the full weight of their support behind the owners if it ever came to be shown that the workers were failing to fulfill their obligations to their employers. In other words, Gandhi's task as he saw it was to lead everyone, workers and owners alike, through the forge of self-purification. It's not surprising that as time dragged on and the dispute wasn't resolved, the workers, for the most part feeling themselves reduced to passive observers of their own struggle, began to lose interest and started giving expression to their desire to go back to work, even without the wage increase.

But for Gandhi such an option was inconceivable, since the workers' pledge not to return to work until their grievances were satisfied had, for him, a sort of religious sanctity. So, faced with the millhands' growing dissent, Gandhi resorted to his talent for historical drama to see him through the critical situation and to insure that his vision of how it should all end would triumph. He told the workers: "I cannot tolerate for a minute that you break your pledge. I shall not take any food, nor use a car till you get 35 percent increase or all of you die fighting for it." His response, then, to the workers' disaffection was a fast to the death. His life was now on the line. This had a double effect. On the one hand, by setting a radical example for the workers, he compelled them to step back in line. After all, if he died it would somehow be their responsibility, since he was putting his life on the chopping-block for their sakes. On the other hand, he was exerting a tremendous amount of pressure on the millowners, since they had a personal stake in his survival: some of them were his personal friends.

Eventually, in the course of the drama of Gandhi's fast, a compromise was reached and the dispute resolved. It is interesting to see how, on the day the lock-out ended, Gandhi, in giving a speech to the millhands, used the example of their pledge-taking as a way of driving home the point that they, the workers, were for all practical purposes spiritually undernourished and were therefore in need of further guidance until such a time as they achieved full spiritual maturity. He said:

> After twenty years' experience, I have come to the conclusion that I am qualified to take a pledge; I see that you are not yet so qualified. Do not, therefore, take an oath without consulting your seniors. If the occasion demands one, come to us, assured that we shall be prepared to die for you, as we are now. But remember that we shall help you only in respect of a pledge you have taken with our concurrence. A pledge taken in error can certainly be ignored. You have yet to learn how and when to take a pledge.

This is the fully ripened patriarchal Gandhi, with his vision of the masses as a sort of vast childlike mob to be pitied and given a helping hand. And in the final analysis, ony *his* hand would do.

Ahmedebad, however, was only one situation. We have to go further to get a fuller, more complete picture of Gandhi's social/political role as a key figure within the Independence movement.

Gandhi's great effectiveness as a nationalist leader grew out of his capacity, even though he was at best an unorthodox Hindu, to fit into the traditional role of the guru, or spiritual leader, by recreating that role in his own image. By dewesternizing himself and by apparently stripping himself of class affiliation and choosing a life of simplicity and renunciation, he seemed, from the perspective of a significant portion of the population, obviously different from many of the other Congress leaders.

And as a proselytizer for Truth—as someone whose chosen path
was to stand above factional interests—his difference from other
leaders was all too easily described at the popular level as the
difference between saint and worldly politicians. The fact that
Gandhi was seen as the "Mahatma" (although he himself didn't
choose the term)—a great spiritual person—proved in the long
run to be immensely valuable to the Congress Party, which was
to emerge as the crucial political formation within the Independence movement.

In order to understand Gandhi's value to the Congress
Party, it's first necessary to recognize that, up until his
appearance as a major nationalist leader, the mass base of the
Congress-led self-determination movement was extremely limited. A large majority of people were suspicious of, even
disinterested in, a movement controlled by the country's elite.
What did the lower castes and classes have in common with rich
people's attempts to wrestle a certain amount of power from the
British?

Gandhi helped change all this. As his national stature grew,
he became a sort of popular symbol, a living guarantee, of the
class-impartiality and democratic nature of the nationalist
movement. As the conscience of that movement, the feeling
went, he could be relied upon to steer it in the right direction if it
veered off course. Subsequently, Gandhi's major political role—
regardless of whatever broader intentions he might have had—
was to mobilize people under the bourgeois-dominated Congress
Party. By stubbornly persisting in the notion that the interests of
the different classes were ultimately harmonious, and by accepting the contingent belief that if class conflict did arise he, as the
conscience of the movement, would be able to singlehandedly
diminish its negative effects, Gandhi became the efficient tool of
a particular class: the bourgeoisie.

We can take Gandhi's position on the untouchables as an
example of how, even when fighting in behalf of the oppressed
against the Congress Party leadership, he was—although he
achieved limited dramatic gains—incapable of laying the social
and political groundwork that would have insured *effective*
elimination of oppression. To the extent that Gandhi's failure in
this area is traceable to his own peculiar brand of willful

romanticism, we have to acknowledge this failure as a representative weakness of his vision.

The name "Harijans" that Gandhi imposed on the untouchables is illustrative of his tendency to idealize reality in a socially dangerous way. Harijan means "children of God," and as such the name suggests something specific about the nature of the people being referred to: that, in terms of human development, they are pre-adolescent, helpless, innocent in the romantic sense of being purer and more immune to evil than "experienced" adults. Gandhi's choice of terms wasn't arbitrary; as we have seen before, he saw the lower classes as children in need of guidance from an intelligent father.

In relation to the untouchable question, Gandhi's self-chosen position was once more that of being everyone's moral instructor. On the one hand, the childlikeness of the untouchables required that they be raised up or spiritually elevated into mature "experimenters with Truth," like Gandhi. In this situation, of course, Gandhi was to be the advisor, the untouchables the followers. On the other hand, there was the problem of the Congress Party leadership, upper caste and primarily from property-owning backgrounds. Gandhi's role in relation to these people, as he saw it, was to persuade them that they weren't adequately sensitized to the plight of the untouchables, or, by extension, to their own moral responsibility to take pity on, and offer a helping hand to, those historically less fortunate than they.

Inevitably his approach down-played the economic or class nature of the relationship between non-caste untouchables and the different castes that made up the rest of the population. Although the untouchables had been legally liberated from slavery in the mid-19th century, in reality this liberation meant little more than a transition from being serfs bound to particular masters to being low-paid discriminated-against (but "free") agricultural laborers. Those who weren't field laborers remained anchored from generation to generation to particular hereditary tasks, like cleaning cremation sites or making leather from the skins of dead animals. The point is that they were alloted those jobs that, although socially necessary, were perceived to be the most menial and debasing. In other words, the untouchables were the sediment, the rock-bottom laboring base of society. What Gandhi failed to perceive was that to effectively release the untouchables from such bondage would require a radical curtailment of the power of the dominant classes, who were in fact the greatest beneficiaries of Indian society's hierarchical structure. What Gandhi substituted for actual social revolution, however, was the idea that people, both at the top and at the bottom of society, could be changed through a consciousness-raising process akin to religious conversion.

But converting people wasn't easy. On the one hand, Gandhi was confronted with those sections of the population who resisted any tampering whatsoever with the existing social structure. On the other hand, he had to deal with radical untouchables who were far more progressive than he was and who demanded the abolition of the whole caste system from top to bottom, a position too revolutionary for Gandhi. In response to this situation, he attempted to steer what at first appeared to be a reasonable compromise course. As time passed, however, it became clear that this compromise process had a serious restraining effect on the untouchable movement as a whole.

One writer, Gail Omvedt, in an article entitled "Gandhi and the Pacification of the Indian National Revolution," shows how Gandhi, in working out his position on untouchability, devoted a good deal of his time to rebutting lower-caste attacks on the caste system. Her aim is to put into perspective the generally-held view that Gandhi was an undeviating supporter of full rights for untouchables. She makes it clear the facts are contrary to such a vision. Where leadership sprang from the ranks of the untouchables themselves, Gandhi resisted it; he was terrified that if the radical goals of militant leaders like Ambedkar were realized, it would have too upsetting an impact on society as a whole.

Once again we are exposed here to Gandhi's patriarchal dimension. He viewed the untouchables as ignorant children, helpless, in need of guidance; *their* projected solutions to the inequities of the caste system were too daredevilish and irresponsible; only *his* solutions made sense. Although he acknowledged that the caste system was corrupt, he maintained it could be reinvigorated. Omvedt shows how in Gandhi's struggle against the oppressiveness of untouchability, he didn't argue for the abolition of the caste system per se, but rather demanded that the untouchables—who, according to Hindu ideology, were so low that they were outside of or "below" the caste system itself—should be absorbed into the *lowest* castes, among those "who were the masses working for the elite." She then goes on to say what should be obvious, that "for Untouchables who were already involved in movements demanding *full* human rights" Gandhi's position was at best "an evasion."

Omvedt also gives another example of Gandhi's contradictions with regard to the untouchable issue. In this instance, the problem at hand was how the untouchables would be integrated into the electoral system. The untouchable leader Ambedkar, representing the opinion of the untouchable community, had one opinion. Gandhi, predictably, had another.

> Ambedkar...was Gandhi's antagonist in his (Gandhi's) major fast over the question of untouchability. This was undertaken in opposition to the decision of the government of India to give a separate electorate to Untouchables, i.e., certain seats would be reserved to them in the legislatures and only Untouchables would vote for their representatives. Gandhi saw this as a major attack on the "unity" of the Hindu community and threatened to fast to death in opposition. While this fast took on the connotation of urging caste Hindus to reform their ideas regarding untouchability (and its compromise was later seen as radical by the orthodox), in fact it was primarily against the Untouchables' demand for separate electorates and primarily against their acknowledged political spokesman, Ambedkar....

> Pressure on Ambedkar to compromise was intense. For all the moral aura surrounding *satyagraha* techniques, which urged that they should win the freely given agreement of opponents, moral blackmail was in fact the primary aspect of this fast-to-death by Gandhi. Ambedkar was well aware of the existence of Untouch-

ables isolated and powerless in villages throughout
India and of the fury that would be unleashed against
them if Gandhi died. He capitulated; a compromise
was reached...which gave the Untouchables an increased number of seats but allowed caste Hindus as
well to vote for Untouchable representatives—and
given the numerical superiority of caste Hindus and
the wealth and organization of the Congress, this
meant that Untouchables favorable to Congress have
invariably been elected.

To say the least, this isn't the typical way that Gandhi's
influence is portrayed by his followers. Gandhi, demystified and
naked in the raw spotlight of history, is definitely different from
the slightly blurry and saintly image of popular legend.

Gandhi was powerful. Yet we have to remember that his
embrace didn't completely engulf the Independence movement.
Throughout the period of the nationalist struggle, there were
incidents that shattered the fabric of Gandhian nonviolence,
revealing the massive and radical nature of the Indian people's
discontent. In the post-Independence period, these incidents
have frequently been depicted as unfortunate deviations from
the generally high moral caliber of the freedom struggle. A
better way to look at these incidents, though, is to see them as
symbolizing the great difficulty that the dominant classes, who
provided the official leadership of the nationalist movement,
had in trying to contain the radical emotions of the people who
formed the foundation, the substratum, of that movement. Such
a perspective will also enable us to see Gandhi more clearly, since
it's an important aspect of his historical position that, at the
edges of his moral authority, there were occurrences that
implicitly denied the legitimacy of that authority.

Here are some cases in point. When Sardar Bhagat Singh,
on 8 April 1929, threw a bomb in the Central Legislative
Assembly in Delhi, his act immediately became for many Indians
a popular symbol of their willingness, if necessary, to fight fire
with fire. Similarly, when in order to finance a bomb factory they
were planning to build, militant nationalists boarded a train on
the Lucknow-Saharanpur line and stole a government strongbox

containing 5000 rupees, it was a sign of a growing consciousness within India that verbal negotiations and "gentlemanly" behavior weren't going to suffice if the freedom movement was going to mature into a full-scale, nation-wide, anti-imperialist movement.

But it wasn't just in militant acts like these, sponsored as they were by revolutionary groups that differed ideologically from the Congress leadership, that the precarious hold of the Congress leaders on the masses of people was displayed. Often the Congress itself was in the position of inadvertantly bringing into being, or uncovering, depths of discontent among the people that it felt intimidated by.

One example of this is the mass non-cooperation movement which, under Gandhi's guidance, was launched by the Congress in 1930 and lasted until 1934. According to Gandhi, the ideological axle of the movement was to be passive resistance; the population, from one end of the country to the other, would simply refuse to cooperate with the British authorities. Such nonviolent resistance, it was thought, would throw a great wrench into the vulnerable machinery of British power. But the reality turned out to be significantly different from the aspiration.

As the mass movement consolidated itself and people began to feel their collective power, they often stepped beyond the limits set for them by their leadership. For instance, In Sholapur key sections of the population (especially the city's textile workers, who played a leading role) came together and effectively dissolved the power of the local British administration and, for a few days, took control of the city. Or again: in Uttar Pradesh, in northern India, the peasants, who had launched a radical no-rent campaign, provided a grassroots militant alternative to Gandhi's more benign conception of non-cooperation. With such a sprawl of unrest spilling across the subcontinent, in the end Gandhi was forced to call off the mass movement that he himself had launched. He bemoaned the fact that people were still not spiritually mature enough, that they were as yet inadequately prepared to assume the responsibilities of true nonviolence. Once again, in his eyes, the population had displayed their unworthiness, their underdevelopment.

Another example of the Congress's precarious hold on the population happened in Bombay in early 1946, on the very eve of Independence, when there occurred the most serious uprising of Indian military personnel in the British armed forces since the nation-shaking Sepoy Mutiny of 1857.

On 18 February 1946, seamen of the Royal Indian Navy mutinied on the ship Talwar, which was docked in the Bombay harbor. This was a coordinated anti-imperialist act directed at British colonial power within India. But what began as a revolt on a single ship soon mushroomed into something far larger and more paralyzing. First it spread to all the ships and flotillas within the harbor, bringing close to 20,000 seamen into the orbit of the revolt. When the British ordered Indian soldiers into the harbor to suppress the mutiny, the soldiers refused to open fire on their brother sailors. This added vital emotional fuel to the uprising. The feeling spread that if all Indians, on shore as well as in the harbor, refused to acknowledge British authority, their respective positions would be reversed and the Indians would usurp power. British troops were called in and ordered to attack the mutineering seamen; a pitched battle was fought but its result was inconclusive. Only one thing was certain: the Royal Indian Navy seamen hadn't yet been defeated.

The British finally responded to the crisis by threatening a full-scale massacre. On 21 February Admiral Godfrey issued a statement to the Indians in which he announced that if they didn't surrender immediately, he would orchestrate the annihilation of the whole Indian navy. Unfortunately for the British, rather than intimidating the Indian sailors the Admiral's proclamation had a reverse effect; it forced them to consciously step up their attempts to secure support from the whole Bombay population. People's response was immediate; a sympathetic general strike was called and Bombay, the "entranceway to India," was shut down for three days. Violent clashes occurred in the streets as British guns swung into action. In the final counting, somewhere between 200 and 300 Indians had been murdered as they persisted in their refusal to accept the dictates of the British. Yet, in spite of the dead, a feeling of freedom was in the air, a sense that the fight had, at last, begun.

By this time the rebellion had escalated to such a point that it represented a threat, not only to the British, but also to the

official leaders of the nationalist movement, who were involved
in trying to negotiate a "peaceful" way to get the British to depart
from the subcontinent so the reins of power could smoothly
pass into their own hands. But now there were dangerous signs
that what was going on in Bombay was infectious. Indian air
force personnel as far south as Bangalore announced their
solidarity with the uprising in Bombay, and police in some major
subcontinent cities were doing the same. The Congress leadership was concerned. They feared such spontaneous outbursts of
mass anger because they knew only too well how these outbursts
could swell into open class warfare, the lower classes pitted
against the more privileged sectors.

Wary of what would happen if the Bombay rebellion went
unchecked, the Congress leadershp intervened with all the
prestige at its disposal. National leaders encouraged the upsurging sailors to call off their mutiny, promising that they (the
national leaders) would take up the seamen's grievances with the
British. From this point on, both the British and the Congress
leaders inaugurated a wholesale attempt to defuse and depoliti-
cize the militant symbolism of the most violent incident of the
Independence struggle. They stated unilaterally that the causes
of the rebellion were minor and rectifiable, having to do only
with wage scales and living conditions on board ship. The high
level of political consciousness that had emerged during the
revolt, as exemplified by the alliance between the insurgent
sailors and Bombay's working classes, was written out of the
story. But even at the moment of surrender, the rebelling naval
men insisted, through their coordinating committee, on the basic
political nature of their mutiny and how this represented the
Indian people's struggle for self-determination. "We surrender
to India and not to the British," they said.

At the time, of course, the full irony of this statement wasn't
realized: that even though they were bowing to the wishes of
other Indians and not to the British authorities, it was still a
surrender, a capitulation not just to the imperialists but also to
the class interests represented by the Congress leadership.

After the mutiny had officially ended, street-rioting continued in Bombay for a number of days. People, although in a
slightly chaotic and confused way, were expressing their unease

at having to submit to the high-sounding language of the national leaders.

They felt that something was wrong, that they were somehow being misled.

5
A FINAL COLLAGE OF IMAGES

1.

Every morning, around seven o'clock, I sit down to write. I have this need to create something solid, an honesty of words, that builds up slowly like sedimentary rock at the bottom of the sea and that's washed clean by the deep waters. I want this manuscript, written on one continent, to be taken to another continent. I want the workers from the American Bosch factory, not far from where I used to live in Massachusetts, to walk alongside the Indian welder on the red dusty road as he goes to work in the morning, or to peer over Laxshmi's shoulder as she crouches in front of her house slicing thin strips from a bamboo pole, as she gets ready to make a basket. It's important that the one be able to look at the other, that each take a sort of physical pride in the other. There should be communication, even if it's only the mental communication of those separated by oceans. I want to be a tiny part of this process, a sort of machine for instantaneously relaying pictures from the one continent to the other. When the cool breeze blows through my window, or the sixteen-year-old girl in the maroon sari next door goes, with her brass vessel, to get water from the stone well on the side of the hill, I want U.S. workers to feel the breeze, see the girl.

Something's happening here that we have to be prepared to accept, to identify with. There are people here who want to transform the countryside, to take over the factories in the cities. They want the land, and the things they build, to be theirs. There's no doubt that this will eventually happen, the signs of it are all over, like fantastic glowing fingerprints that pre-date the crime.

Living here's like living at the bottom of a mountain in a house that's about to be crushed by an avalanche of stones, when on each stone a secret message is written in blood that has flowed straight from the heart of the people.

For instance, in his shop after dark the cabinet-maker looks up from his work and stares out the door. Outside the door, there's a moonlit patch of grass on the dirt path that leads towards the railroad tracks. Looking at it, for a minute he thinks of something fabulous: a world in which people, even those a half planet away, will respect his right to determine his own fate. I know this is what he thought, because he told me. He also said: "Those in power describe the ones who love freedom the most as

dangerous criminals. We live in a time when it's necessary to
look hard for the truth. I hope your fellow countrypeople, and
you too, know this. If not, you won't be able to understand the
future, not just India's, but the world's."

As I write, I think of what he said, and so I put it down. It's
one stone from the avalanche, thrown in your direction. Touch it,
feel the shape of it with your hands, keep it as a gift.

2. (Walking)

A lorry with MYSORE TRANSPORT CORPORATION
painted in bold green letters on its cab door
speeds by;
huge clouds of dust swirl up, a pale orange mist
blowing away from us, to the north
& settling down
on the branches of tamarind trees.
When the lorry passes, there's only a long line of bullock carts
piled with hay,
their drivers holding handkerchiefs over their faces
to keep the dust out of eyes, nostrils, mouths.
We reach the top of the hill & cross the road
& go down the slope on the other side.
In the small valley three boys tend a herd of water buffalo
& beyond them, on the far side
of an old unused irrigation ditch,
men stand in a twelve-foot-deep pit quarrying rock, breaking
                                                          it off
the walls with long iron spikes.
Above them, on the ground surrounding the pit,
four crouched women break the quarried rocks into smaller rocks
with crude wooden-handled hammers.
These women get paid 40¢ for an eight-hour day,
the men get paid more, according to how much rock
they bring up out of the pit—
the highest paid gets $1.25
& that on his best, most productive day, when his body's
in perfect shape.
Six days a week women & men bang stone in the hot sun
& if you ask them if they have any complaints
they laugh in your face.

3.

We get off the bus at the bus stand at the west border of the city. On the left side of the road, there are no buildings except one *pan* shop, a solid-looking square structure painted with red and blue vertical stripes on the outside: a blaze of color. To the right of the shop and further back, two women crouch in the shade of a banyan tree, talking. They're Dambavadi women, in town for their day's begging. One of the women we know. We say hello. Suman continues: "How are you? I saw your daughter a week ago. She said you were in Goa to see your sick brother. How is he?" In an ironic tone, the woman replies: "He's in excellent condition but not in this world. He's dead." She goes on to explain how he'd gone to the hospital for a vasectomy, then stayed for a second, additional operation which the doctors promised would be minor. Afterwards, however, internal bleeding developed; the doctors couldn't stop it and it continued for fifteen days. Finally, he died. She concludes, "They said what they were going to do to him would be easy, but it didn't turn out that way, did it?"

It's ten in the morning. The sun, rising higher, begins to cut into the shade in which the women are sitting. The one whose brother died shrugs her shoulders to indicate that these things happen and there's nothing you can do, except bear it and keep going.

4. (Dusk)
The wind scrapes across
dry
scattered straw.

The ring of blue hills around Vijaynagar
grows bluer
darker by the minute.

Dirt paths leading
in a thousand directions
pass through the village like boulevards

& at night
the jagged stones grow jaggeder
in the earth
in the dark.

Now the old man talks lyrically, excitedly
about ridding the village of the rich,
his voice a whisper,
a single grain of salt falling
like a star through space.
Eyes half closed
it's as if he's singing a grandchild to sleep
or describing the taste
of ripe mango to some
disfigured person, born without a mouth.

5.

In front of the shops on this narrow sidestreet: stacks of
newly woven baskets. Women and men crouch in dark doorways
slicing strips of bamboo from long poles, or weaving them into
baskets. The same activity goes on day after day. The necessary
motions for making a basket have been reduced, through long
practice, to an absolute minimum. There's a casual bantering
between the workers. Voices call from one side of the street to
the other, and from shop to shop. But even while they talk, they
work.

A man comes out of an alley, carrying a tied bundle of
bamboo-lengths. He stands them on end, leaning them toward a
building-front in such a way that they rest against the edge of the
low-hanging brick tile roof. When he needs them, he'll take
them down, one by one.

On the same street, a little further down, a group of about
fifteen men huddle bent-kneed in front of a stone wall, gambling.
One man, his back to the wall, faces the group which is formed in
a semi-circle before him. He's the organizer. On the ground
between him and the rest of the men is a black mat with different
bright-colored numbers and animal designs painted on it. Each
number and animal picture (red-saddled white horse, blue
elephant, golden tiger, etc.) is in its own rectangular box. When
everybody has placed his money on one of the rectangles, the
man spins the gambling-wheel, which is to his right on the
ground. The wheel has pictures and numbers that correspond to
those on the mat. The gamblers watch, waiting to see on what
number or figure the wheel's arm will stop. Other than the

shouts and near-miss sighs of the players, the main sound now is
the quick clicking noise of the wheel's arm as it slaps against the
thin nails that separate the different numbers and pictures.

The players are peasants and unskilled workers. One of
them claps his hands as he wins.

6. (Parts of the Process)
The local, but Canadian-owned
aluminum plant operates on
650 tons of bauxite a day, 5 tons
being needed for each ton
of aluminum produced. In the heat
on the hillside in the mining district
the flesh is like a deepsea diver, saddled
with heavy equipment, walking slow
on the ocean floor. Still, the bodies
have to move quickly, throwing huge shovelsful
of rock onto the backs of trucks.
The sun's a continuous red
electric shock on the skin. All day
while the men dig they talk to each other
& the sound of it's like sections of earth caving in.
Visiting white businessmen, looking on
from a predictable distance,
wonder to themselves
what the ignorant Indians
are saying.

7.
Both of them are Bengali, up-and-coming middle class. He
works for Air India. Suman and I sit with them in their living
room. Our reason for being here is that a few days ago he asked if
I'd take a photograph of their three-year-old son.

The mother, sitting next to Suman, prepares the boy for the
picture. With a damp blue and white towel she scrubs his face
clean. Then she takes off his shirt and shorts and replaces them
with another matching pair, bright yellow. Fully dressed, it's
time now to put on the final cosmetic touch. Holding the boy
between her knees, she puts her left hand on his forehead and

pushes back, so that his face is tilted upwards. Then, after taking some mascara out of a small silver dish with the index finger of her right hand, she puts it on his right eyelid in such a way that a thin wing of mascara crosses the eyelid and tapers off a half inch outside the corner of the eye, on the temple. After this, the other eye is done. Both eyes look huge now; they dominate the boy's chubby face. The final flourish is the application of powder to the boy's chin, cheeks, temples, forehead, nose, and then smoothing it out, making sure it's evenly applied. Now, the face sufficiently whitened and the mascara-blackened eyes standing out even more than before, the boy is ready. Except for one thing. The father, getting up from his chair, stoops down and helps his son put on a pair of sparkling red and white shoes. I look at the boy's face, trying to imagine what he'll look like when he grows up. I do this because his father has said, "When he completes high-school, I will send him to the United States for a good education."

As the father finishes tying the boy's shoes, I have a fantasy: the grown boy is attending a big east-coast American university. He's drunk at some Saturday-night fraternity beer bash. He pulls the photograph I'm about to take out of his wallet and, looking at it, is overcome by a feeling of sentimental nostalgia for the innocent child he once was, but no longer is. When, years later, he returns home, his parents are simultaneously proud of his western education and disturbed by the fact that he now views India and his parents' habits as backward, provincial, a slow-paced bore when compared to the exhilarating speed of the U.S.

The fantasy ends. We go outside into the sunlight and take two photographs. For one of the pictures, the boy stands at attention, arms held tight to his sides, eyes squinting in response to the bright light. For the other, he sits perkily on his blue tricycle, his big wide-open eyes staring straight into the camera's lens.

8. (Universal)
Two men on top
of the power pole, down the road.
The highest one, his white shirt
a small lake of light in the sun,
turns his head slowly

from left to right, looking out
over the wide, hilly landscape
as if, awed, he were seeing it for the first time.
Then he reaches
in his breast pocket, pulls something out:
a cigarette, which he lights.
Taking a drag, he looks straight up
into the sky.
The other man says something
to him, then also begins
looking around.
Above them the sky's huge,
filled with white clouds.
For about three minutes, gazing out over the land,
neither one
does any work, taking in, instead,
each hill, dry streambed, tree, field
laid out below them
far as the eye can see.
Then, refreshed,
they start working again, concentrating
on the cables whose connections
they have to check.

9.

　　Night. We're in the center of a field, in Vijaynagar. Loose
brush has been dragged here and thrown into a big pile. Sticking
out of the pile's center is a scarecrow made of sticks and dry grass.
Someone stoops down, lights a piece of twisted paper and uses it
for a torch, setting the brushpile on fire. Soon ten-foot-high
flames shatter the darkness. People run around the fire, slapping
their hands against their mouths and making a howling noise.
Others beat out a repetitive rhythm on small drums. Many
people are moving at once, either dancing in place or joining the
growing ranks of those running in circles around the fire. Then,
later as the fire subsides and the crowd's energy level diminishes,
someone gives out handfuls of puffed rice and slices of coconut.
Soon the crowd breaks up, and people start to drift off toward
their houses.

This is the beginning of the *holi* festival, with its characteristics of early fertility rites: fire worship, spring as a symbol of
procreation, etc.

The next day: 8 a.m. I look out the window. Three loudly
laughing men walk by, their faces, hair, shirts, pants smeared
with different colored dyes.

As festival, *holi* consists of groups of people wandering
through city and village streets, raising hell and dousing anyone
they meet with liquid dyes. It's a time of uninhibitedness, of
collective psychological release.

I keep looking out the window. There's a shouting sort of
roar coming from beyond the huts. Soon there are over a
hundred men and boys from Hindalga marching into the village,
slapping their mouths and whooping. They're all carrying
bottles filled with different colors. They themselves are drenched
from head to toe with dye. They're like a weird earthbound
rainbow with 200 legs and one gigantic noisy mouth. When they
get close to us (we're outside now), Adriana dashes up to some of
them and empties her own dye bottle on whoever she can get. A
man comes up to me and rubs my face with a sticky pink powder
and then hugs me, first on the right cheek and then on the left.
Then another man does the same. Soon, acting as if he's drunk,
the middle-aged man who smeared me first orders the yelling
and dye-throwing crowd to form a circle. Staggering around the
inside of the circle and singing a bawdy song, slowly he begins to
dance, and as he dances, a partner appears. The one acting drunk
holds a piece of wood carved in the shape of a liquor bottle, and
during the course of the dance he keeps tilting back his head and
putting the bottle to his lips. There are also two other men
dancing with the original dancers now. Both of them have
oily-looking ash-blackened faces, and attached to their heads and
shoulders are branches thick with green leaves. The first two
dancers, the man with the bottle and his partner, now do a dance
that is sexually bold and aggressive, with a lot of bumping and
grinding done with what can only be called a great deal of
playing-to-the-audience slapstick exaggeration. Soon the man
with the bottle comes and drags me into the circle's center, and
holding hands, we improvise a dance like something out of
Zorba the Greek. Then all five of us begin jumping around more

or less independently of each other, but with a sort of collectively unified chaos. As we dance, we clap our hands and shout while the circle of people surrounding us shouts back at us in a call-and-response fashion....

Later in the morning, I remember something that someone told me the other day: that last year during *holi* the peasants in a particular village, having gotten themselves emotionally worked up, accosted the son of a much disliked landlord and assaulted him, sending him to the hospital.

It wasn't an isolated incident. *Holi* is known for social eruptions with economic overtones.

The "inner person" is always looking for a way to come out.

10. (The Spirit of the Poor Peasantry)

A fine red dust
on the petals of these flowers.
Blown by the wind
it's scattered everywhere.
It moves
but never disappears.

11.

He's sixty years old, a night watchman in a small electronics plant. He has no particular story to tell. Talking casually and smiling a lot, he casts around from one part of experience to another. Almost precisely because he hasn't coordinated what he has to say, he's extremely informative. He offers up bits and pieces of his life, not with any individual pride or anger, but with the calm self-effacingness of a man who assumes that whatever he has to offer is typical, predictable, common.

"I don't have any fields," he says, "I have nothing to pass on to my sons. For my father it was a little different. He had fields, but by the time I'd grown up he lost them." The white beard-stubble around his mouth is broken by a smile, not a sad or sarcastic smile, just an ordinary one. Soon he's talking about things that don't have to do with him in particular.

"It looked like things were going to change. Some landless people in the village where I now live were given land by the government. It was only a little bit, but at least it was land. But they didn't have the money to buy the equipment to farm it. In the end, it all came to nothing. From my father's time until now, things haven't changed much."

To deepen the conversation, to try to extend it, I mention something about China, about how much more successful their attempts at land reform seem to have been. I want to elicit his opinion on what the solution to all these problems is. But he cuts me off almost before I begin.

"Yes, I know about China," he says. "People aren't starving there, from what I hear. Some of the farmers and workers here are beginning to say we're going to have to get ourselves together like they did there, before anything changes. They're right, I guess. Something like that will have to happen, or else things will just go on the way they've been."

And again he smiles, his sixty-year-old face lit up, not with political fury, but with a calm—almost detached—understanding of the world he lives in.

12.   (The Basket-Weaver Woman Talks)

"The 6th day of the month is a pile
of broken wooden axles
in my head.
Nothing works right.
Last night the electricity failed,
this morning our hen wandered off
& it took us three hours to find her,
50 bamboo poles cost 60 rupees
& on top of that you have to pay
to have them carted home.
Also there's my 16-year-old granddaughter,
still not married.
These are only
my petty complaints.
Worse than everything are the local officials
who give big speeches
written for them by Achari, the famous landlord.
These men were nursed long ago
by mother cobra, eater
of mice & other small rodents.
When I talk about this, my breath gets so hot

it could shrivel up those little red flowers
on the ground here, in front of us."

13.

Suman and Shamabai's aunt are in Shamabai's tiny one-
room hut, helping her to deliver. Her labor pains began only
about an hour ago, but, in her own words, "When my pains start,
I give birth quick."

The aunt instructs Shamabai to put her feet against the wall
and push; after ten minutes a baby girl is born. But Shamabai's
work isn't done; she must keep pushing to help the release of the
afterbirth. At last it comes out. With a scissors, Suman cuts the
umbilical cord about six inches from the baby's navel. Shamabai
then tells Suman to take the cut piece of cord and rub it on the
child's upper lip, under her arms, on her genital area and legs. It
will prevent excess hair from growing on the body, Shamabai
says. Suman laughs and replies, "Does that mean you don't have
hair, did it work for you?" Shamabai laughs back: "Do I have
hair! Kiss me between the legs and you'll see whether or not I
have hair!"

Next, the aunt takes a small copper coin and bandages it to
the end of the piece of umbilical cord that's still sticking out from
the baby's stomach. After this is done tumeric and talcum
powder are applied to the unbandaged part of the cord. The coin
is used because it's believed that the copper helps the healing
process. The powder and tumeric are used because they help the
cord to dry out and fall off.

Then the baby has to be cleaned, in order to remove the birth-
film from her body. Suman does this. First, a mixture of eggwhite
and chickpea flour is rubbed on the baby, then she's washed with
soap and water.

Now a final ritual has to be performed. A banana leaf is
placed on the floor and put on the leaf are a gold earring, a
five-*paise* piece, a few grains of uncooked rice, and a little
tumeric. The baby is then lowered onto the leaf and lifted up
three times for good fortune.

When this is over, Suman takes the afterbirth, which earlier
she'd put in a clay vessel, and goes outside and digs a hole and
buries it. When she returns to the hut, Shamabai and her aunt are

sitting in the corner next to the baby smoking *beedies* (cigarettes). When the two women finish smoking, Suman and Shamabai's aunt wash Shamabai with oil and water and then tell her to rest, which she grudgingly agrees to do. The baby's asleep. Shamabai's other two children, Saluchanna and Ganpati, who were running in and out of the room while their mother was giving birth, sit next to her as she stretches out on the floor.

Later in the evening, at 8:30, Suman goes back to check on Shamabai. As she goes in the door, she sees Shamabai sitting in the corner, wiping her eyes. "Are you crying?" Suman asks. "Crying? No," Shamabai answers, "I'm just a little tired. Why should I be crying? I've just given birth to a woman; that's no cause for crying."

One of the reasons for Shamabai's fatigue is that in the afternoon, after resting for awhile, she got up and washed some clothes. Then there were Ganpati and Saluchanna, who wanted to talk to her.

"Just because you give birth," she says, "life doesn't stop."

14. (Season)

The fallen paraplegic twitches
in the dust.
Hot, dusty breeze brushes
the bull's back. A cart's
wooden wheels creak.

In the countryside, small dunes
of dust, on the petals of flowers.
In the city, dust gathering
in the doorway of the shop
where the pot-mender welds
a brass pot.

Dust. Reddish, powdery. Blowing & drifting.

Heatwave. Streambeds
dry up.
Wells, with hard, caked mud at the bottom.
Flies whining.
No rain,
no crops.

At night, the landlord, drinking
imported lager, remembers
European opera houses.

Days pass. Grinning children scoop up handfuls of dust.
The fifty-year-old coolie limps forward, a spittle
of light foaming at the corners of his mouth.
In the accountant's notebooks
all the numbers shrivel up, turn to dust.

In Hindalga & Vijaynagar & Ganeshpur & Belgaum—
necks
knuckles
kneebones
shoulderblades
eyes.

Side by side with the living, the dead march
yelling for revenge.

15.

Night. Next door, Holika shouts at one of her girls. Then, there's silence. Vijaynagar, now, is drifting off to sleep, under the stars.

Later. No sounds. Village of mute huts. Some of the people must be having visions in their sleep. Possibly someone sees, as part of the landscape of their particular dream, the radiant whiteness of a jasmine flower. Someone else might see fingers clawing endlessly at a tiny, barren plot of dirt.

The next day. We leave. Before going, a number of emotional farewells. Meeda Mamma stands on the side of the hill, waving goodbye.

We go to the train station in Belgaum. Before reaching the station, one of the last things we see is a noisey crowd of workers blocking traffic on a main street, as they surround a car in which are seated some officials from a local factory.

16.

There are many stories to be told. Each is a fragment of the life of the total population. Some of them, slightly more dramatic than others, sum up the people's inner toughness, their desire, not only to survive, but to survive with dignity, pride.

Here's one such story.

In December 1975, two peasant leaders from the state of Andhra Pradesh were executed by the Indian government. Both had been convicted at the beginning of 1972 for the slaying of a landlord in an area known for the deprived status of its peasantry. For a long time, this area had been characterized by an escalating friction between poor and rich.

A person who was kept for a few days in a cell next to the condemned men, in the September prior to their deaths, reported that although the time of their executions was drawing near, they weren't in despair. They had arranged to have their eyes donated to an eye bank, and in reference to this they would say, "Although we will not be able to see the success of our revolution, we are leaving behind our eyes so that they can see it."

Somewhere those eyes still live: meteors burning.

Notes

Part I

page 15-16: Quotes in paragraph beginning 'The image of universal Indian slowness.' Clark Blaise and Bharti Mukerjee, *Days and Nights in Calcutta* (Doubleday and Company, Inc.: New York, 1977), pp. 11, 13, 19.

page 17: Naipaul's statement about a peasantry that can't comprehend the idea of change. V.S. Naipaul, *India: A Wounded Civilization* (Alfred A. Knopf: New York, 1977), p. 8.

page 17: Ginsberg's comment about India as a wonderworld. Allen Ginsberg, *Indian Notebooks* (City Lights: San Franccisco, 1970).

page 77: Sangpapa's story. *Economic and Political Weekly*, Vol. 13, No. 2, pp. 51-52.

page 79: Paragraph beginning 'One example of such failure.' See Hari Sharma, 'The Green Revolution in India: The Prelude to a Red One', in Hari Sharma and Kathleen Gough (editors), *Imperialism and Revolution in South Asia* (Monthly Review Press: New York, 1973), pp. 77-96.

page 81: Information on Naxalites, in paragraph beginning 'One example of the growth.' See Inquilab Zindabad, 'The Red Sun is Rising,' in *Imperialism and Revolution in South Asia*, pp. 360-61.

page 82: Details about the Srikakulum revolt in paragraph beginning 'The most famous of these cases.' Ibid., 361. Also see Lasse and Lisa Berg, *Face to Face: Fascism and Revolution in India* (Ramparts Press: Berkeley, 1971), pp. 224-26.

page 83: Quote: 'Peasant revolts have in fact...' Kathleen Gough, 'Indian Peasant Uprisings,' *Bulletin of Concerned Asian Scholars*, Vol. 8, No. 3, p. 3.

page 83: Details on the Telengana peasant revolt in paragraph beginning 'Although at first the Telengana movement.' See H. Alvi, 'Peasants and Revolution' in *Imperialism and Revolution in South Asia*, pp. 326-28.

page 85: Information on Kilvenmani. *Face to Face: Fascism and Revolution in India*, pp. 17-18.

page 88: Swadeshi Cotton Mills. *Economic and Political Weekly,* Vol. 13, No. 9, pp. 442-445.

page 89: Information on Thane district in paragraph beginning 'Such harsh measures.' *Times of India,* January 7, 1978.

Part II

page 108: Information on Mohenjo-daro and Harappa in paragraph beginning 'Caste began as far back.' D.D. Kosambi, *The Culture and Civilization of Ancient India* (Vikas Publishing House, New Delhi, 1976), pp. 54-55.

page 108: Mythological references to Indra and Agni in paragraph beginning 'The invading Aryans.' S. Radhakrishan and C. Moore (editors), *A Sourcebook in Indian Philosophy* (Princeton Paperbacks, New Jersey, 1967), pp. 5-9.

page 109: Paragraph beginning 'And so the Aryans.' S.A. Shah (editor), *Towards National Liberation* (Montreal), p. 26.

page 110: For more information on the concept of *jati*, see Alan R. Beal's *Golapur: A South Indian Village* (Holt, Rinehart, and Winston, New York, 1962), pp. 33-44.

page 116: Caste violence in Villupurum, *Economic and Political Weekly*, Vol. 13, No. 41, pp. 1721-1725.

page 120: Quotes from the Laws of Manu, in paragraph beginning 'At the same time.' *A Sourcebook in Indian Philosophy* pp. 189-190.

page 126: Quote starting 'In childhood the female must be subject to her father,' in paragraph beginning 'At the center of sexual relations in India.' Ibid., p. 190.

page 127: Quote starting 'is disgraced,' in paragraph beginning 'Such things happen.' Ibid., p. 191.

Part III

page 135: Quote beginning 'India was in the throes of famine.' Anand Mohan, *Indira Gandhi: A Personal and Political Biog raphy* (Hawthorn Books: New York, 1967), p. 199.

page 135: Paragraph beginning 'Immediately after Independence.' Paresh Chattopadhyay, 'State Capitalism in India,' in A.A. Shah (editor), *Towards National Liberation: Essays on the Political Economy of India* (Montreal, 1973), p. 62.

page 136: Paragraph beginning 'The thinking behind this strategy.' Ibid., p. 60 and p. 68. Also see Chattopadhyay's 'Trends in Indian Economic Development' in *Imperialism and Revolution in South Asia*, p. 119.

page 138: Information on the disintegrating economic situation, in paragraph beginning 'During the period.' See Raijt San's 'The New Economics' in *Towards National Liberation*, pp. 97 and 99. For information on the rapid development of the private sector, see Chattopadhyay's 'State Capitalism in India,' also in *Towards National Liberation*, p. 67. Growing unemployment is discussed in Meghnad Desai's 'India: Contradictions of Slow Capitalist Development' in (Blackburn, editor) *Explosion in a Subcontinent* (Penguin: Baltimore, 1975), p. 21.

page 139: Information on agricultural laborers in paragraph beginning 'Poverty was everywhere.' Chattopadhyay's 'Trends in Indian Economic Development' in *Imperialism and Revolution in South Asia*, p. 111.

page 140: Information on foreign investments and technological collaboration agreements, in paragraph beginning 'In 1957 the number of government-approved schemes.' See Prabhat Patnaik's 'Imperialism and the growth of Indian Capitalism' in *Explosion in a Subcontinent*, p. 61. Also see 'State Capitalism in India' in *Towards National Liberation*, p.60.

page 140: U.S. and British investments and aid, in paragraph beginning 'It's also necessary to note.' See Chattopadhyay's 'Trends in Indian Economic Development' in *Imperialism and Revolution in South Asia*, pp. 121-22.

page 140: Burmah Shell, Caltex and Standard Vacuum, in paragraph beginning 'One of the first major U.S. breakthroughs.' Heimsath Mansingh, *A Diplomatic History of Modern India* (Allied Publishers: Calcutta, 1971), pp. 370-71.

page 141: Standard Oil of Indiana, in paragraph beginning 'Another example.' Harry Magdoff, *The Age of Imperialism* (Monthly Review, New York, 1969), pp. 128-29.

page 142: Two-phased Green Revolution, in paragraph beginning 'By far the area.' Desias's 'India: Contradictions of Slow Capitalist Development' in *Explosion on a Subcontinent*, p. 245.

page 143 Poverty level percentages, in paragraph beginning 'Some of the negative.' Hari Sharma's 'The Green Revolution in India: Prelude to a Red One,' in *Imperialism and Revolution in South Asia*, p. 94.

page 143: U.S. Public Law 480, in paragraph beginning :The legal foundation.' *A Diplomatic History of Modern India*, p. 377

page 143: Paragraph beginning 'The method by which U.S. agriculture surplus.' Ibid., p. 378.

page 144: U.S. control of approximately half the Indian currency in circulation, in paragraph beginning 'On the surface.' 'Imperialism in India' (Committee of Concerned Asian Scholars, Ithaca, New York). The Vietnam example comes from Madhavan's 'ADB: A Case Study in Bootlicking' in *Towards National Liberation*, p. 96.

page 144: U.S. prices 30-50% higher than world market prices. 'Imperialism in India' (Ithaca), p. 15.

page 145: 1967 elections, in paragraph beginning 'In the 1967 elections.' 'India: Emerging Contradictions of Slow Capitalist Development' in *Explosion in a Subcontinent*, pp. 11-12.

page 146 Congress Party split in 1969, in paragraph beginning 'A good example.' 'The Emergency in India,' *Bulletin of Concerned Asian Scholars*, Vol. 7, No. 4, p. 12.

page 147: Quote about Indira Ghandi as a fiery leader in paragraph beginning 'It could only be beneficial.' Ibid., p. 12.

page 148: For information on the different Indian police forces in paragraph beginning 'Over the years,' see leaflet published by the Indian Student Association of the University of California.

page 148: Oppression in West Bengal, in paragraph beginning

'In West Bengal.' 'Emergency in India' in *Bulletin of Concerned Asian Scholars*, Vol. 7, No. 4, p. 12.

page 149: Information on railway workers' strike, in paragraph beginning 'Another example.' David Selbourne, *An Eye To India: The Unmasking of a Tyranny* (Penguin: Great Britain, 1977), p. 18.

page 150: Case of Sandip Kumar Dev. *New India Bulletin*, Vol. 2, Nos. 3-4 (March-August 1977), p. 21.

page 150: Case of Sipra Roy. Ibid., p. 23.

page 151-152: Items and data having to do with Indian economic situation. Statistics on food grain availability can be found in 'Emergency in India,'*Bulletin of Concerned Asian Scholars*, Vol. 7, No. 4, p. 7. Information on consumer prices is in Ibid., p. 7. Government estimates on number of unemployed can be found in *New India Bulletin*, Vol. 3, No. 1-2 (January-April 1978), p. 11.

page 152: The quote on Narayan, in paragraph beginning 'Precisely for these reasons.' *New York Times*, November 30, 1974.

page 153: Information on middle class intellectuals in the J.P. movement, in paragraph beginning 'Although Narayan's leadership.' Devi Prasad's 'The People's Resistance in Bihar' (Indians for Democracy: Lansing, Michigan), p. 7.

page 153: Students with the J.P. movement, in the paragraph beginning 'The role that students played.' Ibid., p. 9. Also p. 6.

page 154: The two quotes on the Bihar base of the J.P. movement. See 'The Emergency in India,' *Bulletin of Concerned Asian Scholars*, Vol.7, No. 4.

page 155: The quote about the J.P. movement being 'a movement of the people...It should not become a party.' Devi Prasad, 'The People's Resistance in Bihar' (Indians for Democracy, Lansing, Michigan), p. 7.

page 155: The J.P. movement's slogans, in paragraph beginning

240 NOTES ON INDIA

'Because of the serious.' 'The Emergency in India' *Bulletin of Concerned Asian Scholars,* Vol. 7, no. 4, p. 15.

page 156: Quote beginning 'The most powerful woman in the world...' Ibid., p. 2.

page 157: Quote about the 'last vestiges of democracy' in the paragraph beginning 'But suprisingly.' From an April 9, 1976 article in *The New York Times,* 'Dismay in India.'

page 157: Quote beginning 'There was little public reaction.' See 'The Emergency in India,' *Bulletin of Concerned Asian Scholars,* Vol. 7, No. 4, p. 2.

page 158: Information on bonuses in the paragraph beginning 'For instance, the Emergency.' *New India Bulletin,* Vol. 1, no. 5. (May-June, 1976), p. 5. Arrest of 2000 labor people: *Eye to India,* p. 181. 480,000 workers laid off: *New India Bulletin,* p. 5. Indira Gandhi's quote about increased production: *Eye to India,* p. 250.

page 159: Information on the Chas Nala mining tragedy, in the paragraph beginning 'The night before the disaster.' 400 workers killed: *Eye to India,* pp. 249-52. Quote about workers being 'engulfed': Ibid., p. 249.

page 162: Information about 500,000 people from Delhi being relocated, in paragraph beginning 'By April, 1976.' Ibid., p. 269.

page 162: 150,000 people jailed during the Emergency. *New India Bulletin,* Vol. 3, No. 1-2 (January-April, 1978), p. 10.

page 162: Quote concerning the need for censorship, in paragraph beginning 'In order to justify.' *Eye to India,* p. 391.

page 163: Information on jailbreaks, in paragraph beginning 'Increasingly, there were incidents.' *Lok Awaz,* Vol. 3, No. 8(May 28, 1976). Also *Eye to India,* p. 294.

page 163: Information on resistance in the countryside, in paragraph beginning 'There was also.' *New India Bulletin,* Vol. 2, No. 1(November-December, 1976), p. 13.

page 164: Story of Gucharn Singh, in paragraph beginning 'Another story.' *New India Bulletin,* Vol. 2, no. 3-4, (March-April, 1977).

page 165: Demolition near Turkman gate, in paragraph beginning 'The slum-housing demolition project.' *Eye to India*, p. 279-80.

page 166: Quote from Associated Press. *New India Bulletin*, Vol. 1, No. 4 (March-April, 1976), p. 6.

page 166: Resistance to forced sterilization in Uttar Pradesh, in the paragraph beginning 'The event at.' *New India Bulletin*, Vol. 2, no. 1 (November-December, 1976), p. 8.

page 167: Poem. *New India Bulletin*, Vol. 1, No. 3 (January-February, 1976), p. 11.

page 167-168: Long quote on strikes. *Eye to India*, pp. 289-90.

page 173: Information on Indian press censorship being favorable to the U.S., in the paragraph beginning 'Yet the situation wasn't.' Ibid., p. 157.

page 173: World Bank quote about vigorous measures, in paragraph beginning 'By summer/autumn 1976.'*Eye to India*, p. 24. The reference to Business Week is taken from an article in *New India Bulletin*, Vol. 1, No. 5 (May-June, 1976), p. 11.

page 174: The foodgrain deal, in paragraph beginning 'In the spring.' *Lok Awaz*, Vol. 3, No. 8 (May 28, 1976), p. 3.

page 176: Quote concerning Soviet assistance, in paragraph beginning 'Although it can be said.' Amiya Kumar Bagchi, 'Foreign Capital in India,' *Imperialism and Revolution in South Asia*, p. 62. Next quote in same paragraph is from N.K. Chandra's 'USSR and Third World: Unequal Distribution of Gains' in the *Economic and Political Weekly Annual Number 1977*, Vol. 12, No. 6,7 and 8, p. 349.

page 176: Paragraph beginning '1971 was a crucial turning point.' 'Soviet Social Imperialism in India (A CPI—ML Publication),'reprinted by the Indian People's Association in North America (Quebec, Canada), p. 29.

page 177: Quote beginning 'The changed position.' Ibid., p. 30.

page 177: Information on India's increasing dependence on Soviet support, in the paragraph beginning 'The question is.' *New India Bulletin*, Vol. 3, No. 1-2 (January-April, 1976), p. 45. Soviet military aid six times greater than that of the U.S. Ibid. p. 5.

242   NOTES ON INDIA

page 178: Switch-trading, in paragraph beginning 'One example.' 'USSR and Third World,' *Economic and Political Weekly Annual Number 1977*, Vol. 12, No. 6, 7 and 8, p. 369.

Part IV

page 191: Queen of Sheba, in paragraph beginning 'As a matter of fact.' Gibson's *Spain and the New World* (Harper and Row: New York, 1966), pp. 7-13.

page 192: Emerson's quote: 'as sublime as heat and night.' Steven Whicher (ed.), *Selections from Ralph Waldo Emerson* (Houghton Mifflin and Company, Boston, 1957), p. 144.

page 192: Ibid., p. 196.

page 192: The quote from *Upanishads* was originally pointed out to me by S. Mokashi Punekar, writer and professor. Adyakki Lokkama's poem was translated by professor C.R. Yaravintelimath and myself.

page 194: The long quote beginning 'Increasingly trade contacts' is taken from Romila Thapur's 'Communalism and Ancient Indian History' which is printed in the pamphlet *Communalism and the Writing of Indian History* (People's Publishing House: New Delhi, 1977). The succeeding four quotes are also taken from the same article.

page 197: The Allen Ginsberg quote, in the paragraph beginning 'In the 60s.' Allen Ginsberg, *Howl and Other Poems* (City Lights Books, San Francisco, 1956), p. 17.

page 197: Gary Snyder's poem. Gary Snyder, *The Back Country* (New Directions, New York, 1957), p. 94.

page 198: The quote in the paragraph beginning 'Underdeveloped and with still tangible traces.' Allen Ginsberg, Ankor Wat (Fulcrum Press, London, 1968), p. 18.

page 203: On this page, and the pages that follow, details having to do with the Ahmedabad labor dispute are taken from Erikson's *Gandhi's Truth: On the Origins of Militant Nonviolence* (W.W. Norton and Company: New York, 1969), pp. 322-363. Although the details are taken from Erikson's book, the interpetation of those details is mine, not his.

page 203: Gandhi's *moksha* quote, in the paragraph beginning 'To Gandhi.' Mohandas Gandhi, *An Autoboigraphy: The Story of my Experiments with Truth* (Beacon Press: Boston, 1957), p. XII.

page 204: The quote about Gandhi's unwillingness to abolish class distinctions, in the paragraph beginning 'Gandhi applied this perspective.' Gail Omvedt quotes this assessment in her 'Gandhi and the Pacification of the Indian National Revolution' in *Bulletin for Concerned Asian Scholars*, Vol. 5, No. 1, p. 8.

page 209: Paragraph beginning 'One writer.' Ibid., pp. 2-8.

page 209: Quote about the masses working for the elite, in the paragraph beginning 'Once again.' Ibid., p. 7.

page 210: Long quote about the friction between Ambedkar's politics and Gandhi's. Ibid., p. 7.

page 211: Information about the bombing of the Central Legislative Assembly and also the train robbery. V.D. Mahajan's *India Since 1526* (S. Chand and Company: New Delhi, 1976), Part 2, p. 456.

page 212: Information on the non-cooperation movement, in the paragraph beginning 'One example' and also in the paragraph that follows. M. Farooqui, 'India's Freedom Struggle and the Communist Party' (Communist Party Publication: New Delhi, 1974), pp. 29-31.

page 213: Royal Indian Navy Mutiny. Ibid., pp. 41-42. Also see Omvedt's 'Gandhi and the Pacification of the Indian National Revolution' in *Bulletin for Concerned Asian Scholars*, Vol. 5, No. 1, pp. 5-6.

Part V

page 232: Peasant leaders, sentenced to death, in paragraph beginning 'In December, 1975.' *New India Bulletin*, Vol. 2, No. 1 (November-December, 1978), p. 11.

Glossary

bhakeri: flat bread, made out of rye flour and water.

dahl: yellow lentils biled to souplike consistancy; one of the main foods in Indian diet.

haldi: tumeric; seasoning and powder; also used for ceremonial or religious purposes.

kum-kum: colored paste or powder; used by women to make the traditional mark (*bindi*) on their foreheads; also used for ceremonial or religious purposes.

lungi: three yards of material wrapped around waist in skirt-like fashion; worn mostly by men.

moksha: spiritual liberation; enightenment; the highest form of transcendence.

paise: a coin; smallest denomination of the rupee; equivalent to a penny.

pan shop: small shop that sells cigarettes, tobacco, candy, gum and other such items; gets its name from its main saleable item; betal nuts mixed with certain spices and wrapped in a *pan* leaf; this mixture of betal nuts and *pan* leaf is called *pan* and is regularly eaten by many Indians.

satyagraha: nonviolence; the power of truth; the will towards truth.